"I thoroughly enjoyed **First to the Wall**. This is a must read for any swimmer who wants to be great! The stories and the various swimmers throughout the last 100 years were inspiring, educational, humorous, as well as informative. *...If one is to become great in any endeavor, one must know the history of what one is trying to surpass and the trials and tribulations one must go through in order to be first to the wall."*

~ Jerry Heidenreich, *1972 Munich Games*
Four-time Olympic Medal Winner

"From motivational quotes to entertaining anecdotes, **First to the Wall** is filled with fascinating stories of Olympic swimming history. Swimming fans of all ages will enjoy the tales of medal winners from countries all over the world. The charts accompanying each chapter will give competitive swimmers a chance to compare times with those achieved in the finals at each Olympiad. **First to the Wall** brought back many fond memories of Olympic performances and of the champions I've watched throughout my swimming and coaching careers."

~ Rick Waterhouse, *Coach*
Terrapin Swim Team, Concord California

"The Olympic Games are all about what's good in this world - not the Olympics themselves, but the time honored traditions and what we learn from them. I look at the past performances in this book, **First to the Wall**, and they send shivers down my spine and I am continually inspired by them. The Olympic experience is a time when the human spirit triumphs over all and the winner is everyone. May the Olympic fever burn brightly in all of you as you read **First to the Wall**."

~ Jeff Float, *Gold Medalist (Los Angeles 1984)*

"**First to the Wall** is a wonderful tribute to all Olympic swimmers and a well deserved credit to their hard work, perseverance and years of dedication. The research, writing and remarkable photography make this a tremendous resource for swimmers and all fans of the Olympic Games."

~ Janey Decker Miller, *Director of Olympic Sports*
Gold Medal Management

First to the Wall
100 Years of Olympic Swimming

Kelly Gonsalves
Susan LaMondia

FreeStyle Publications, Inc.
East Longmeadow, Massachusetts

Published in the United States by

FREESTYLE PUBLICATIONS, INC.
P.O. Box 154
EAST LONGMEADOW, MA 01028-2309

Library of Congress Catalog Card Number:
99-91016

ISBN 0-9674171-0-4

Permission for cover photograph graciously granted by
Olympic Champion Amy Van Dyken

Cover Photograph © Morse Photography

Manufactured in the United States of America

Acknowledgments

~ With thanks to the many people who gave their time and encouragement and without whom this book would not have been possible.

~ To Matt Fenn, for his patience in letting us "move the furniture."

~ To Isabelle Fraser (Pioneer Valley Aquatic Club), for her years of dedication to competitive swimming.

~ To Preston Levi, Director of the Henning Library at the International Swimming Hall of Fame, whose assistance and time was given so generously.

~ To Marty Lynch for his attention to grammar.

~ To photographer Tim Morse, who thankfully has a special place in his heart for the sport of swimming.

~ To Eve Athens for encouraging her children to always reach for their dreams.

~ To the following Olympians who took the time to share their stories and whose good wishes made this project all the more special:

Theresa Andrews - 1984	Nancy Hogshead - 1984
Brooke Bennett - 1996	Lenore Kight -1932 &1936
Mike Bruner - 1976	Claudia Kolb - 1964 & 1968
Steve Clark - 1960 & 1964	Ada Kok - 1964 & 1968
Alva Colouhoun - 1960	Debbie Meyer - 1968
Ann Curtis - 1948	Karen Moe - 1972
John Davies - 1948 & 1952	John Naber - 1976
George DiCarlo - 1984	Eric Namesnik -1992 & 1996
Jeff Farrell - 1960	Sandra Neilson - 1972
Jeff Float - 1980 & 1984	Aileen Riggin - 1920 & 1924
Alan Ford - 1948	Murray Rose - 1956 & 1960
Bruce Furniss - 1976	Carrie Steinseifer - 1984
Brian Goodell - 1976	Éva Székely - 1948, 1952 & 1956
Jed Graef - 1964	Dara Torres - 1984, 1988 & 1992
Whitney Hedgepeth -1988 & 1996	Amy Van Dyken - 1996
Mark Henderson -1996	Michael Wenden — 1968
John Henricks - 1956 & 1960	Sharon Wichman – 1968
Jerry Heidenreich - 1972	David Wilkie - 1972 & 1976

Table of Contents

Dedication

*To our entire family for the love
and support only a family can give,
especially our husbands,
Gil and Tom,
and our daughters,
Nicole, Kendall,
Kristen, Katelyn, Allyson,
who endured the countless
hours of work.*

Foreword

The first celebration of the "modern" Olympic Games was held in Athens, Greece, in 1896. Little about these early swimming events resembles what we know today as the Olympic Swimming Competition.

Modern competitive swimmers enjoy such "luxuries" as temperature controlled and regulation size, indoor and outdoor pools. The use of lane lines, starting blocks, electronic timing devices, water resistant swimsuits, goggles and age-group swim programs have all evolved over the last century of Olympic swimming.

Through all this there is one common denominator. At the start of the race stand the athletes who have come to represent their countries. The race begins and all fight to the finish striving to reach their goals. When the race is over, there alone stands the swimmer who is — **first to the wall.**

Chapter 1

Olympiad I – 1896
Athens, Greece

forty thousand spectators lined the shore of the Bay of Zea, in Athens. They were there to witness history, the first swimming events to be held in Olympic competition.

Bay of Zea, Greece. Site of first Olympic swimming course.

Courtesy of ISHOF

OFF THE $\mathcal{Wall}$

Too Cold For Comfort!

American swimmer, Gardner Williams, who trained and saved his money for the expensive journey to Greece, jumped into the  icy waters only to scramble out, moments later, yelling, "I'm freezing!"

A small boat took the competitors out to the *approximate* distance for each of the events. The swimmers plunged into the open sea, using any stroke that would return them to shore as quickly as possible. Not only did they battle 12-foot waves, but the weather in Greece was unusually cold and the water was a frigid 55 degrees Fahrenheit.

ALFRÉD HAJÓS-GUTTMANN
HUNGARY

The world's first Olympic swimming gold medalist was eighteen year-old Alfréd Hajós-Guttmann. Known as "The Hungarian Dolphin," he won both the 100m and 1200m swimming events.

"Three small boats took us out to the open sea, which was quite rough. My body had been smeared with a half-inch layer of grease, for I was more cunning after the 100m event, and tried to protect myself against the cold.

Courtesy of ISHOF

We jumped into the water at the start of a pistol, and from that point on the boats left the competitors to the mercy of the waves, rushing back to the finish line to inform the jury of the successful start. I must say that I shivered from the thought of what would happen if I got a cramp from the cold water.

My will to live completely overcame my desire to win. I cut through the water with a powerful determination and only became calm when the boats came back in my direction, and began to fish out the numbed competitors who were giving up the struggle. At that time I was already at the mouth of the Bay. The roar of the crowd increased...I won ahead of the others with a big lead."– A.H. Guttmann

When Hajós-Guttmann was thirteen his father drowned in the Danube River, which might explain his determination to become a strong swimmer. After his swimming career was over, he became an architect and designed aquatic sites.

PAUL NEUMANN
AUSTRIA

Paul Neumann was also a swimming gold medalist in the first modern Olympic Games. He held Austria's title as "National River Swimming Champion."

Neumann won the 500m freestyle title in 1896. His stroke style, then considered unusual, was described as follows; "He lay flat on his stomach and breast, face partially down using a double over-arm stroke." This description sounds similar to what is known as the butterfly stroke today.

Courtesy of ISHOF

This accomplished Austrian later moved to the United States and became a doctor.

L A N E   L I N E S

Freestyle for Sailors

Open only to members of the Greek Navy, was the 100m freestyle for sailors. Ioannis Malokinis won this race with a time nearly one minute slower than Guttmann's time in the 100m freestyle event! This event was short-lived and was never seen again in Olympic competition.

1896 OLYMPIC SWIMMING FINALS

INDIVIDUAL EVENTS

	Gold	Silver	Bronze	Fourth	Fifth	Sixth	Seventh	Eighth
Men 100m Freestyle								
	Alfréd Hajós Guttmann	Otto Herschmann						
	HUN – 1:22.2 o	AUT – 1:22.8						
Men 400m Freestyle (500 meters)								
	Paul Neumann	Antonios Pepanos	Eustathios Choraphas					
	AUT – 8:12.6	GRE – 9:57.6	GRE					
Men 1500m Freestyle (1200 meters)								
	Alfréd Hajós Guttmann	Ioannis Andreou	Eustathios Choraphas					
	HUN – 18:22.2	GRE – 21:03.4	GRE					
Men 100m Freestyle For Sailors – Discontinued Event								
	Ioannis Malokinis	Spiridon Chasapis	Dimitrios Drivas					
	GRE – 2:20.4	GRE	GRE					

w World Record   *o* Olympic Record   *p* Preliminary Heat   *dq* Disqualified   *e* Equal to World Record   *eo* Equal to Olympic Record
dns Did Not Start   *dnf* Did Not Finish   *ac* Also Competed   *r* Relay Lead-off Split   *E* Estimated

OLYMPIAD I – 1896 - ATHENS, GREECE

Chapter 2

Olympiad II - 1900
Paris, France

The 1900 Olympic Games were held over the course of five months in Paris, France. That is a long time between events! Recorded times for swimming in this Olympiad were quite spectacular and for a very good reason. The events were held in the River Seine, and swum *with* the current.

JOHN ARTHUR JARVIS
GREAT BRITAIN

John Arthur Jarvis called himself, "The Amateur Swimming Champion of the World." During the 1900 Olympic Games, Jarvis was credited with winning the 1,000m (now the 1500m freestyle event) and the 4,000m freestyle race. This was the first and last time the 4,000m free event was in the Olympic swimming program.

Jarvis with his many swimming awards.

Courtesy of ISHOF

Returning to Olympic competition in 1906, Jarvis collected a silver and bronze medal for individual events. He also anchored Great Britain's 4X250m (now 4X 200m) freestyle relay team, to a third place finish and a second bronze medal.

Jarvis was one of the first "teachers" of life saving, earning himself the title of "Professor Jarvis." He did, in fact, save many lives, including a famous rescue of twin sisters.

FREDERICK LANE
AUSTRALIA

Frederick Lane won two gold medals for Australia at the 1900 Olympic Games in Paris. Lane took one gold in the 200m freestyle race and another in the one and only *obstacle course* event.

Courtesy of ISHOF

Lane was the first man to clock one minute flat in a 100-yard race. He later broke the one minute barrier with a 59.6.

Unfortunately, Lane's times came before the existence of the world-wide system of "record ratification," so his times were not listed, denying him a much-deserved place in the record books.

OTTO WAHLE
AUSTRIA

Otto Wahle represented his homeland, Austria, in the 1900 and 1904 Olympic Games, winning a total of three Olympic medals.

Wahle subsequently came to the United States and coached American Olympic swimmers in the 1912 and 1920 Olympiads. He contributed greatly to the development of the United States' competitive swimming program.

Belly 1900 Flops

The events listed below were all in the Olympic program in Paris, but were never again swum in Olympic competition.

The Obstacle Course Event

Swimmers had to conquer three obstacles during the course of this race. The swimmers had to clamber over a pole, cross over a line of boats and lastly, swim beneath another string of boats.

Frederick Lane of Australia was the winner of this one-time event. Lane, who had spent his youth around the Sydney docks, knew his boats. During the obstacle race, Lane crossed over the stern while his competitors climbed over the middle, wider sections of the boats.

Underwater Swimming Event
underwater swimming

This event was scored by "meters swum," two points per meter, in addition to one point awarded for each second the swimmer remained *under* the water. Charles de Vendeville of France won the event with a high point score of 188.4. He stayed under the water for 1:08.4 minutes and swam 60 meters.

4,000 Meter Freestyle
4,000m freestyle

John Jarvis of Great Britain, won this event in a time of 58.24 (minutes) establishing himself as the greatest distance swimmer of his day.

200 Meter Swimming
200m swimming

As the first "team swimming" event in the modern Olympics, this event may have sparked the idea of the relay. It was, however, greatly different.

OFF THE **Wall**

No Horsing Around

For his victories at the 1900 Games, Frederick Lane was presented with a bronze statue of a horse that weighed 50 pounds!

This event had twenty competitors and each team of swimmers was awarded points as each of its five members finished. The team with the lowest combined score won the title.

The team from Germany won with members placing 1st, 2nd, 4th, 6th and 19th. The British Team had been given the wrong starting time and unfortunately, missed the event entirely!

1900 OLYMPIC SWIMMING FINALS

| Gold | Silver | Bronze | Fourth | Fifth | Sixth | Seventh | Eighth |

INDIVIDUAL EVENTS

1896 - Event Not Held On Olympic Program

Men 200m Freestyle

Gold	Silver	Bronze	Fourth	Fifth	Sixth
Frederick Lane	Zoltán Halmay	Karl Ruberl	Robert Crawshaw	Maurice Hochepied	F. Stapleton
AUS – 2:25.2 or	HUN – 2:31.4	AUT – 2:32.0	GBR – 2:45.6	FRA – 2:53.0	GBR – 2:55.0

Men 1500m Freestyle (1000 Meters)

Gold	Silver	Bronze	Fourth	Fifth	Sixth
John Arthur Jarvis	Otto Wahle	Zoltán Halmay	Max Hainle	Louis Martin	Leuillieux
GBR – 13:40.2	AUT – 14:53.6	HUN – 15:16.4	GER – 15:22.6	FRA – 16:34.4	FRA – 16:53.2

Men 4000m Freestyle – Discontinued Event

Gold	Silver	Bronze	Fourth	Fifth	Sixth
John Arthur Jarvis	Zoltán Halmay	Louis Martin	Thomas Burgess	Eduard Meijer	Fabio Mainoni
GBR 58:24.0	HUN 1:08:55.4	FRA 1:13:08.4	FRA 1:15:07.6	NED 1:16:37.2	ITA 1:18:25.4

w World Record *o* Olympic Record *p* Preliminary Heat *dq* Disqualified *e* Equal to World Record *eo* Equal to Olympic Record
dns Did Not Start *dnf* Did Not Finish *ac* Also Competed *r* Relay Lead-off Split *E* Estimated

OLYMPIAD II – 1900 – PARIS, FRANCE

1900 OLYMPIC SWIMMING FINALS

Gold	Silver	Bronze	Fourth	Fifth	Sixth	Seventh	Eighth	1896 – Event Not Held On Olympic Program

Men 200m Backstroke

	Gold	Silver	Bronze	Fourth	Fifth
	Ernst Hoppenberg	Karl Ruberl	Johannes Drost	Thomas Burgess	de Romand
	GER – 2:47.0	AUT – 2:56.0	NED – 3:01.0	FRA – 3:12.6	FRA – 3:38.0

Obstacle Race – Discontinued Event

	Gold	Silver	Bronze	Fourth	Fifth	Sixth
	Frederick Lane	Otto Wahle	Peter Kemp	Karl Ruberl	F. Stapleton	William Henry
	AUS – 2:38.4	AUT – 2:40.0	GBR – 2:47.4	AUT – 2:51.2	GBR – 2:55.0	GBR – 2:58.0

Underwater Swimming – Discontinued Event

	Gold	Silver	Bronze	Fourth	Fifth	Sixth
	Charles de Vendeville	André Six	Peder Lykkeberg	de Romand	Tisserand	Hans Anioi
	FRA	FRA	DEN	FRA	FRA	GER
	60 – Meters	60 – Meters	28.50 - Meters	47.50 – Meters	30.75 – Meters	36.95 – Meters
	1:08.4 – Time	1:05.4 – Time	1:30.0 – Time	50.2 – Time	48.0 - Time	30.0 - Time
	188.4 – Points	185.4 – Points	147.0 – Points	145.0 – Points	109.0 - Points	103.9 - Points

200m Team Swimming - Discontinued Event

	Gold	Silver	Bronze	Fourth
	GER	FRA	FRA	FRA
	32 points	51 points	61 points	65 points

Chapter 3

Olympiad III - 1904
St. Louis, Missouri, United States

The 1904 Games were held in St. Louis, Missouri, in the United States. Only thirteen countries were represented in these Olympic Games because travel was so expensive. Due to the popularity of the World's Fair also being held in St. Louis during this time, home interest in these Games was minimal. Only 2,000 people attended the 85-event program. A total of 50 swimmers representing four different countries participated in the swimming events.

Courtesy of ISHOF

The swimming events were held in an artificial lake and a wooden raft was used as the starting platform. This was the first time Olympic swimming events were held in still water. Attached to the raft was a lifeboat, in case a rescue was necessary. This "starting platform" sank with the weight of the competitors. To make matters worse, the raft shifted backwards with the movement of the swimmers taking their start. The competitors almost fell flat on their faces just trying to plunge into the water. Once in the lake, the swimmers had difficulty swimming straight because there were no lane lines and the turn markers kept drifting.

CHARLES DANIELS
UNITED STATES

The first American to win an Olympic swimming event was Charles Daniels. Born on March 24,1885, he is considered the founding father of the "American Crawl".

In 1905, this swimming champion set an incredible total of fourteen world records in a four day period. Daniels won a total of eight medals ending his Olympic career at the 1908 Games with a world record time in the 100m freestyle.

Charles Daniels - America's first Olympic Swimming Champion.

Courtesy of ISHOF

ZOLTÁN HALMAY
HUNGARY

Zoltán Halmay of Hungary was the *eventual* winner of the 50yd freestyle race in St. Louis. In the *first* swimming of this race the U.S. judge shockingly declared the American, Scott Leary the winner, even though Halmay had touched him out by a foot.

A fight erupted involving everyone in sight. The matter was eventually resolved by means of a "swim-off" with Halmay winning once again. He went on to capture the 100yd title as well.

Courtesy of ISHOF

Halmay competed in four Olympiads, including the "Intercalated Games of 1906," winning a total of nine swimming medals. That record was unsurpassed until Mark Spitz toppled it in 1972. Halmay's times were considered phenomenal during his era. Even more incredible was that he did it all using *only* his arms—he swam without a kick!

Belly 1904 Flops

400 Meter Breaststroke
400m breaststroke

The 400m breaststroke event made its first appearance in Olympic competition in 1904. **Georg Zacharies** of Germany won the race. This event made its next Olympic appearance in 1912 and again for the last time in 1920.

880 Yard Freestyle
880 yard freestyle

The "side-stroking" German swimmer, **Emil Rausch**, was the gold medal winner of this event. Along with this gold, Rausch won another in the one-mile (1500m) race. He was the last man to win an Olympic gold medal using the sidestroke technique.

Plunge For Distance
plunge for distance

Swimmers started with a standing dive and plunged through the water motionless, without the benefit of kicking or stroking. The swimmers remained underwater up to sixty seconds or until their head surfaced. Officials would then measure the length of their dive.

William Dickey of the United States won this event with a plunge of (62) feet and (6) inches. The British plunger W. Taylor, who held his nation's record of (78) feet and (9) inches, did not travel to the St. Louis Games.

4 X 50 Yard Freestyle Relay
4x50 yard freestyle relay

As the German team lined up for the first ever Olympic relay race, the Americans complained, stating that the race was for "clubs" only. The German team was comprised of members from various swim clubs. The American officials ruled against the Germans and they were not allowed to compete. Subsequently, the first four places were all American club teams with the New York Athletic Club taking the gold. American officials' partiality was very evident during these Games.

OFF THE **Wall**

Lights Out!

During the 1908 Olympic Games, Hungarian, Zoltán Halmay was a member of the 4 X 200 free relay team. The Hungarian team seemed to have the race well in hand. Then the unthinkable happened. While swimming his leg Halmay began to lose consciousness in the last 50 meters! He managed to struggle to the finish line, but had to be hauled from the pool before he drowned. The Hungarians still managed to take a silver medal.

1904 OLYMPIC SWIMMING FINALS

INDIVIDUAL EVENTS

	Gold	Silver	Bronze	Fourth	Fifth	Sixth	Seventh	Eighth
Men 50m Freestyle (50 yards)						1896-1900 – Event Not Held On Olympic Program		
	Zoltán Halmay	J. Scott Leary	Charles Daniels	David Gaul	Leo Goodwin	Raymond Thorne		
	HUN – 28.2 Swim-off - 28.0	USA – 28.2 Swim-off - 28.6	USA	USA	USA	USA		
Men 100m Freestyle (100 yards)					1900 – Event Not Held On Olympic Program			
	Zoltán Halmay	Charles Daniels	J. Scott Leary	Francis Gailey	David Hammond	Leo Goodwin		
	HUN – 1:02.8	USA	USA	USA	USA	USA		
Men 200m Freestyle (220 yards)								
	Charles Daniels	Francis Gailey	Emil Rausch	Edgar Adams				
	USA – 2:44.2	USA – 2:46.0	GER – 2:56.0	USA				
Men 400m Freestyle (440 yards) - World Record (5:22.2 440 yards)					1900 – Event Not Held On Olympic Program			
	Charles Daniels	Francis Gailey	Otto Wahle	Leo Goodwin				
	USA – 6:16.2	USA – 6:22.0	AUT – 6:39.0	USA				
Men 880y Freestyle (880 yards) - Discontinued Event								
	Emil Rausch	Francis Gailey	Géza Kiss	Edgar Adams	Jamison Handy	Otto Wahle		
	GER – 13:11.4	USA – 13:23.4	HUN	USA – *ac*	USA – *ac*	AUT - *ac*		

w World Record *o* Olympic Record *p* Preliminary Heat *dq* Disqualified *e* Equal to World Record *eo* Equal to Olympic Record
dns Did Not Start *dnf* Did Not Finish *ac* Also Competed *r* Relay Lead-off Split *E* Estimated

OLYMPIAD III – 1904 – ST. LOUIS, U.S.A.

1904 OLYMPIC SWIMMING FINALS

	Gold	Silver	Bronze	Fourth	Fifth	Sixth	Seventh	Eighth
Men 1500m Freestyle (1 mile)								
	Emil Rausch	Géza Kiss	Francis Gailey	Otto Wahle	Edgar Adams	Louis deBreda Handle	John Meyers	
	GER – 27:18.2	HUN – 28:28.2	USA – 28:54.0	AUT	USA – dnf	USA – dnf	USA – dnf	
Men 100m Backstroke (100 yards) 1896-1900 – Event Not Held On Olympic Program								
	Walter Brack	Georg Hoffmann	Georg Zacharias	William Orthwein	David Hammond	Edwin Swatek		
	GER – 1:16.8	GER	USA	USA – ac	USA – ac			
Men 400m Breaststroke (440 yards) 1896-1900 – Event Not Held On Olympic Program								
	Georg Zacharias	Walter Brack	H. Jamison Handy	Jörg Hoffmann				
	GER – 7:23.6	GER	USA	GER				
Men Plunge For Distance – Discontinued Event 1896-1900 – Event Not Held On Olympic Program								
	William Dickey	Edgar Adams	Leo Goodwin	N. Samuels	Charles Pyrah			
	USA	USA	USA	USA	USA			
	M – 19:05	M – 17.53	M – 17.37	M – 16.76	M – 14.02			
	FT./IN. – 62-6	FT./IN. – 57-6	FT./IN. – 57-0	FT./IN. – 55-0	FT./IN. – 46.0			
Men 200y Freestyle Relay – Discontinued Event 1896-1900 - Event Not Held On Olympic Program **RELAY EVENT**								
	Josephy Ruddy, Leo Goodwin, Louis Handley, Charles Daniels	David Hammond, Wm. Tuttle, H. Goetz, Ray Thorne	A. Reyburn, G. Evans, M. Schwartz, W. Orthwein	Edgar Adams, David Bratton, G. Van Cleaf, David Hesser				
	USA - NY Athletic Club	USA - Chicago Athletic Club	USA - Missouri Athletic Club	USA - NY Athletic Club				
	Team #1 - 2:04.6			Team #2				

Chapter 4

The Interim Games - 1906
Athens, Greece

In 1906, "The Interim Games" were held to mark the tenth anniversary of the modern games. There seems to be some question as to whether these games were "official." They were called the "Intercalated Games at Athens" and were unnumbered because they didn't fall into the regular four-year Olympic cycle.

These Games were a great success, drawing huge crowds including members of various royal families. Pierre de Coubertin, the founding father of the Modern Olympics, felt

OFF THE Wall

ONE GALLON WINE

Changing Water Into Wine

Officials stopped the U.S. Olympic Team, en route to the Games by train, in Italy. The mineral water the American's were carrying was mistaken for illegal gin (alcohol) and taken away. The Italian Officials, wanting to be fair, gave the team native wine in trade!

that these 'Interim Games' helped get the "Olympic Movement" back on track.

Olympic newcomer **Otto Scheff** of Austria captured two Olympic medals in 1906 and came back in 1908 to win yet another. **Henry Taylor** of Great Britain makes his Olympic debut in 1906. The Interim Games also saw the return of Olympic swimming champions **Charles Daniels, Zoltán Halmay** and **John Jarvis** in their quest for more medals. *See the chart section for the medal winners.*

L A N E   L I N E S

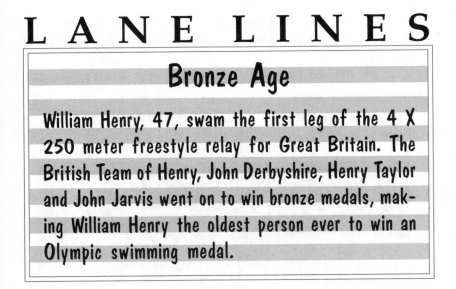

Bronze Age

William Henry, 47, swam the first leg of the 4 X 250 meter freestyle relay for Great Britain. The British Team of Henry, John Derbyshire, Henry Taylor and John Jarvis went on to win bronze medals, making William Henry the oldest person ever to win an Olympic swimming medal.

1906 OLYMPIC SWIMMING FINALS

INDIVIDUAL EVENTS

Gold	Silver	Bronze	Fourth	Fifth	Sixth	Seventh	Eighth

Men 100m Freestyle - World Record (1:05.8 Zoltán Halmay HUN)

Gold	Silver	Bronze	Fourth	Fifth	Sixth	Seventh	Eighth
Charles Daniels	Zoltán Halmay	Cecil Healy	Paul Radmilovic	John Derbyshire	Hjalmar Johansson		
USA – 1:13.4	HUN – 1:14.2	AUS	GBR	GBR	SWE		

Men 400m Freestyle - World Record (5:19.0 440 yards)

Gold	Silver	Bronze	Fourth	Fifth	Sixth	Seventh	Eighth
Otto Scheff	Henry Taylor	John Arthur Jarvis	Alajos Bruckner	Paul Radmilovic	Cecil Healy		
AUT – 6:23.8	GBR – 6:24.4	GBR – 6:27.2	HUN	GBR	AUS		

Men 1500m Freestyle

Gold	Silver	Bronze	Fourth	Fifth	Sixth	Seventh	Eighth
Henry Taylor	John Arthur Jarvis	Otto Scheff	Max Pape	Emil Rausch	Ernst Bahnmeyer	Oskar Schiele	Leopold Mayer
GBR – 28:28.0	GBR – 30:07.6	AUT – 30:53.4	GER – 32:34.6	GER – 32:40.6	GER – 33:29.4	GER – 33:52.4	AUT – 34:41.0

w World Record   *o* Olympic Record   *p* Preliminary Heat   *dq* Disqualified   *e* Equal to World Record   *eo* Equal to Olympic Record
dns Did Not Start   *dnf* Did Not Finish   *ac* Also Competed   *r* Relay Lead-off Split   *E* Estimated

INTERCALATED GAMES – 1906 – ATHENS, GREECE

1906 OLYMPIC SWIMMING FINALS

| Gold | Silver | Bronze | Fourth | Fifth | Sixth | Seventh | Eighth |

RELAY EVENT

Men 800m Freestyle Relay (4 X 250m)   1896-1904 – Event Not Held On Olympic Program

Gold	Silver	Bronze	Fourth	Fifth	Sixth	Seventh	Eighth
József Ónody, Henrik Hajós, Géza Kiss, Zoltán Halmay	Ernst Bahnmeyer, Oskar Schiele, Emil Rausch, Max Pape	William Henry, John Derbyshire, Henry Taylor, John Arthur Jarvis	Frank Bornamann, Joseph Spencer, Maquard Schwartz, Charles Daniels	Harald Julin, Robert Andersson, Charles Norelius, H. Johansson	Edmund Bernardt, Leopold Mayer, Simon Orlik, Otto Scheff		
HUN – 16.52.4	GER – 17:16.2	GBR	USA	SWE	AUT - *dnf*		

Chapter 5

Olympiad IV - 1908
London, England

The Olympic Games finally broke through as a world event at the 1908 London Games. There were 2,056 athletes representing twenty-two nations. A total of 36 women competed in these Games, but swimming was not yet an event on the women's Olympic program. The British Men's Swimming Team reigned, taking all but one gold.

Olympic 1ST

At the London Games, a 100m pool was constructed in the middle of Shepherd's Bush Stadium, where most of the Olympic events were held. This was the first time Olympic Swimming events were held in an actual pool! Later, the 50m pool would become the standard.

The Olympic swimming program consisted of six events including the 4X200m free relay event. It was at these Games that swimming as a sport began to organize on an international level and the International Swimming Federation was created.

SIR FRANK BEAUREPAIRE
AUSTRALIA

Sir Frank Beaurepaire of Australia won his first two Olympic medals at the 1908 London Games. He went on to earn four more Olympic medals, competing through 1924.

Beaurepaire was suspended from the 1912 Games for professionalism. His crime—lecturing on swimming and lifesaving, which were part of his job as a physical education teacher.

Beaurepaire's dream was to see the Olympic Games come to his country. In 1956, the Olympic Games were awarded to Melbourne, Australia, and Beaurepaire was elected "Lord Mayor," for a second time, to host the event. Unfortunately, Sir Frank passed away just seven months before the opening of those Games.

PAUL RADMILOVIC
GREAT BRITAIN

Competing in five Olympiads from 1908 to 1928, was Paul Radmilovic of Great Britain. "Raddy," as he was known, competed in both swimming and water polo events during his Olympic career.

Outside of the pool, Radmilovic was a scratch golfer and an outstanding "footballer" (soccer player).

Courtesy of ISHOF

He was active in international swimming for 35 years and swam a quarter-mile daily until his death at the age of 78.

HENRY TAYLOR
GREAT BRITAIN

"Happy" Henry Taylor, whose Olympic career spanned four Olympiads, made his first Olympic appearance at the Intercalated Games in 1906.

An orphan, Taylor was raised by his brother. He trained whenever he could, even during his lunch breaks as a cotton mill worker. He would train in any water he could find—in the canals and even in the baths on "dirty water day."

Courtesy of ISHOF

"Happy" Henry Taylor - the "Aquatic Marvel."

At the 1908 Olympic Games, Taylor was clocked at 22:48.4 minutes in the 1500m freestyle race, a time that was recognized as the first international world record for this event. He won a total of eight Olympic medals during his reign as the "Aquatic Marvel."

1908 OLYMPIC SWIMMING FINALS

Gold	Silver	Bronze	Fourth	Fifth	Sixth	Seventh	Eighth

INDIVIDUAL EVENTS

Men 100m Freestyle - World Record (1:05.8 Zoltán Halmay HUN)

Gold	Silver	Bronze	Fourth	Fifth	Sixth	Seventh	Eighth
Charles Daniels	Zoltán Halmay	Harald Julin	Leslie Rich				
USA – 1:05.6w	HUN – 1:06.2	SWE – 1:08.0	USA				

Men 400m Freestyle — World Record (5:19.0 440 yards)

Gold	Silver	Bronze	Fourth	Fifth	Sixth	Seventh	Eighth
Henry Taylor	Francis Beaurepaire	Otto Scheff	William Foster				
GBR – 5:36.8	AUS – 5:44.2	AUT – 5:46.0	GBR				

Men 1500m Freestyle

Gold	Silver	Bronze	Fourth	Fifth	Sixth	Seventh	Eighth
Henry Taylor	Thomas Battersby	Francis Beaurepaire	Otto Scheff				
GBR – 22:48.4w	GBR – 22:51.2	AUS – 22:56.2	AUT – dnf				

w World Record *o* Olympic Record *p* Preliminary Heat *dq* Disqualified *e* Equal to World Record *eo* Equal to Olympic Record
dns Did Not Start *dnf* Did Not Finish *ac* Also Competed *r* Relay Lead-off Split *E* Estimated

1908 OLYMPIC SWIMMING FINALS

Gold	Silver	Bronze	Fourth	Fifth	Sixth	Seventh	Eighth
Men 100m Backstroke – World Record (1.25.0)					1906 – Event Not Held On Olympic Program		
Arno Bieberstein	Ludvig Dam	Herbert Haresnape	Gustav Aurisch				
GER – 1:24.6 w	DEN – 1:26.6	GBR – 1:27.0	GER				
Men 200m Breaststroke				1896-1906 – Event Not Held On Olympic Program			
Frederick Holman	William Robinson	Pontus Hanson	Ödön Toldi				
GBR – 3:09.2 w	GBR – 3:12.8	SWE – 3:14.6	HUN – 3:15.2				

RELAY EVENT

Men 800m Freestyle Relay

Gold	Silver	Bronze	Fourth
John Derbyshire, Paul Radmilovic, William Foster, Henry Taylor	Harry Hebner, Leo Goodwin, Charles Daniels, Leslie Rich	József Munk, Imre Zachár, Béla Las-Torres, Zoltán Halmay	Francis Beaurepaire, Fred Springfield, Reginald "Snowy" Baker, Theodore Tartakover
GBR – 10:55.6w	USA – 11:02.8	HUN – 10:59.0	AUS/NZE

Chapter 6

Olympiad V - 1912
Stockholm, Sweden

The Games of 1912 were held in Stockholm, Sweden and 28 countries were represented. The swimming events were held in an "open air facility." A 100m pool was built into the Stockholm Harbor.

These Games hold the esteemed honor of being the first to see women competing in an Olympic swimming event. Pierre de Coubertin had not seen women in his vision of the Olympic Games. Unfortunately, James Sullivan of the United States, an active supporter of the AAU (American Athletic Union), shared de Coubertin's views.

Sullivan was able to block the Union's sponsorship of a National Championship for American women and in doing so, kept the U.S. women swimmers from participating in these Games.

These men were not the only roadblocks for women swimmers. Rose Scott of Australia, then considered a "feminist," resigned her office as President of the New South

Olympic 1ST

Women make first Olympic Splash!

In prior years the women's Olympic competition had been limited to tennis and other events that, shall we say, were "less revealing!"

Wales Ladies Swimming Association because the Sydney Club planned to send Sarah Durack and Mina Wylie to the 1912 Games.

Ms. Scott felt it was disgusting that men be allowed to attend and "watch" the competition. Men attended and even cheered, as both Durack and Wylie went on to capture medals.

SARAH "FANNY" DURACK
AUSTRALIA

Sarah "Fanny" Durack was the first woman to win an Olympic gold medal in any swimming event. She swam the

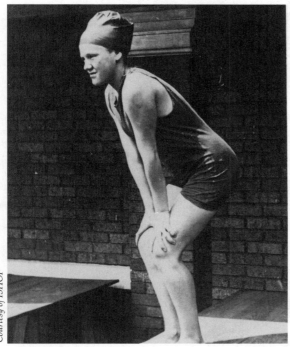

100m freestyle final to win in exactly the same time that Alfréd Hajós-Guttmann did in 1896.

In an earlier heat she set a world record in the 100m freestyle (1:19.8). At one time, Durack held every world record in women's swimming from 50 yards to one mile. Fanny set eleven world records between 1912 and 1918.

Courtesy of ISHOF

"Fanny"Durack, the first woman to win a gold medal in Olympic Swimming.

JENNIE FLETCHER
GREAT BRITAIN

Jennie Fletcher was Great Britain's first woman Olympic medalist. She received a bronze medal in the 100m free and a gold as part of England's relay team.

Great Britain's 400m freestyle relay team (l-r): Bella Moore, Jennie Fletcher, Annie Spiers, & Irene Steer.

Jennie was at her peak during the 1908 Olympic Games, but due to the lack of women competitors, her event was canceled. Ms. Fletcher held the world record for the 100y freestyle event for seven years. She broke that record herself eleven times in a three–year period.

When asked about her most memorable moment, she replied, "...when King Gustav of Sweden placed the classic laurel wreath on my head, put the gold around my neck and said, "Well done, England."

HARRY J. HEBNER
UNITED STATES

Courtesy of ISHOF.

Harry Hebner, America's first Olympic 100m backstroke gold medalist.

The first American swimmer to capture the gold medal in the 100m backstroke was Harry J. Hebner. Hebner was also a member of the silver medal relay team.

Hebner began his Olympic career in 1908 taking the bronze in the backstroke event. He ended his Olympic career in 1920 as a member of the water polo team and carried his country's flag during the opening ceremonies.

GEORGE HODGSON
CANADA

Canada's lone swimmer at the 1912 Olympic Games was George Hodgson. He earned gold in the 400m and the 1500m freestyle events, setting Olympic records in both. These records would stand until the 1924 Games.

Swimming the 1500m race Hodgson did something amazing — he broke three world records without ever leaving the pool! The first record came at the 1000m mark and the second at 1500 meters. Hodgson continued on until he reached his third record at one mile.

Hodgson enlisted in the Royal Naval Air Service in World War I and took part in a famed sea rescue, earning a medal of a different kind, the Silver Sea Gallantry medal.

In 1920 Hodgson competed in the Olympics but did not medal, considering himself lucky just to finish. An avid swimmer throughout his life, he swam three times a week into his late 80's.

Courtesy of ISHOF

Canada's George Hodgson broke three world records during one race.

SCORE
BOARD

Germany's Walter Bathe was one of two swimmers to collect two individual gold medals at the 1912 Stockholm Games. He won both the 200m and 400m breaststroke events.

Bathe's teammates Wilhelm Lutzow and Kurt Malisch followed him to the finish in the 200m breaststroke final. This is the only time Germany has swept this event in Olympic competition.

1912 OLYMPIC SWIMMING FINALS

| Gold | Silver | Bronze | Fourth | Fifth | Sixth | Seventh | Eighth |

INDIVIDUAL EVENTS

Women 100m Freestyle - World Record (1:20.6 Daisy Curwen GBR)   1896-1908 – Event Not Held On Olympic Program

Gold	Silver	Bronze	Fourth	Fifth	Sixth
Sarah "Fanny" Durack p - 1:19.8 w	Wilhelmina Wylie	Jennie Fletcher	Margarete "Grete" Rosenberg	Annie Speirs	Daisy Curwen
AUS – 1:22.2	AUS – 1:25.4	GBR – 1:27.0	GER – 1:27.4	GBR – 1:27.4	GBR – dns

Men 100m Freestyle - World Record (1:02.4 Kurt Bretting GER)   Olympic Record (1:05.6 Charles Daniels USA 1908)

Gold	Silver	Bronze	Fourth	Fifth	Sixth
Duke Paoa Kahanamoku p - 1:02.4 e	Cecil Healy	Kenneth Huszagh	Kurt Bretting	Walter Ramme	William Longworth
USA - 1:03.4	AUS – 1:04.6	USA – 1:05.6	GER – 1:05.8	GER – 1:06.4	AUS – dns

Men 400m Freestyle - World Record (5:23.0 Frank Beaurepaire AUS)

Gold	Silver	Bronze	Fourth	Fifth
George Hodgson	John Hatfield	Harold Hardwick	Cecil Healy	Béla Las-Torres
CAN – 5:24.4 o	GBR – 5:25.8	AUS - 5:31.2	AUS - 5:37.8	HUN – 5:42.0

w World Record   *o* Olympic Record   *p* Preliminary Heat   *dq* Disqualified   *e* Equal to World Record   *eo* Equal to Olympic Record
dns Did Not Start   *dnf* Did Not Finish   *ac* Also Competed   *r* Relay Lead-off Split   *E* Estimated

OLYMPIAD V – 1912 – STOCKHOLM, SWEDEN

1912 OLYMPIC SWIMMING FINALS

Gold	Silver	Bronze	Fourth	Fifth	Sixth	Seventh	Eighth
Men 1500m Freestyle - World and Olympic Record (22:48.4 Henry Taylor GBR 1908)							
George Hodgson CAN – 22:00.0w	John Hatfield GBR – 22:39.0	Harold Hardwick AUS – 23:15.4	Malcolm Champion NZE - dnf	Béla Las-Torres HUN - dnf			
Men 100m Backstroke - World Record (1:15.6 Otto Fahr GER) Olympic Record (1:24.6 Arno Bieberstein GER 1908)							
Harry Hebner p – 1:20.8 o USA – 1:21.2	Otto Fahr GER - 1:22.4	Paul Kellner GER - 1:24.0	András Baronyi HUN - 1:25.2	Otto Gross GER - 1:25.8			
Men 200m Breaststroke - World Record (3:00.8 Felicien Coubert FRA) Olympic Record (3:09.2 Frederick Holman GBR 1908)							
Walter Bathe GER – 3:01.8 o	Wilhelm Lützow GER – 3:05.0	Kurt Mählisch GER – 3:08.0	Percy Courtman GBR – 3:08.8	Thor Henning SWE – dnf			
Men 400m Breaststroke							
Walter Bathe GER – 6:29.6 o	Thor Henning SWE – 6:35.6	Percy Courtman GBR – 6:36.4	Kurt Malisch GER – 6:37.0	Wilhelm Lützow GER - dnf			

1906-1908 – Event Not Held On Olympic Program

1912 OLYMPIC SWIMMING FINALS

RELAY EVENTS

Gold	Silver	Bronze	Fourth	Fifth	Sixth	Seventh	Eighth

Women 400m Freestyle Relay

1896-1908 – Event Not Held On Olympic Program

Gold	Silver	Bronze	Fourth	Fifth	Sixth	Seventh	Eighth
Isabella Moore, Jennie Fletcher, Annie Speirs, Irene Steer	Wally Dressel, Louise Otto, Hermine Stindt, Margarete Rosenberg	Margarete Adler, Klara Milch, Josephine Sticker, Berta Zahourek	Greta Johansson, Karin Lundgren, Sonja Johnsson, Vera Thulin				
GBR – 5:52.8 w	GER – 6:04.6	AUT – 6:17.0	SWE				

Men 800m Freestyle Relay - World and Olympic Record (10:55.6 GBR 1908)

Gold	Silver	Bronze	Fourth	Fifth	Sixth	Seventh	Eighth
Cecil Healy, Malcolm Champion, Leslie Boardman, Harold Hardwick	Kenneth Huszagh, Harry Hebner, Perry McGillivray, Duke Paoa Kahanamoku	William Foster, Thomas Battersby, John Hatfield, Henry Taylor	Oskar Schiele, Georg Kunisch, Kurt Bretting, Max Ritter				
AUS/NZE 10:11.6 w	USA – 10:20.0	GBR – 10:28.2	GER – 10:37.0				

Chapter 7

Olympiad VI - 1916
Berlin, Germany

he 1916 Olympic Games were to be held in Berlin, Germany. World War I, which had started in August of 1914, was only half over. There would be no Sixth Olympiad.

Olympiad VII - 1920
Antwerp, Belgium

n 1920, eight years since the last competition, the Olympic Games resumed in Antwerp, Belgium. Central Europe and Russia, still recovering from the war, did not send athletes to this Olympiad.

These Games marked the arrival of American women as competitors—and what a debut they

Olympic 1ST

The Olympic Flag was introduced with its five inter-locking rings. Each ring represented the original five major continents that were committed to participating in the Games at this time. The colors of red, blue, yel-low, green and black were chosen so that each nation could find its own flag's color represented.

The Olympic Creed was also introduced at these Games. Both the Flag and the Creed remain a part of the Olym-pic tradition today.

made! The U.S. women made a clean sweep of medals in the two individual swimming events held. Their relay team in the 4X100m freestyle event touched an incredible 29 seconds faster than the silver medal British Team.

The United States Men's Team was equally amazing. They captured gold in every event, with the exception of the two breast-stroke events, and won a convincing victory in their freestyle relay.

ETHELDA BLEIBTREY
UNITED STATES

Ethelda Bleibtrey was the first woman from the United States to win an Olympic title. She won the 100m freestyle event, defeating her next competitor by over three seconds, setting a world record mark in the process. She would follow-up with two more gold medals, sweeping the women's events.

The swimming events at the 1920 Olympics were held in a "tidal estuary" (the narrow area where a river meets the sea), and according to Bleibtrey, "they were swimming in mud, not water." With that in mind, her times were even more incredible.

Bleibtrey initially started swimming to counteract the effects of childhood polio. She began swimming competitively only to keep her friend and fellow swimmer, Charlotte Boyle company. Before long Ethelda won every national championship from 50 yards on up, remaining undefeated throughout her amateur career.

Bleibtrey would become more notorious for her adventures outside of the Olympic arena. She was a "trail blazer," breaking the rules, laws and traditions that were considered taboo for women in her day.

Courtesy of ISHOF

Ethelda Bleibtrey - America's first female Olympic Swim Champion.

In the early 1900's, women were expected to dress modestly on the public beaches. The attire included a heavy "bathing costume," made up of "foundation garments" (bra/girdle/corset), stockings (worn with high laced shoes), a hat and the all-essential "modest skirt" (which was worn by men as well).

In 1919, Bleibtrey was issued a citation and jailed for "Nude Swimming" on Manhattan Beach—she had removed her stockings before entering the water. Shame on you Ethelda! All this notoriety won her public favor and before long women were "liberated" from having to swim with stockings.

That was not the end of Bleibtrey's brush with the law. In 1928, she turned "pro" and was on what was known as a "tank tour." During one show the tank leaked all over the theater in which they were performing. The owners cut Bleibtrey from the remaining weeks of the tour and sued her, causing her great financial difficulty.

At about the same time the New York Daily News was campaigning to open the Central Park Reservoir for public swimming. New York had a shortage of public swimming facilities. They "arranged" for Ethelda to be arrested for swimming in the reservoir.

Arrested she was, transported to the New York City Police Station by paddy wagon and thrown in jail for the night! Bleibtrey was paid $1,000 for the stunt and New York opened its first large public swimming facility soon after. It was all for the good of swimming, of course!

Ethelda Bleibtrey, with help, went on to form the United States Olympians Association and to teach and coach swimming. She is truly one of America's great pioneers for women's swimming and women in general.

OFF THE

Courtesy of ISHOF

"Slowpolka" to Belgium

For all the glory the U.S. Olympic Team earned in 1920, what they may remember most was the trip to Belgium. The team was scheduled to sail on the "Great Northern," one of the fastest and finest troop ships. Unfortunately, the ship broke down just prior to departure.

The "Princess Matioke," a funeral ship, was available. Athletes boarded amongst harbor docks lined with the 1800 caskets of American war dead that had just been taken from the ship.

The sleeping quarters smelled like formaldehyde and the ship was infested with rats. The men slept in the hold of the ship, curling up in triple-decker hammocks that hung from chains. The women were somewhat better off with accommodations on the upper deck.

It was rumored that the athletes passed the time throwing bottles at the "little rodents". They nicknamed the ship "Princess Slowpolka" because the miserable trip took almost two weeks!

The conditions of this ship were so poor that members of the Olympic team, led by swimmer Norman Ross, later staged a "sit-in," refusing to return home on board the "Princess."

DUKE KAHANAMOKU
UNITED STATES

Duke Kahanmoku was, by most accounts, America's first "super star" swimming champion. He was born of Hawaiian royalty, the son of Princess Ruth, in Honolulu, Hawaii.

Kahanamoku participated in four Olympiads, ('12, '20, '24, '32) three as a swimmer and one as a member of the water polo team, at the age of 41. Had the 1916 Games been held and had he not been stricken by illness in 1928, his Olympic career may have been even more amazing.

Duke "crawled" over the surface of the water like no one had done before and he did it in times that few could believe. In 1911, as an unknown swimmer, he bettered the world records in the 50y and 100y freestyle events by over one and one–half and four and one–half seconds respectively. His 100y time made him the first man to officially break the one-minute barrier, eventually lowering his time to 53 seconds.

These times were so startling that the A.A.U. (American Athletic Union) refused to sanction them. Documentation was gathered showing that a registered surveyor had measured the course before the race and three times afterwards.

Duke with Ethelda Bleibtrey (R), Charlotte Boyle, and his surfboard!

Courtesy of ISHOF

The documentation also confirmed that the swim was done against the tide and swimmers had no advantage. Duke's closest competitor in the 100y race finished an incredible 10 yards behind him.

This evidence was still not enough for President Wahle of the A.A.U. He felt that Kahanamoku should prove himself against the swimmers of the "mainland" before his records could be sanctioned.

Duke would have to prove himself time and time again. In the 100m freestyle event at the Stockholm Games, he won his two preliminary heats easily, but due to a misunderstanding he and fellow Americans Kenneth Huszagh and Perry McGill missed the semi-final heat.

SCORE
BOARD

The men's 200m and 400m breaststroke events in Antwerp were carbon copy races. The same four swimmers had exactly the same finishes in each race.

GOLD   Håkan Malmroth
        Sweden

SILVER Thor Henning
        Sweden

BRONZE Arvo Aaltonen
        Finland

FOURTH Jack Howell
        U.S.A.

Officials recognized that a final without the now favored Hawaiian would be ridiculous and decided to hold a special heat. Duke and Huszagh made the final, both swam to medals and all three of these Americans would swim to a silver medal in the 4X200m free relay.

In Belgium, at the 1920 Olympic Games, Duke became caught up in another controversy through no fault of his own. He won the 100m freestyle event on his birthday, and set a new world record over that distance. The Australians protested that their man had been boxed in (there were still no lane lines at this time). It was ordered that the final be repeated. This race ended in the exact same order as the first.

Kahanamoku's contributions to water sports were many. He was an outstanding surfer and is believed to have brought that sport to Australia and other countries in his travels as a Red Cross instructor.

Kahanamoku is also credited with inventing board (wind) surfing and was one of the first known to surf behind the wake of a motorboat. In 1925 at Newport Beach, California, a yacht capsized and Duke, utilizing his surfboard, rescued eight of the passengers from the ocean. Unfortunately, 17 others drowned.

The popular athlete worked in Hollywood for some years, appearing in several films. Duke Kahanamoku returned home and served as Sheriff of Honolulu for two decades.

NORMAN ROSS
UNITED STATES

Norman Ross was a triple gold medalist at the 1920 Games. He, too, was involved in the 100m freestyle lane controversy at Antwerp, having been the one to unintentionally interfere with the Australian swimmer. Ross, after being disqualified, was not in the water when the final was held again.

Olympic 1ST

You're Outta Here!

American Norman Ross, had the first "D.Q." in an Olympic Swimming event.

OUT!

Courtesy of ISHOF

Triple gold medalist - Norman Ross

Ross made a name for himself out of the water as well. He was the rebellion leader who rallied his fellow Olympic teammates to stage a "sit-in," in protest for better accommodations for the voyage home. Their effort was successful and the "Princess" sailed home without the 1920 Olympic Team.

1920 OLYMPIC SWIMMING FINALS

Gold	Silver	Bronze	Fourth	Fifth	Sixth	Seventh	Eighth

INDIVIDUAL EVENTS

Women 100m Freestyle - World Record (1:16.2 Sarah "Fanny" Durack AUS)   Olympic Record (1:19.8 S. Durack AUS 1912)

Gold	Silver	Bronze	Fourth	Fifth	Sixth	Seventh	Eighth
Ethelda Bleibtrey	Irene Guest	Frances Schroth	Constance Jeans	Violet Walrond	Jane Gylling	Charlotte Boyle	
USA – 1:13.6 w	USA – 1:17.0	USA – 1:17.2	GBR – 1:22.8	NZE	SWE	USA – dnf	

Men 100m Freestyle - World Record (1:01.4 Duke Kahanamoku USA)   Olympic Record (1:02.4 Duke Kahanamoku USA 1912)

Gold	Silver	Bronze	Fourth	Fifth	Sixth	Seventh	Eighth
Duke Paoa Kahanamoku	Pua Kela Kealoha	William Harris	William Herald	Norman Ross			
USA – 1:00.4 w *1:01.4	USA – 1:02.2 *1:02.6	USA – 1:03.2 *1:03.0	AUS – *1:03.8	USA – dq			

Women 400m Freestyle – World Record (4:43.6 300m)   1896-1912 – Event Not Held On Olympic Program

Gold	Silver	Bronze	Fourth	Fifth	Sixth	Seventh	Eighth
Ethelda Bleibtrey	Margaret Woodbridge	Frances Schroth	Constance Jeans	Eleanor Uhl	Jane Gylling	Violet Walrond	
USA – 4:34.0 w	USA – 4:42.8	USA – 4:52.0	GBR – 4:52.4	USA	SWE	NZE	

w World Record *o* Olympic Record *p* Preliminary Heat *dq* Disqualified *e* Equal to World Record *eo* Equal to Olympic Record
dns Did Not Start *dnf* Did Not Finish *ac* Also Competed *r* Relay Lead-off Split *E* Estimated

* Second final was held because William Herald of Australia had been fouled (interference) by American Norman Ross.

OLYMPIAD VII – 1920 – ANTWERP, BELGIUM

1920 OLYMPIC SWIMMING FINALS

Gold	Silver	Bronze	Fourth	Fifth	Sixth	Seventh	Eighth
Men 400m Freestyle - World Record (5:14.6 Norman Ross USA)					Olympic Record (5:24.4 George Hodgson CAN 1912)		
Norman Ross	Ludy Langer	George Vernot	Fred Kahele	Francis Beaurepaire			
USA – 5:26.8	USA – 5:29.0	CAN – 5:29.6	USA	AUS – *dnf*			
Men 1500m Freestyle - World and Olympic Record (22:00.0 George Hodgson CAN 1912)							
Norman Ross	George Vernot	Francis Beaurepaire	Fred Kahele	Eugene Bolden			
USA – 22:23.2	CAN – 22:36.4*E*	AUS – 23:04.0*E*	USA – 23:59.1*E*	USA – 24:04.3*E*			
Men 100m Backstroke - World Record (1:15.6 Otto Fahr GER)					Olympic Record (1:20.8 Harry Hebner USA 1912)		
Warren Paoa Kealoha *p* – 1:14.8 *w*	Ray Kegeris	Gérard Blitz	Percy McGillivray	Harold Kruger			
USA – 1:15.2	USA – 1:16.8	BEL – 1:19.0	USA – 1:19.4	USA			
Men 200m Breaststroke - World Record (2:56.6 Percy Courtman GBR)					Olympic Record (3:01.8 Walter Bathe GER 1912)		
Håkan Malmroth	Thor Henning	Arvo Aaltonen	Jack Howell	Ivan Stedman	Per Cederblom		
SWE – 3:04.4	SWE – 3:09.2	FIN – 3:12.2	USA	AUS	SWE - *dnf*		
Men 400m Breaststroke – Discontinued Event							
Håkan Malmroth	Thor Henning	Arvo Aaltonen	Jack Howell	Per Cederblom			
SWE – 6:31.8	SWE – 6:45.2	FIN – 6:48.0	USA – 6:51.0	SWE			

1920 OLYMPIC SWIMMING FINALS

RELAY EVENTS

	Gold	Silver	Bronze	Fourth	Fifth	Sixth	Seventh	Eighth

Women 400m Freestyle Relay   Olympic Record (5:52.8 GBR 1912)

	Gold	Silver	Bronze
	USA – 5:11.6"	GBR – 5:40.8	SWE – 5:43.6
	Margaret Woodbridge, Frances Schroth, Irene Guest, Ethelda Bleibtrey	Hilda James, Constance Jeans, Charlotte Radcliffe, Grace McKenzie	Aina Berg, Emy Machnow, Karin Nilsson, Jane Gylling

Men 800m Freestyle Relay - World and Olympic Record (10:11.6 AUS/NZE 1912)

	Gold	Silver	Bronze	Fourth	Fifth
	USA – 10:04.4w	AUS – 10:25.4	GBR – 10:37.2	SWE – 10:50.2	ITA
	Perry McGillivray, Pua Kela Kealoha, Norman Ross, Duke Paoa Kahanamoku	Henry Hay, William Herald, Ivan Stedman, Francis Beaurepaire, *p* – Keith Kirkland	Leslie Savage, Edward Percival Taylor, Henry Harold Annison	Robert Andersson, Frans Möller, Orvar Trolle, Arne Borg	Mario Massa, Agostino Frassinetti, Antonio Quarantotto, Gilio Bisagno

Chapter 8

Olympiad VIII - 1924
Paris, France

he eighth Olympiad, held in Paris, France, saw the popularity of the Games grow enormously. Forty-four countries were represented with competitors numbering 3,092.

American swimmers again took center stage. Following in the successful wake of "The Duke," this United States team was dominated by Hawaiians (eight men and one woman, Mariechen Wehselau).

Courtesy of ISHOF

The United States Olympic Men's Swim Team swam to gold in every event, with the exception of the 1500m freestyle, where they were completely shut out. The American Women's Swim Team collectively won nine of the possible twelve individual medals offered on the Olympic Women's Swim Program. They also went on to seize the 4X100m freestyle relay title, thrashing the second place team by over 18 seconds.

Unlike the nightmarish voyage of 1920, the Americans were actually able to train on board ship. The swimmers wore a harness and were suspended from a cable, "swimming in place" in the small canvass pool below deck.

Courtesy of ISHOF

Training aboard ship

These Americans, however, had problems of their own. The United States Olympic Committee and assorted American officials (probably parents as well!), were overly concerned about shielding their young women swimmers from the "immoral" influences and temptations of Paris. Their solution was to house the women far outside the city, forcing them to spend five to six hours daily, traveling to and from the Olympic pool site.

L A N E   L I N E S

Divide and Conquer!

After the controversies in the pool at the 1920 Games, "lane dividers" were introduced and would become a standard in Olympic competition.

SYBIL BAUER
UNITED STATES

Sybil Bauer came to the 1924 Olympic Games holding *every* existing world record for the backstroke, at *every* distance. Prior to the Paris Games, Bauer broke Stubby Kruger's 440y backstroke world record by *four seconds*, becoming the first woman ever to break an existing men's world record in swimming. That meet, unfortunately, was not sanctioned and the time was not official.

Bauer easily captured the gold in Paris, beating out her closest competitor by four seconds. During her six years of competitive swimming she set 23 world records. Bauer was, without a doubt, the world's first dominant women's backstroker.

At the peak of her career, Sybil Bauer was stricken with cancer. She was engaged to Ed Sullivan, a Chicago sports writer who would go on to host the incredibly popular "Ed Sullivan Show."

At her funeral six world class swimmers, including Johnny Weissmuller, served as pallbearers. At the time of her death, twenty-two year old Sybil Bauer still held eight existing national and world records.

ANDREW CHARLTON
AUSTRALIA

Andrew "Boy" Charlton grew up in the slums just outside of Sydney, Australia. Tom Adrian, a well-known swimmer turned coach, adopted Charlton. At the age of five Charlton won his first race and at fifteen, he held his first world record.

Charlton and Adrian traveled to the Paris Games by ocean liner. On the way, Adrian suffered a nervous breakdown and was rescued after jumping into the sea. There was speculation Charlton's performance would suffer after this traumatic incident.

Andrew "Boy" Charlton - holder of five Olympic medals

"Boy" not only won the 1500m event, but broke Arne Borg's two day-old record by over one minute! Charlton collected a total of five Olympic medals attending the 1924 and 1928 Games.

GERTRUDE EDERLE
UNITED STATES

The remarkable Gertrude Ederle, was a triple medalist at these Games, earning a bronze in both the 100m and 400m freestyle and a gold medal as a member of the women's 4 X 100m free relay squad.

Ederle, however, earned her true fame outside of the Olympic arena. Born on October 23, 1906, in New York City, she became, at twelve, the youngest person ever to break a world record. In 1925, after the Olympic Games, she gave up her amateur status and turned toward a new goal.

Primarily a distance swimmer, she announced her plans to become the first woman ever to swim the English Channel. Up until this time only six people, all men, had accomplished this grueling swim.

The *London Daily News* responded to her announcement with the following; "Even the most uncompromising champion of the rights and capacities of women, must admit that in contests of physical skill, speed and endurance, they must remain the weaker sex."

On August 6, 1926, just after 7:00 a.m., Gertrude Ederle started her historic swim from the French shore. She arrived in England 14 hours and 31 minutes later. Her swim destroyed the current men's record by more than TWO HOURS and stood as a record for women for some 38 years.

Ederle became a national hero and came home to a ticker tape parade in New York City, where an estimated two million people lined the streets to catch a glimpse of her.

Courtesy of ISHOF

Ederle's ticker tape parade

Unfortunately, hard times hit for Ederle. The Channel swim had damaged both her eardrums leaving her deaf. She spent some time touring the vaudeville circuit, performing in a huge collapsible swimming tank, but this soon proved too much for her.

Ederle suffered a nervous breakdown and later, spent four years in a cast recovering from a back injury. In 1933, summoning all of the strength, courage and spirit she possessed, Gertrude was able to rebound from these hardships and went on to teach deaf children to swim.

WARREN KEALOHA
UNITED STATES

On his first day of competitive swim *practice*, Warren Kealoha unofficially broke a world record for the 100y backstroke.

In 1920, at the age of 16, Warren made his first Olympic appearance, winning the first of his two Olympic titles. However, before he could be awarded the gold medal, a debate took place over whether Warren's unusual backstroke style was legal. Satisfied that Kealoha's method was legitimate, the judges allowed his victory to stand. Kealoha's unusual stroke is the same technique used around the world today.

Warren Kealoha - first swimmer to win gold in the 100m backstroke in two consecutive Games.

It was a family affair for the Kealohas at the 1920 Olympic Games. Pua Kealoha, Warren's brother earned a relay gold medal, as well as a silver medal in the 100m freestyle.

Warren repeated his golden performance once again in 1924, becoming the first to win gold in the 100m backstroke at two consecutive Olympiads.

ETHEL LACKIE
UNITED STATES

Seventeen-year-old Ethel Lackie was a double gold medalist at the Paris Games. In an American sweep of the 100m freestyle final, Lackie blazed past American teammates Mariechen Wehselau and Gertrude Ederle in the last 25 meters of the race. She won her second gold as a member of the 4X100m freestyle relay team.

Lackie and American teammate Johnny Weissmuller were both coached by the beefy William Bachrach of Chicago's Illinois Athletic Club. Both swimmers swam to victory in the 100m freestyle events at the 1924 Games, making "Big Bill" the first person to coach both the men's and women's champion in this event at the same Olympiad.

Lackie would go on to break the 100y freestyle world record in 1926. She became the first woman to swim this event in under 1:01.00. The one-minute barrier would not be broken until 1934.

Olympic 1ST

British Invasion

Lucy Morton was the first British woman to win an individual Olympic swimming title. Her victory in the 200m breaststroke event prevented an all-American gold sweep.

Phyllis Harding of Great Britain was the first female swimmer to compete in four Olympiads. She medaled at the 1924 competition, winning silver in the 100m backstroke.

AILEEN RIGGIN
UNITED STATES

Fourteen year-old Aileen Riggin of the United States made her first appearance at the 1920 Games, at all of four feet, eight inches and seventy pounds. She won gold in the springboard diving event, thus making her the youngest champion of these Games.

Young Olympian to Master's Swimmer

Upon her return to the Games in 1924, Riggin was the first athlete to compete in two different sports at the same Olympiad. The versatile Riggin became the first athlete to win medals in *both* swimming and diving at the same Olympic Games. She captured the silver medal for springboard diving and a bronze medal in the 100m backstroke event.

Photos donated by Aileen Riggin-Soule

In 1922, Aileen Riggin starred in the first slow motion and underwater coaching/training films ever made. After turning professional she toured the world, performing with Gertrude Ederle and Helen Wainwright. Ms. Riggin went on to help Billy Rose with his first "Aquacade," a spectacular water show, and appeared in two Hollywood musicals as well. The multi-talented Riggin authored numerous articles that appeared in national publications on swimming, diving and women in sport.

Aileen Riggin Soule also competed in the 90-94 age group of U.S. Master Swimming, and held Masters records. Riggin has one piece of advice to offer Olympic hopefuls, "Stick with it! Never give up!"

HELEN WAINWRIGHT
UNITED STATES

Helen Wainwright was another U.S. swimmer and diver, one of only three athletes in Olympic history to win medals in both categories. Wainwright dove her way to silver in the springboard event at the 1920 Games, and returned in 1924 to take a silver medal in the 400m freestyle final.

By 1926 Wainwright had turned professional, and traveled the tank tours with Olympic teammates and friends Aileen Riggin and Gertrude Ederle.

Courtesy of ISHOF

400m U.S. sweep. (l-r) gold: Martha Norelius, silver: Helen Wainwright, and bronze: Gertrude Ederle

During WWII, Wainwright donated her numerous medals and trophies for the metal needed in the war effort, with two exceptions: her Olympic and National medals.

1924 OLYMPIC SWIMMING FINALS

INDIVIDUAL EVENTS

	Gold	Silver	Bronze	Fourth	Fifth	Sixth	Seventh	Eighth
Women 100m Freestyle - World Record (1:12.8 Gertrude Ederle USA) Olympic Record (1:13.6 Ethelda Bleibtrey USA 1920)								
	Ethel Lackie	Mariechen Wehselau p – 1:12.2 w	Gertrude Ederle	Constance Jeans	Irene Tanner	Maria Vierdag		
	USA – 1:12.4	USA – 1:12.8	USA – 1:14.2	GBR – 1:15.4	GBR – 1:20.8	NED		
Men 100m Freestyle - World Record (57.4 Johnny Weissmuller USA) Olympic Record (1:00.4 Duke P. Kahanamoku USA 1920)								
	Johnny Weissmuller	Duke Kahanamoku	Samuel Kahanamoku	Arne Borg	Katsuo Takaishi	Orvar Trolle		
	USA – 59.0 o	USA – 1:01.4	USA – 1:01.8	SWE – 1:02.0	JPN – 1:03.0	SWE		
Women 400m Freestyle – World Record (5:53.2 G. Ederle USA) Olympic Record (300m 4:34.0 E. Bleibtrey USA 1920)								
	Martha Norelius	Helen Wainwright	Gertrude Ederle	Doris Molesworth	Gwitha Shand	Irene Tanner		
	USA – 6:02.2 o	USA – 6:03.8	USA – 6:04.8	GBR – 6:25.4	NZE – dnf	GBR		
Men 400m Freestyle - World Record (4:54.7 Arne Borg SWE) Olympic Record (5:24.4 George Hodgson CAN 1912)								
	Johnny Weissmuller	Arne Borg	Andrew "Boy" Charlton	Åke Borg	John Hatfield	Lester Smith		
	USA – 5:04.2 o	SWE – 5:05.6	AUS – 5:06.6	SWE – 5:26.0	GBR – 5:32.0	USA		

w World Record *o* Olympic Record *p* Preliminary Heat *dq* Disqualified *e* Equal to World Record *eo* Equal to Olympic Record
dns Did Not Start *dnf* Did Not Finish *ac* Also Competed *r* Relay Lead-off Split *E* Estimated

OLYMPIAD VIII – 1924 – PARIS, FRANCE

1924 OLYMPIC SWIMMING FINALS

	Gold	Silver	Bronze	Fourth	Fifth	Sixth	Seventh	Eighth

Men 1500m Freestyle - World Record (21:15.0 Arne Borg SWE)   Olympic Record (22:00.0 George Hodgson CAN 1912)

	Gold	Silver	Bronze	Fourth	Fifth	Sixth	Seventh	Eighth
	Andrew "Boy" Charlton	Arne Borg	Francis Beaurepaire	John Hatfield	Katsuo Takaishi	Åke Borg		
	AUS – 20:06.6w	SWE – 20:41.4	AUS – 21:48.4	GBR – 21:55.6	JPN – 22:10.4	SWE		

Women 100m Backstroke - World Record (1:22.4 Sybil Bauer USA)   1896-1920 - Event Not Held On Olympic Program

	Gold	Silver	Bronze	Fourth	Fifth	Sixth	Seventh	Eighth
	Sybil Bauer	Phyllis Harding	Aileen Riggin	Florence Chambers	Jarmila Müllerová	Ellen King		
	USA – 1:23.2 o	GBR – 1:27.4	USA – 1:28.2	USA – 1:30.8	CZE – 1:31.2	GBR		

Men 100m Backstroke - World Record (1:12.4 Warren Kealoha USA)   Olympic Record (1:14.8 Warren Kealoha USA 1920)

	Gold	Silver	Bronze	Fourth	Fifth	Sixth	Seventh	Eighth
	Warren Paoa Kealoha	Paul Wyatt	Károly Bartha	Gérard Blitz	Austin Rawlinson	Giyo Saito		
	USA – 1:13.2 o	USA – 1:15.4	HUN – 1:17.8	BEL – 1:19.6	GBR – 1:20.0	JPN		

Women 200m Breaststroke - World Record (3:20.4 Irene Gilbert GBR)   1896-1920 – Event Not Held On Olympic Program

	Gold	Silver	Bronze	Fourth	Fifth	Sixth	Seventh	Eighth
	Lucy Morton	Agnes Geraghty	Gladys Carson	Vivan Pettersson	Irene Gilbert	Laury Koster	Hjördis Topel	
	GBR – 3:33.2 o	USA – 3:34.0	GBR – 3:35.4	SWE – 3:37.6	GBR – 3:38.0	LUX – 3:39.2	SWE – 3:47.6	

Men 200m Breaststroke - World Record (2:50.4 Erich Rademacher GER)   Olympic Record (3:01.8 Walter Bathe GER 1912)

	Gold	Silver	Bronze	Fourth	Fifth	Sixth	Seventh	Eighth
	Robert Skelton p - 2:56.0 o	Joseph de Combe	William Kirschbaum	Bengt Linders	Robert Wyss	Thor Henning		
	USA – 2:56.6	BEL – 2:59.2	USA – 3:01.0	SWE – 3:02.2	SUI – 3:05.6	SWE		

1924 OLYMPIC SWIMMING FINALS

RELAY EVENTS

	Gold	Silver	Bronze	Fourth	Fifth	Sixth	Seventh	Eighth	Olympic Record (5:11.6 USA 1920)

Women 400m Freestyle Relay

Gold	Silver	Bronze	Fourth	Fifth	Sixth
Gertrude Ederle, Euphrasia Donnelly, Ethel Lackie, Mariechen Wehselau	Florence Barker, Grace McKenzie, Irene Vera Tanner, Constance Jeans	Aina Berg, Vivan Pettersson, Gulli Everlund, Hjördis Töpel	Vibeke Möller, Hedevig Rasmussen, Karen Maud Rasmussen, Agnete Olsen	Ernestine Lebrun, Gilberte Mortier, Bibienne Pellegry, Marguerite Protin	Mietje Baron, Alida Bolten, Geertruida Klapwijk, Maria Vierdag
USA – 4:58.8 "w"	GBR – 5:17.0	SWE – 5:35.6	DEN – 5:42.4	FRA – 5:43.4	NED – 5:45.8

Men 800m Freestyle Relay - World and Olympic Record (10:04.4 USA 1920)

Gold	Silver	Bronze	Fourth	Fifth	Sixth
J. Wallace O'Connor, Harrison Glancy, Ralph Breyer, Johnny Weissmuller, p – Richard Howell	Maurice Christie, Ernest Henry, Francis Beaurepaire, Andrew "Boy" Charlton, p – Ivan Stedman	Georg Werner, Orvar Trolle, Åke Borg, Anne Borg, p – Thor Henning, Gösta Persson	Torahiko Miyahata, Katsuo Takaishi, Kazuo Noda, Kazuo Onoda	John Thomson, Albert Dicken, Harold Annison, Edward Percival Peter, p – Leslie Savage	Guy Middleton, Henri Padou, Edouard Vanzeveren, Emile Zeibig
USA – 9:53.4 w	AUS – 10:02.2	SWE – 10:06.8	JPN – 10:15.2	GBR – 10:29.4	FRA

Chapter 9

Olympiad IX - 1928
Amsterdam, The Netherlands

hundreds of pigeons, an "ancient games" symbol of peace, were released, adding drama to the opening ceremony in Amsterdam. Forty-six countries were represented with a total of 3,014 athletes participating.

The United States swimmers captured six of a possible eleven gold medals, with the remaining five awarded to five different countries. This was a sign of things to come.

Olympic 1ST

An En"light"ening Tradition Begins

The burning of the "Olympic Flame" throughout Olympic competition had its start in Amsterdam and continues on as tradition today.

ARNE BORG
SWEDEN

Though Arne Borg collected three medals at the 1924 Olympic Games his *golden moment* finally came in Amsterdam, where he swam to gold in the 1500m freestyle final.

In Spain, a year prior to the 1928 Olympic Games, Borg set a world record time of 19:07.2 in the 1500m free event.

Arne Borg takes his start.

What is even more amazing is he swam this race right after having had a few teeth knocked out in a water polo match! Ouch!

Borg, like American swimming sensation Johnny Weissmuller, was popular at home and abroad and both were known for their fun loving antics. When Borg was called up for military service during peacetime, he chose to travel to Spain for a planned vacation. In spite of his popularity, Borg was sent to prison. While there, he received so many gifts of food and wine that he gained seventeen pounds by his release!

During his peak years Borg was considered the world's premier distance swimmer. From 1921 to 1929 this prolific record breaker set 30 individual world records.

GEORGE KOJAC
UNITED STATES

George Kojac was a double gold medalist at the 1928 Olympic Games. He led the sweep for the United States in the 100m backstroke event and was a member of the 4X200m freestyle relay team that set a world record (9:36.2). During his swimming career Kojac would hold a grand total of 23 world records.

Upon graduating from Rutgers University he went on to attend Columbia Medical School, sacrificing the 1932 Games to concentrate on his studies.

George Kojac's time in the 100m backstroke at the 1928 Olympic Games was the *only* men's swimming time not broken during the 1932 Games. Dr. George Kojac went on to represent his country again, this time as a surgeon in the military.

MARTHA NORELIUS
UNITED STATES

In 1924, at fifteen years of age, Martha Norelius won her first gold medal in the 400m freestyle final, defeating team-

SCORE
BOARD

Seventeen-year-old Maria "Sis" Braun of Holland touched out Ellen King of Great Britain for the win in the 100m backstroke event. Braun had set a new world record for this event during her preliminary heat (1:21.6). The youngster from Holland also collected a silver medal in the 400m freestyle event.

mates Gertrude Ederle and Helen Wainwright. She returned in 1928 and became the first woman to capture gold medals, in the same event, in consecutive Games. This feat in the women's 400m freestyle event has never been repeated.

This Swedish born, U.S. raised, athlete spent the summer of 1927 setting world records—29 to be exact! Johnny Weissmuller set a *mere* 16 world records that same summer.

Norelius was superstitious and believed she couldn't swim without her trademark "cap." On one occasion, during a National 500y event, she was still putting on

Norelius in training.

Courtesy of ISHOF

her cap when the starting pistol went off. Diving in well after the other swimmers, she still managed to win the event. Her father's comment; "She knew she had plenty of time."

Martha ended her amateur career in 1929 after being suspended by the AAU for swimming with professionals during an exhibition in Miami. As a "pro" she won $10,000 in the ten mile Wrigley Marathon that was held in Toronto. It was here that she met her future husband, Joe Wright, a Canadian Olympian.

Albina Osipowich - United States

Albina Osipowich of the United States captured the 100m freestyle title at the 1928 Olympic Games. This swimming pioneer also collected a second gold medal at these Games, as a member of the 4 X 100m freestyle relay team.

medal
count
2

HILDEGARD SCHRADER
GERMANY

Hildegard Schrader was the first woman to win a gold medal for Germany in an individual Olympic swimming event. She didn't break a world record, but she did manage to break one of the straps of her swimsuit in an *exciting* 200m *breaststroke* final! The modest Hildegard stayed in the pool until the problem strap was fixed. Schrader insisted, "I would have gone faster, if I had not been so embarrassed."

Schrader equaled the world record in the 200m breaststroke during a preliminary heat at the 1928 Olympic Games. She later became the first woman to break the three-minute barrier for the 200y breaststroke event (2:57.8).

L A N E   L I N E S

"Argentinian Upset"

Alberto Zorrilla won Argentina's first Olympic swimming gold medal in the 400m freestyle. Billed as a duel between "Boy" Charlton and Arne Borg, the unknown Zorrilla pulled ahead of the two superstars from an outside lane in the last 50 meters to claim victory.

PETER JOHN WEISSMULLER
UNITED STATES

In 1950, the Associated Press Poll voted Peter John Weissmuller "The Greatest Swimmer of the Past 50 Years"— twenty-two years after his last Olympic competition.

Johnny Weissmuller, as he was better known, was the first International Swimming Hall of Fame honoree. During his career he set 51 world records, 107 American records and held 56 national titles. A two-time Olympian, (1924 & 1928 Games), Weissmuller raced to five Olympic gold medals and earned a bronze medal with the 1928 water polo team as well.

Courtesy of ISHOF

The great Johnny Weissmuller.

Coach Bill Bachrach first saw Weissmuller, a spindly, awkward fifteen year old, swim at Chicago's Illinois Athletic Club. "Big Bill's" recruitment pitch to Weissmuller went like this, "Swear to me you'll work a year with me without questions and I'll take you on. You won't swim against anybody. You'll just be a slave and you'll hate my guts, but in the end you just might break every record there is." Weissmuller agreed with the conditions and trained for over a year. He grew into a 6'3", 195 pound, superstar.

In July of 1922, Weissmuller became the first man to break one minute for the 100m freestyle event (59.6). His time of 51 seconds for the 100y freestyle, set on April 5, 1927, remained a world record for seventeen years.

Weissmuller's accomplishments are even more amazing when you consider he set all his records without the benefit of flip turns, modern lane lines, and starting blocks.

Johnny Weissmuller, always a crowd pleaser, was known for entertaining the fans with comical dives between swimming events. It wasn't surprising that he ended up in Hollywood, making twelve Tarzan movies and earning close to $2,000,000 over two decades.

OFF THE *Wall*

King of the Jungle?

In 1959, Weissmuller found out just how famous "Tarzan" was throughout the world. He was attending a celebrity golf tournament in Cuba. As he and his entourage were departing for the golf course Cuban rebels surrounded their vehicle. The rebels disarmed Weissmuller's bodyguards and pointed their rifles at the Americans.

Weissmuller exited his car, slowly rising to his full 6'-3" and began to pound his chest with his fist letting out a wail in true "Tarzan" fashion. The stunned rebels suddenly broke into laughter and began calling out, "Tarzan, Tarzan! Bienvenido! Welcome to Cuba." They put down their weapons and began shaking the legendary star's hand and asking for his autograph. "Tarzan" and company were then given a personal escort to the golf course!

1928 OLYMPIC SWIMMING FINALS

INDIVIDUAL EVENTS

Gold	Silver	Bronze	Fourth	Fifth	Sixth	Seventh	Eighth
Women 100m Freestyle - World Record (1:10.0 Ethel Lackie USA) Olympic Record (1:12.2 Mariechen Wehselau USA 1924)							
Albina Osipowich USA – 1:11.0 o	Eleanor Garatti USA – 1:11.4	Margaret Joyce Cooper GBR – 1:13.6	Jean McDowell GBR – 1:13.6	Susan Laird USA – 1:14.6	Charlotte Lehmann GER – 1:15.2		
Men 100m Freestyle - World Record (57.4 J.Weissmuller USA) Olympic Record (59.0 Johnny Weissmuller USA 1924)							
Johnny Weissmuller USA – 58.6 o	István Bárány HUN – 59.8	Katsuo Takaishi JPN – 1:00.0	George Kojac USA – 1:00.8	Walter Laufer USA – 1:01.0	Walter Spence CAN – 1:01.4	Alberto Zorrilla ARG – 1:01.6	
Women 400m Freestyle – World Record (5:49.6 Martha Norelius USA) Olympic Record (6:02.2 Martha Norelius USA 1924)							
Martha Norelius USA – 5:42.8 w	Maria "Sis" Braun NED – 5:57.8	Josephine McKim USA – 6:00.2	Sarah Stewart GBR – 6:07.0	Frederica van der Goes RSA – 6:07.2	Irene Tanner GBR – 6:11.6		
Men 400m Freestyle - World Record (4:50.3 Arne Borg SWE) Olympic Record (5:04.2 Johnny Weissmuller 1924)							
Alberto Zorrilla ARG – 5:01.6 o	Andrew "Boy" Charlton AUS – 5:03.6	Arne Borg SWE – 5:04.6	Clarence "Buster" Crabbe USA – 5:05.4	Austin Clapp USA – 5:16.0	Raymond Ruddy USA – 5:25.0		

w World Record **o** Olympic Record **p** Preliminary Heat **dq** Disqualified **e** Equal to World Record **eo** Equal to Olympic Record
dns Did Not Start **dnf** Did Not Finish **ac** Also Competed **r** Relay Lead-off Split **E** Estimated

1928 OLYMPIC SWIMMING FINALS

	Gold	Silver	Bronze	Fourth	Fifth	Sixth	Seventh	Eighth
Men 1500m Freestyle - World Record (19:07.2 Arne Borg SWE) Olympic Record (20:06.6 Andrew "Boy" Charlton AUS 1924)	Arne Borg	Andrew "Boy" Charlton	Clarence "Buster" Crabbe	Raymond Ruddy	Alberto Zorrilla	Garnet Ault		
	SWE–19:51.8 o	AUS – 20:02.6	USA – 20:28.8	USA – 21:05.0	ARG – 21:23.8	CAN – 21:46.0		
Women 100m Backstroke - World Record (1:22.0 Willy van den Turk NED) Olympic Record (1:23.2 Sybil Bauer USA 1924)	Maria "Sis" Braun	Ellen King	Margaret Joyce Cooper	Marion Gilman	Eleanor Holm	Lisa Lindstrom	Elizabeth Stockley	
	p - 1:21.6 w							
	NED–1:22.0	GBR – 1:22.2	GBR – 1:22.8	USA – 1:24.2	USA – 1:24.4	USA – 1:24.4	NZE – 1:25.8	
Men 100m Backstroke - World Record (1:09.0 George Kojac USA) Olympic Record (1:13.2 Warren Paoa Kealoha USA 1924)	George Kojac	Walter Laufer	Paul Wyatt	Toshio Irie	Ernst Küppers	John Besford		
	USA – 1:08.2 w	USA – 1:10.0	USA – 1:12.0	JPN – 1:13.6	GER – 1:13.8	GBR – 1:15.4		
Women 200m Breaststroke - World Record (3:11.2 Lotte Mühe GER) Olympic Record (3:33.2 Lucy Morton GBR 1924)	Hildegard Schrader	Mietje "Marie" Baron	Lotte Mühe	Else Jacobsen	Margaret Hoffman	Brita Hazelius		
	p - 3:11.2 e							
	GER – 3:12.6	NED – 3:15.2	GER – 3:17.6	DEN – 3:19.0	USA – 3:19.2	SWE – 3:23.0		
Men 200m Breaststroke - World Record (2:48.0 Erich Rademacher GER) Olympic Record (2:56.0 Robert Skelton USA 1924)	Yoshiyuki Tsuruta	Erich Rademacher	Teofilo Yldfonzo	Erwin Sietas	Eric Harling	Walter Spence		
	JPN – 2:48.8 o	GER – 2:50.6	PHI – 2:56.4	GER – 2:56.6	SWE – 2:56.8	CAN – 2:57.2		

1928 OLYMPIC SWIMMING FINALS

Gold	Silver	Bronze	Fourth	Fifth	Sixth	Seventh	Eighth

RELAY EVENTS

Women 400m Freestyle Relay - Olympic Record (4:58.8 USA 1924)

Gold	Silver	Bronze	Fourth	Fifth	Sixth	Seventh	Eighth
Adelaide Lambert, Eleanor Garatti, Albina Osipovich, Martha Norelius p – Josephine McKim, Susan Laird	Margaret Cooper, Sarah Stewart, Irene Tanner, Ellen King	Kathleen Russell, Rhoda Rennie, Marie Bedford, Frederica van der Goes	Charlotte Lehmann, Reni Erkens-Küpper, Hertha Wunder, Irmintraut Schneider	Bibienne Pellegry, Anne Dupire, Marguerite Ledoux, Claire Horront p – Georgette Roty	Elisabeth Smits, Geertje Baumeister, Maria Vierdag, Maria Braun		
USA - 4:47.6 w	GBR - 5:02.8	RSA - 5:13.4	GER - 5:14.4	FRA - 5:33.0	NED – dq		

Men 800m Freestyle Relay - World and Olympic Record (9:53.4 USA 1924)

Gold	Silver	Bronze	Fourth	Fifth	Sixth	Seventh	Eighth
Austin Clapp, Walter Laufer, George Kojac, Johnny Weissmuller, p – Paul Samson, David Young	Hiroshi Yoneyama, Nobuo Arai, Tokuhei Sada, Katsuo Takaishi	F. Munroe Bourne, James Thompson, Garnet Ault, Walter Spence	András Wanié, Rezsö Wanié, Géza Sziagritz-Tarródy, István Bárány	Aulo Gustafsson, Sven Pettersson, Eskil Lundahl, Arne Borg	Reginald Sutton, Joseph Whiteside, Edward Percival Peter, Albert Dicken	José González Espuglas, Estanislao Artal Garriga, Ramon Artigas Rigual, Francisco Segala Torres	
USA - 9:36.2 w	JPN - 9:41.4	CAN - 9:47.8	HUN - 9:57.0	SWE - 10:01.8	GBR - 10:15.8	ESP	

Chapter 10

Olympiad X - 1932
Los Angeles, California, United States

The 1932 Olympic Games, held in Los Angeles, California, were attended by a staggering 1.25 million people, among them Hollywood's biggest names.

Los Angeles featured the "Olympic Village" concept that would serve as a model for future games. At these Games only the male athletes, benefited from the village accommodations. Women were housed at the Chapman Park Hotel.

The Japanese Men's Olympic Swim Team blew just about everyone out of the water, taking eleven of sixteen possible medals. Of the seventeen-member squad, eleven were teen-agers. A writer for the L.A. Times wrote, "When those kids get their full growth they'll probably have to carry anchors to give their foe a chance."

There were many theories regarding this "sudden" Japanese dominance. Norio Nomura, manager of the Japanese team credited the U.S. swimmers with their success. He recalled seeing American swimming manuals around the pools in Japan as far back as 1918.

Olympic 1ST

Come on in, the Water's Fine!

Los Angeles introduces the first temperature controlled Olympic pool.

In 1932, everyone was

talking about the Japanese Crawl, Nomura said their techniques came from watching Johnny Weissmuller.

There were other factors contributing to their success. Many felt the Japanese were in better condition. Japan had a shortage of indoor pools, and because of this had to resort to dry land conditioning. Aerobic exercises and stretching, not widely practiced in these early years, were already part of the Japanese training program.

Whatever the reasons, the Japanese swam to their dominance as a team with no one individual emerging as a "superstar." Four different Japanese men won individual events, three of them breaking world records.

THE MEN'S SWIM TEAM
JAPAN

Courtesy of ISHOF

Kusuo "Kid"amura

Kusuo Kitamura at 14, was the youngest champion of these Olympic Games in any event, with his win in the 1500m freestyle. This same victory made him the youngest gold medalist ever in any men's Olympic event. His Olympic record would remain intact until the 1952 Games.

Yoshiyuki Tsuruta's gold in the 200m breaststroke event in 1928 was Japan's first Olympic swimming medal. He returned in 1932 to capture his second consecutive title in this event.

SCORE

B O A R D

Japanese Sweeps!

100m Backstroke

GOLD   Masaji Kiyokawa

SILVER   Toshio Irie

BRONZE   Kentaro Kawatsu

200m Breaststroke

GOLD   Yoshiyuki Tsuruta

SILVER   Reizo Koike

BRONZE   Teofilo Yldefonzo

Yasuji Miyazaki upset the Americans in the 100m freestyle final. This 15 year-old established a new Olympic record (58.0) in an earlier heat. Miyazaki collected a second gold medal at these Games as a member of the 800m freestyle relay team that demolished the Olympic record by over 37 seconds.

In spite of their youth and talent, Japanese domination in Olympic swimming was short lived. The men's team went on to capture three gold medals at the 1936 Olympic Games. However, in the nine subsequent Olympics they would only see two victories. Swimmer Kiyokawa said it best; "We didn't actually fall apart, the rest of the world caught up with us."

Japanese sweep of 200m breaststroke. (l-r) T. Yldefonzo, Y. Tsuruta, R. Koike

CLARENCE "BUSTER" CRABBE
UNITED STATES

American Clarence "Buster" Crabbe kept the Japanese Swim Team from sweeping gold in every event. Crabbe took the 400m freestyle in an exciting battle with Jean Taris of France. The race was so close that legendary Olympian Johnny Weissmuller, who had been seated in the first row of the spectator section, hurdled the fence to move in for a closer look at the finish.

Crabbe had planned on pursuing a career in law, but after the race with Taris he would later say, "My life was entirely changed because of 1/100th of a second...nothing was ever the same again."

George Kojac counting laps for teammate Buster Crabbe

Crabbe had swum at the 1928 Olympic Games. In the transatlantic crossing to the Netherlands, he lost ten pounds and was weak. He managed to capture a bronze in the 1500m freestyle and place fourth in the 400m free event.

At the 1928 Games the swimmers practiced in the Utrecht, the canals of the Rhine River, instead of the Olympic pool. Crabbe spoke of this experience, "The Utrecht had little fish in the water and they got into our swim suits." Not the typical training experience!

Crabbe later went on to star in over 150 films. He is most famous for his roles as Flash Gordon, Buck Rogers, and Tarzan.

WILLEMIJNTJE "WILLY" DEN OUDEN HOLLAND

Fourteen year-old Willy den Ouden captured silver medals for both the 100m freestyle event and as the anchor of the Netherlands Women's 4 X 100m free relay team at the L.A. Games.

Ms. den Ouden returned to the Olympic Games in 1936, as the current world record holder of the 100m freestyle event (1:04.6), a record that would stand for twenty years. Surprisingly, den Ouden finished fourth in the 100m free final, but went on to win gold as a member of the Netherlands 400m free relay squad.

The popular swimmer set thirteen individual world records during her distinguished career. Den Ouden was the first female swimmer to break the one-minute barrier for 100 yards.

CLARE DENNIS AUSTRIA

Clare Dennis, 16, of New South Wales, won the 200m breaststroke final at the 1932 L.A. Games. During an earlier heat

OFF THE Wall

A Perfect "$100"

During the diving competition at the 1936 Games a gentleman dressed in regular street clothes executed an exquisite bellyflop into the diving pool. It was later learned this unofficial diver was a German sportswriter. He may not have scored a ten for his dive but he collected $100 on a bet.

she broke the Olympic record. American Buster Crabbe, who had watched the teenager swim this preliminary round, had some suggestions for her.

During the final, Dennis followed Crabbe's recommendations. After plunging into the pool she took three full strokes before surfacing (no longer allowed) and was first to touch the wall at each turn in order to psyche out the other competitors. Dennis not only won but also broke her own Olympic record set in an earlier heat by almost two seconds (3:06.3).

Dennis' win at the 1932 Olympic Games prevented the United States Women's Team from a golden sweep of the swimming events.

ELEANOR HOLM
UNITED STATES

When it came to "making a splash," no one did it quite like Eleanor Holm! Her Olympic career began in 1928 when, at the age of 15, she placed fifth in the 100m backstroke. She returned in 1932 with a decisive win in that same event.

After the 1932 Olympic Games, Eleanor married a famous singer and orchestra leader. She led a very active social life on the "night club circuit," and her swimming career was still in full swing. Eleanor set a world record in the 100m backstroke in 1935, and another in 1936 in the 200m backstroke event.

She was a member of three U.S. Olympic teams, but holds the dubious distinction of being "suspended" from the 1936 Olympic Team.

Holm was expected to repeat her 1932 gold medal perfor-

Courtesy of ISHOF

Backstroke champion - Eleanor Holm

mance in Berlin. However, her antics during the nine-day voyage on board ship to the Games lead to the demise of her amateur career.

The "independent Eleanor" didn't adjust well to the restrictions set down for the athletes on board the ship. She broke training and defied the U.S. Olympic officials by attending a "champagne party." Holm never denied the allegations of drinking and gambling and was removed from the team along with the other athletes who broke the rules.

Eleanor Holm, who hadn't lost in seven years, was forced to sit in the stands and watch as 16 year-old Nida Senff of Holland took home the gold.

LENORE KIGHT
UNITED STATES

The match-up of world record holder Helene Madison and Lenore Kight may well have been the race of the Games. A crowd of 15, 000 spectators witnessed this exciting duel in the 400m freestyle final!

As they approached the last turn the swimmers were neck and neck. Madison came out of the turn faster, but

Kight fought hard, narrowing the gap. The fans, now on their feet, were shouting wildly, as they waited for the swimmers to reach the wall. Madison touched first with Lenore only one 1/10th of a second behind her, both breaking the world and Olympic records!

Lenore poolside at Berlin in 1936 and sixty years later with her Olympic medal.

Lenore Kight-Wingard would go on to set seven freestyle world records and earn 20 national freestyle crowns. She made the 1936 Olympic Team and added a bronze medal to her achievements.

Photos donated by Lenore Kight-Wingard

When asked recently what accomplishments she is most proud of, Lenore said, "Teaching many, many children how to swim."

Olympic 1ST

Hideko Maehata won a silver medal for the 200m breaststroke event at the 1932 Games, becoming the first Japanese woman to win an Olympic medal.

At the 1936 Games, Maehata captured gold in the same event, becoming Japan's first woman to win gold.

HELENE MADISON
UNITED STATES

The sports writers dubbed 5' 10" Helene Madison "Queen of the Waters." The statuesque American earned three gold medals at the 1932 Olympic Games.

Madison was the fastest female swimmer on the planet, setting world records at 20 distances from 100y to one mile. It was nine years before her 1000y and one-mile marks were bettered. She was the first female swimmer to swim 100y in one minute flat.

Retiring at the age of 19, she had one of the shortest careers in swimming history. No one since has equaled, collectively, her amazing feats.

Courtesy of ISHOF

For three years running Helene Madison dominated every freestyle event at the U.S. Women's Nationals and held 17 official world freestyle records in 1932.

1932 OLYMPIC SWIMMING FINALS

INDIVIDUAL EVENTS

	Gold	Silver	Bronze	Fourth	Fifth	Sixth	Seventh	Eighth
Women 100m Freestyle - World Record (1:06.6 Helene Madison USA) Olympic Record (1:11.0 Albina Osipowich USA 1928)								
	Helene Madison	Willemijntje den Ouden	Eleanor Saville Garatti	Josephine McKim	Frances Bult	Jennie Maakal		
	USA – 1:06.8 o	NED – 1:07.8	USA – 1:09.3	USA – 1:09.3	AUS – 1:09.9	RSA – 1:10.8		
Men 100m Freestyle - World Record (57.4 J. Weissmuller USA) Olympic Record (58.6 Johnny Weissmuller USA 1928)								
	Yasuji Miyazaki p – 58.0 o	Tatsugo Kawaishi	Albert Schwartz	Manuella Kalili	Zenjiro Takahashi	Ramond Thompson		
	JPN – 58.2	JPN – 58.6	USA – 58.8	USA – 59.2	JPN – 59.2	USA – 59.5		
Women 400m Freestyle - World Record (5:31.0 Helene Madison USA) Olympic Record (5:42.8 Martha Norelius USA 1928)								
	Helene Madison	Lenore Kight	Jennie Maakal	Margaret Joyce Cooper	Yvonne Godard	Norene Forbes		
	USA – 5:28.5 w	USA – 5:28.6	RSA – 5:47.3	GBR – 5:49.7	FRA – 5:54.4	USA – 6:06.0		
Men 400m Freestyle - World Record (4:47.0 Jean Taris FRA) Olympic Record (5:01.6 Alberto Zorrilla ARG 1928)								
	Clarence "Buster" Crabbe	Jean Taris	Tsutomu Oyokota	Takashi Yokoyama	Noboru Sugimoto	Andrew "Boy" Charlton		
	USA – 4:48.4 o	FRA – 4:48.5	JPN – 4:52.3	JPN – 4:52.5	JPN – 4:56.1	AUS – 4:58.6		

w World Record   *o* Olympic Record   *p* Preliminary Heat   *dq* Disqualified   *e* Equal to World Record   *eo* Equal to Olympic Record
dns Did Not Start   *dnf* Did Not Finish   *ac* Also Competed   *r* Relay Lead-off Split   *E* Estimated

OLYMPIAD X – 1932 – LOS ANGELES, U.S.A.

1932 OLYMPIC SWIMMING FINALS

Gold	Silver	Bronze	Fourth	Fifth	Sixth	Seventh	Eighth
Men 1500m Freestyle - World Record (19:07.2 Arne Borg SWE)						Olympic Record (19:51.8 Arne Borg SWE 1928)	
Kusuo Kitamura	Shozo Makino	James Cristy	Noel Philip Ryan	Clarence "Buster" Crabbe	Jean Taris		
JPN – 19:12.4 o	JPN – 19:14.1	USA – 19:39.5	AUS – 19:45.1	USA – 20:02.7	FRA – 20:09.7		
Women 100m Backstroke - World Record (1:18.2 Eleanor Holm USA) Olympic Record (1:21.6 Maria "Sis" Braun NED 1928)							
Eleanor Holm	Philomena "Bonny" Mealing	Elizabeth Valerie Davies	Phyllis Harding	Joan McSheehy	Margaret Joyce Cooper	Maria Philipsen-Braun	
p – 1:18.3 o	AUS – 1:21.3	GBR – 1:22.5	GBR – 1:22.6	USA – 1:23.2	GBR – 1:23.4	NED - *dns*	
Men 100m Backstroke - World and Olympic Record (1:08.2 George Kojac USA 1928)							
Masaji Kiyokawa	Toshio Irie	Kentaro Kawatsu	Robert Zehr	Ernst Küppers	Robert Kerber		
JPN – 1:08.6	JPN – 1:09.8	JPN – 1:10.0	USA – 1:10.9	GER – 1:11.3	USA – 1:12.8		
Women 200m Breaststroke - World Record (3:03.4 Else Jacobsen DEN)					Olympic Record (3:11.2 Hilde Schrader GER 1928)		
Clare Dennis	Hideko Maehata	Else Jacobsen	Margery Hinton	Margaret Hoffman	Anne Govednik	Jane Cadwell	
AUS – 3:06.3 o	JPN – 3:06.4	DEN – 3:07.1	GBR – 3:11.7	USA – 3:11.8	USA – 3:16.0	USA – 3:18.2	
Men 200m Breaststroke - World Record (2:44.0 Leonard Spence CAN)				Olympic Record (2:48.8 Yoshiyuki Tsuruta JPN 1928)			
Yoshiyuki Tsuruta	Reizo Koike	Teofilo Yldefonzo	Erwin Sietas	Jikirum Adjaluddin	Shigeo Nakagawa		
JPN – 2:45.4	p – 2:44.9 o	PHI – 2:47.1	GER – 2:48.0	PHI – 2:49.2	JPN – 2:52.8		

1932 OLYMPIC SWIMMING FINALS

RELAY EVENTS

Women 400m Freestyle Relay - World and Olympic Record (4:47.6 USA 1928)

Gold	Silver	Bronze	Fourth	Fifth	Sixth	Seventh	Eighth
USA – 4:38.0 w	NED – 4:47.5	GBR – 4:52.4	CAN – 5:05.7	JPN – 5:06.7			
Josephine McKim, Helen Johns, Eleanor Saville Garatti, Helene Madison	Maria Vierdag, Maria Oversloot, Cornelia Laddé, Willemijntje den Ouden	Elizabeth Valerie Davies, Helen Varcoe, Margaret Joyce Cooper, Edna Hughes	Irene Pirie, Irene Mullen, Ruth Kerr, Betty Edwards	Kazue Kojima, Hatsuko Morioka, Misao Yokota, Yukie Arata			

Men 800m Freestyle Relay - World and Olympic Record (9:36.2 USA 1928)

Gold	Silver	Bronze	Fourth	Fifth	Sixth	Seventh	Eighth
JPN – 8:58.4 w	USA – 9:10.5	HUN – 9:31.4	CAN – 9:36.3	GBR – 9:45.8	ARG – 10:13.1	BRA – 10:36.5	
Yasuji Miyazaki, Masonori Yusa, Takashi Yokoyama, Hisakichi Toyoda	Frank Booth, George Fissler, Marola Kalili, Manuella Kalili	András Wanié, László Szabados, András Székely, István Bárány	George Larson, George Burrows, Walter Spence, F. Munro Bourne	Joseph Whiteside, Robert Leivers, Martyn Ffrench-Williams, Reginald Sutton	Carlos Kennedy, Leopoldo Tahier, Roberto Peper, Alfredo Rocca	Manoel Lourenço Silva, Isaac Dos Santos Moraes, Manoel Rocha Villar, Benevenuto Martins Nunes	

Chapter 11

Olympiad XI - 1936
Berlin, Germany

a relay of 3,000 men brought the Olympic Flame across seven countries to Berlin, Germany, the site of the 1936 Olympic Games. Germany's Adolf Hitler hoped to use the Olympic Games to further his political agenda. The U.S. team proudly marched past Hitler, refusing to dip the American flag.

The concept of the Olympic Village, originated at the Los Angeles Games, was improved upon in Berlin. The village was made up of 150 cottages. Each country's village was tailored to its particular customs and needs. The Finns had sauna baths, the Japanese steam baths, and the French were given wine with their meals.

In the pool, the "butterfly stroke" made its first Olympic appearance. The stroke was used in the breaststroke event and not until 1956 would it become an event of its own.

The Japanese Men's Swim Team continued to reign. For the second consecutive Olympiad they swam to a world record in the 800m free relay event.

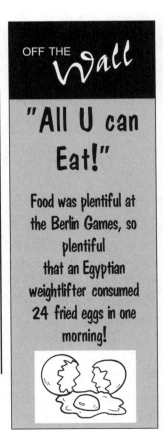

OFF THE **Wall**

"All U can Eat!"

Food was plentiful at the Berlin Games, so plentiful that an Egyptian weightlifter consumed 24 fried eggs in one morning!

In the women's events the Dutch dominated, winning gold in four out of the five events offered on the women's Olympic swim program.

FERENC CSIK HUNGARY

Hungarian Ferenc Csik, swimming in an outside lane, broke up what appeared to be a Japanese sweep of the men's 100m freestyle final. The four top finishers, Csik, Masanori Yusa, Shigeo Arai and Masaharu Taguchi touched the wall within a half second of each other.

Csik, 22, a medical student, also captured a bronze medal as a member of Hungary's 800m free relay team. He went on to become an Army surgeon and in 1945 was killed, during an air raid while attending a wounded soldier.

TETSUO HAMURO JAPAN

Tetsuo Hamuro is one of Japan's most renowned breaststrokers. A field of butterfly breaststrokers dominated the lineup for the 200m event in 1936. Hamuro, swimming the conventional breaststroke, was the surprise victor.

Hamuro held world records in both the 100m and 200m long course events. Before retiring from swimming in 1940 for military service,

Courtesy of ISHOF

Hamuro would hold ten National Championships and national records for the 50m, 100m, 200m breaststroke and a medley relay. His national records stood the test of time—nineteen years!

RAGNHILD HVEGER
DENMARK

Ragnhild Hveger is perhaps the greatest swimmer never to have won Olympic gold. In 1936, at the age of 15, she took silver in the 400m freestyle final. The cancellation of the 1940 and 1944 Olympic Games denied Ragnhild, while in her prime, the opportunity to show the world what she could do.

Courtesy of ISHOF

Ragnhild Hveger - the "Golden Torpedo."

During those years she broke over 40 world records. In 1940, Hveger set a new world record for the eighth time in the 400m freestyle, with a time of 5:00.1. It would be sixteen years before a women would break the five minute barrier in this event. Her 200m, 800m and 1500m free world record times stood for 15 years.

Known as Denmark's "Golden Torpedo," Hveger retired in 1945 and did not attempt to compete in the 1948 Olympic Games. At the age of 31, she came back to represent Denmark at the Helsinki Games of 1952.

Sixteen years after her first Olympic competition, Hveger led the 400m freestyle event for three-quarters of the race. She finished fifth, but her world record (5:00.1) remained unbroken.

LANE LINES

The Young & the Restless

Inge Sörenson of Denmark won a bronze medal for the 200m breaststroke at the age of 12 years and 24 days, making her the youngest person to win an Olympic swim medal. Martha Geneger of Germany, the silver medalist in the same event, was only 14 years old. At 22, an "old woman" by this field of competitors, was gold medalist Hideko Maehata of Japan.

ADOLPH KIEFER
UNITED STATES

Adolph Kiefer was the first to break the one-minute barrier in the 100y backstroke event. In Berlin, Kiefer easily won the 100m backstroke final and was considered by many the greatest backstroker ever.

From 1935 to 1943 Kiefer won nine consecutive AAU outdoor 100m backstroke

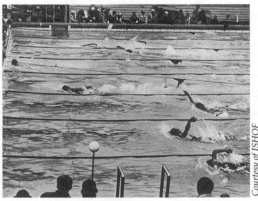

Kiefer's 1936 100m backstroke victory

Courtesy of ISHOF

championships. The cancellation of the 1940 and 1944 Games denied Kiefer the opportunity to further his Olympic accomplishments.

During that time, Kiefer became a Lieutenant in the U.S. Navy. After surveying shipwrecks world wide, Lieutenant Kiefer noted a high number of unnecessary fatalities due to drowning. He completely revamped the naval swim instruction program, a contribution that has made an everlasting impact.

Adolph Kiefer's records stood for 15 years, some four years after his retirement in 1950.

HENDRIKA MASTENBROEK
HOLLAND

"Rie" Mastenbroek, a versatile seventeen-year-old, captured four Olympic medals at the 1936 Games. In both her 400m and 100m freestyle races she came from behind to win.

During the 100m backstroke Mastenbroek became entangled in the lane ropes causing her to slow down,

Olympic 1ST

"Rie" Mastenbroek was the first swimmer in one Olympiad to:

Win 3 Gold Medals & to win 4 Medals total.

Courtesy of ISHOF

Mastenbroek and Coach Ma Braun

yet she still managed to capture a silver medal. She was the anchor for the Netherlands' gold medal winning relay team.

Mastenbroek held three world records in freestyle events and six in the backstroke events during her career. Her feat of three Olympic gold medals during one Olympiad would not be matched until the 1964 Olympic Games.

JACK MEDICA
UNITED STATES

At the 1936 Olympic Games, Jack Medica trailed Japan's Shumpei Uto during most of the 400m freestyle final. With only 10 meters to go, Medica blazed ahead for the win. He also won two silver medals at these Games in the 1500m and 800m free relay events.

Courtesy of ISHOF

400m freestyle ceremony (L-R) Bronze: S. Makino, Gold: J. Medica & Silver: S. Uto

At the University of Washington, Medica was literally a one-man swim team. At the collegiate championships swimmers were allowed to compete in three individual events. Medica won all three of his races, but because he was the only member of his team, could not take part in the relay events. Nevertheless he placed an incredible third in the standings behind powerhouses Michigan and Iowa.

SCORE
BOARD

Terada's 20 Second Triumph

Swimmer	Cntry	1500m tm
Noburo Terada	JPN	19:13.7
Jack Medica	USA	19:34.0
Shumpei Uto	JPN	19:34.5

Medica's victories took valuable points away from Yale and Iowa, allowing Michigan to win the Nationals. Michigan coach Matt Mann awarded the Washington superstar a Michigan varsity letter in appreciation.

Jack Medica went on to coach swimming at Columbia University and the University of Pennsylvania.

KATHERINE L. RAWLS
UNITED STATES

OFF THE *Wall*

Back to the Wall!

Holland's backstroker Dina Senff missed her touch at the turn, returned to the wall, kicked off and managed to just beat out teammate Rie Mastenbroek for the victory!

Katherine L. Rawls, an Olympic swimmer and diver, earned bronze as a member of the 1936 American free relay squad. In addition, at the 1932 and 1936 Olympic Games she won silver medals in the springboard competition.

In 1933 Rawls became the first woman to win four national titles at one meet and in 1938 repeated this achievement.

During WWII, Katherine Rawls, now Mrs. Theodore Thompson, was one of the first 21 women selected to pilot fighting planes to combat zones for the Air Transport Command.

1936 OLYMPIC SWIMMING FINALS

INDIVIDUAL EVENTS

	Gold	Silver	Bronze	Fourth	Fifth	Sixth	Seventh	Eighth

Women 100m Freestyle - World Record (1:04.6 W. den Ouden NED) Olympic Record (1:06.8 Helene Madison USA 1932)

Gold	Silver	Bronze	Fourth	Fifth	Sixth	Seventh
Hendrika "Rie" Mastenbroek	Jeannette Campbell	Gisela Arendt	Willemijntje den Ouden	Catherina Wagner	Olive McKean	Katherine Rawls
NED – 1:05.9 o	ARG – 1:06.4	GER – 1:06.6	NED – 1:07.6	NED – 1:08.1	USA – 1:08.4	USA – 1:08.7

Men 100m Freestyle - World Record (56.4 Peter Fick USA) Olympic Record (58.0 Yasuji Miyazaki JPN 1932)

Gold	Silver	Bronze	Fourth	Fifth	Sixth	Seventh
Ferenc Csik	Masanori Yusa	Shigeo Arai	Masaharu Taguchi	Helmut Fischer	Peter Fick	Arthur Lindegren
HUN – 57.6	JPN – 57.9	JPN – 58.0	p – 57.5 o JPN – 58.1	GER – 59.3	USA – 59.7	USA – 59.9

Women 400m Freestyle — World Record (5:16.0 W. den Ouden NED) Olympic Record (5:28.5 Helene Madison USA 1932)

Gold	Silver	Bronze	Fourth	Fifth	Sixth	Seventh
Hendrika "Rie" Mastenbroek	Ragnhild Hveger	Lenore Wingard Kight	Mary Lou Petty	Piedade Coutinho Azevedo	Grete Frederiksen	Catherina Wagner
NED – 5:26.4 o	DEN – 5:27.5	USA – 5:29.0	USA – 5:32.2	BRA – 5:35.2	DEN – 5:45.0	NED – 5:46.0

Men 400m Freestyle - World Record (4:38.7 Jack Medica USA) Olympic Record (4:48.4 Buster Crabbe USA 1932)

Gold	Silver	Bronze	Fourth	Fifth	Sixth	Seventh
Jack Medica	Shumpei Uto	Shozo Makino	Ralph Flanagan	Hiroshi Negami	Jean Taris	Robert Leivers
USA – 4:44.5 o	JPN – 4:45.6	JPN – 4:48.1	USA – 4:52.7	JPN – 4:53.6	FRA – 4:53.8	GBR – 5:00.9

w World Record   *o* Olympic Record   *p* Preliminary Heat   *dq* Disqualified   *e* Equal to World Record   *eo* Equal to Olympic Record
dns Did Not Start   *dnf* Did Not Finish   *ac* Also Competed   *r* Relay Lead-off Split   *E* Estimated

OLYMPIAD XI – 1936 – BERLIN, GERMANY

1936 OLYMPIC SWIMMING FINALS

	Gold	Silver	Bronze	Fourth	Fifth	Sixth	Seventh	Eighth
Men 1500m Freestyle - World Record (19:07.2 Arne Borg SWE)	Noboru Terada	Jack Medica	Shumpei Uto	Sunao Ishiharada	Ralph Flanagan	Robert Leivers	Heinz Arendt	
Olympic Record (19:12.4 Kusuo Kitamura JPN 1932)	JPN – 19:13.7	USA – 19:34.0	JPN – 19:34.5	JPN – 19:48.5	USA – 19:54.8	GBR – 19:57.4	GER – 19:59.0	
Women 100m Backstroke - World Record (1:15.8 Rie Mastenbroek NED)	Dina "Nida" Senff p – 1:16.6 o	Hendrika "Rie" Mastenbroek	Alice Bridges	Edith Motridge	Tove Bruunström	Lorna Frampton	Phyllis Harding	
Olympic Record (1:18.3 Eleanor Holm USA 1932)	NED – 1:18.9	NED – 1:19.2	USA – 1:19.4	USA – 1:19.6	DEN – 1:20.4	GBR – 1:20.6	GBR – 1:21.5	
Men 100m Backstroke - World Record (1:04.8 Adolph Kiefer USA)	Adolph Kiefer	Albert Vandeweghe	Masaji Kiyokawa	Taylor Drysdale	Kiichi Yoshida	Yasuhiko Kojima	Percival Oliver	
Olympic Record (1:08.2 George Kojac USA 1928)	USA – 1:05.9 o	USA – 1:07.7	JPN – 1:08.4	USA – 1:09.4	JPN – 1:09.7	JPN – 1:10.4	AUS – 1:10.7	
Women 200m Breaststroke - World Record (3:00.4 Hideko Maehata JPN)	Hideko Maehata p – 3:01.9 o	Martha Geneger	Inge Sörensen	Johanna "Hanni" Hölzner	Johanna Waalberg	Doris Storey	Jeannette Kastein	
Olympic Record (3:06.3 Clare Dennis AUS 1932)	JPN – 3:03.6	GER – 3:04.2	DEN – 3:07.8	GER – 3:09.5	NED – 3:09.5	GBR – 3:09.7	NED – 3:12.8	
Men 200m Breaststroke - World Record (2:37.2 Jack Kasley)	Tetsuo Hamuro	Erwin Sietas	Reizo Koike	John Herbert Higgins	Saburo Ito	Joachim Balke	Teofilo Yldefonzo	
Olympic Record (2:44.9 Reizo Koike JPN 1932)	JPN – 2:41.5 o	GER – 2:42.9	JPN – 2:44.2	USA – 2:45.2	JPN – 2:47.6	GER – 2:47.8	PHI – 2:51.1	

1936 OLYMPIC SWIMMING FINALS

RELAY EVENTS

Gold	Silver	Bronze	Fourth	Fifth	Sixth	Seventh	Eighth

Women 400m Freestyle Relay - World Record (4:32.8 NED) — Olympic Record (4:38.0 USA 1932)

Gold	Silver	Bronze	Fourth	Fifth	Sixth	Seventh
NED – 4:36.0 w	GER – 4:36.8	USA – 4:40.2	HUN – 4:48.0	CAN – 4:48.0	GBR – 4:51.0	DEN – 4:51.4
Johanna Selbach, Catherina Wagner, Willemijntje den Ouden, Hendrika "Rie" Mastenbroek	Ruth Halbsguth, Leni Lohmar, Ingeborg Schmitz, Gisela Arendt, p – Ursula Pollack	Katherine Rawls, Bernice Lapp, Mavis Freeman, Olive McKean, p – Elizabeth Ryan	Ilona Ács, Ágnes Bíró, Véra Harsányi, Magdolna Lenkei	Mary McConkey, Zilpha Grant, Margaret Pirie, Phyllis Dewar	Margaret Jeffery, Edna Hughes, Irene Milton-Stone, Olive Wadham	Ragnhild Hveger, Tove Bruunström, Elvi Svendsen, Eva Arendt

Men 800m Freestyle Relay - World Record (8:52.2 JPN) — Olympic Record (8:58.4 JPN 1932)

Gold	Silver	Bronze	Fourth	Fifth	Sixth	Seventh	Eighth
JPN – 8:51.5 w	USA – 9:03.0	HUN – 9:12.3	FRA – 9:18.2	GER – 9:19.0	GBR – 9:21.5	CAN – 9:27.5	SWE – 9:37.5
Masanori Yusa, Shigeo Sugiura, Masaharu Taguchi, Shigeo Arai	Ralph Flanagan, John Macionis, Paul Wolf, Jack Medica, p – Ralph Gilman, Charles Hutter	Árpád Lengyel, Oszkár Abay-Nemes, Ödön Gróf, Ferenc Csik	Alfred Nakache, Christian Talli, René Cavalero, Jean Taris	Werner Plath, Wolfgang Heimlich, Hermann Heibel, Helmut Fischer	Martyn Ffrench-Williams, Romund Gabrielsen, Robert Leivers, Norman Wainwright	F. Munroe, Bourne, Robert Hamerton, Robert Hooper, Robert Pirie	Björn Borg, Sten Olov Bolldén, Sven Petterson, Gunnar Werner

Chapter 12

Olympiads XII & XIII
1940 & 1944

The decade that should have celebrated three Olympic Games saw only one. The devastation of World War II prevented the observance of both the 1940 and 1944 Olympic Games. Even though these Games were canceled they are acknowledged by the numerals XII and XIII.

Olympiad XIV - 1948
London, England

The Olympic Games returned in 1948 bringing with them a renewed spirit celebrated by 59 countries and 4,099 athletes.

The United States Men's Swim Team was awesome capturing gold in every event. This phenomenal accomplishment is unlikely to be repeated in Olympic competition again. The Americans won 11 of 16 possible medals. Only three swimmers on the 18-man squad failed to reach the finals.

Olympic 1ST

Greta Andersen won Denmark's first ever Olympic gold medal for swimming, in the 100m freestyle final. Her teammate, Karen Harup, followed up with Denmark's second, for the 100m back event.

GRETA ANDERSEN
DENMARK

Greta Andersen obtained Olympic fame as a sprinter, winning gold in the 100m freestyle, but later became known globally as "The World's Greatest Distance Swimmer." She held records from 100 yards to the 50-mile mark in a career that spanned 20 years.

In 1956, Andersen set a 10-mile world record of four hours and 25 minutes in California's Salton Sea. She set another world record by swimming around Atlantic City, New Jersey (25 miles), in 10 hours and 17 minutes.

Courtesy of ISHOF

Greta Andersen celebrated English Channel swimmer

Greta was also one of the most celebrated English Channel swimmers, crossing the Channel six times during her career. She held the women's speed records for both directions and would lose up to 25 pounds during one of these cold water swims.

Greta Andersen won more money than any other woman professional swimmer in history by the time she retired. At the end of her swimming career she opened a swim school and health club in Los Alamitos, California.

ANN CURTIS
UNITED STATES

Ann Curtis was the only American woman to win a gold medal in an individual event at the 1948 Games.

Courtesy of ISHOF

Gold medalist Ann Curtis with silver medalist Karen Harup (DEN), and bronze medalist Cathy Gibson (GBR).

In addition to her 400m freestyle title, Curtis also anchored the United States' 400m free relay team. Coming from behind for the win, she clocked a 1:04.4, beating Willy den Ouden's 12-year world record (1:04.6). However, it was an unofficial time since it was off a relay start. Curtis also collected a silver medal for the 100m freestyle event.

Ann Curtis went on to win a total of 31 National Championships, a record that would not be broken for over 30 years.

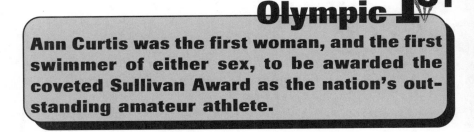

Olympic 1ST

Ann Curtis was the first woman, and the first swimmer of either sex, to be awarded the coveted Sullivan Award as the nation's outstanding amateur athlete.

ALAN FORD
UNITED STATES

Alan Ford broke Johnny Weissmuller's sixteen-year old world record in the 100y freestyle in 1943. He also holds the proud distinction of being the first swimmer to break the 50-second barrier in the 100y freestyle event, the swimming equivalent of the four-minute mile.

Courtesy of ISHOF

He subsequently lowered the 100y mark to 49.4 seconds in 1945, a record that stood for seven years. Ford held the world record on two occasions for the 100m freestyle event.

Alan Ford was one of the many athletes whose swimming career was affected by the war. "Word War II killed any Olympic dreams," said Ford. After serving in the navy, his wife encouraged his comeback. That comeback included a silver medal in the 100m freestyle at the 1948 London Games.

Ford's advice to today's Olympic hopefuls, "Keep things in perspective. Use swimming as a means for an education and world travel. You still must make a living when the headlines are over."

Allen Stack - USA

Allen Stack, American backstroker and world record holder in the 100m event, won the final touching out teammate Robert Crowell with a time of 1:06.4.

JOHN MARSHALL
AUSTRALIA

John Marshall captured silver and bronze medals at the 1948 Olympic Games as a distance freestyler. Yale University's coach, Robert Kiphuth, was so impressed with Marshall's talent that he arranged for him to study at Yale.

The Australian would go on to break 19 world records after working with Kiphuth. He competed again at the 1952 and 1956 Olympic Games. 1n 1956, at the age of 25, he swam the "new" butterfly event (200m) and placed fifth.

John Marshall died tragically the following year in an automobile accident.

JAMES P. McLANE
UNITED STATES

In 1948, Jimmy McLane captured three Olympic medals at the age of 17. He returned to the Games in 1952 as a member of the gold medal winning 800m freestyle relay team.

At the age of thirteen, McLane won the Outdoor National long distance title, becoming the youngest men's champion in history. He was considered a pioneer in the youth swimming movement in the United States.

Jimmy was one of swimming's true tacticians. He arrived at each meet with a plan that included knowing his opponents' strategy. McLane scouted the great Australian swimmer, John Marshall, whom he would meet in the 1500m freestyle final in London.

He observed that Marshall preferred to swim close to the lane divider on his breathing side. McLane, swimming in the lane next to Marshall during the final, pulled out ahead immediately and proceeded to use his forceful kick to douse and impede the Australian the entire way! McLane captured the gold and Marshall went home with silver. Jimmy truly enjoyed the planning and strategy of competition.

Courtesy of ISHOF

Gold medal winning 800m free relay squad: (l-r) Smith, McLane, Ris and Wolf.

WILLIAM SMITH, JR.
UNITED STATES

When William Smith was six years old he was stricken with typhoid fever. To build his strength he began swimming in irrigation ditches on a sugar plantation in his native Hawaii.

Smith served his country in WW II and completed his education at Ohio State. At the 1948 Olympic Games, Smith out swam teammate James McLane by over two seconds taking gold in the 400m freestyle. Smith also anchored the United States' 800m free relay team to victory.

After the 1948 Games, Smith returned to Honolulu and became the Director of Water Safety for the Honolulu Department of Parks and Recreation.

LANE LINES

No "Kneed" to Worry

American, Walter Ris, was not favored in the 100m freestyle final having been plagued with a chronic knee problem. Ris managed to catch the competition in the last 10 meters to win with a new Olympic record.

Courtesy of ISHOF

The first seven of the eight finalists in the 200m breaststroke race all used the butterfly stroke. Joseph Verdeur led a United States sweep of this event, followed by teammates Keith Carter and Robert Sohl. He is considered a pioneer of the butterfly stroke (used in breaststroke event) prior to it becoming an individual event internationally.

1948 OLYMPIC SWIMMING FINALS

INDIVIDUAL EVENTS

	Gold	Silver	Bronze	Fourth	Fifth	Sixth	Seventh	Eighth
Women 100m Freestyle - World Record (1:04.6 W. den Ouden NED) Olympic Record (1:05.9 Rie Mastenbroek NED 1936)								
	Greta Andersen	Ann Curtis	Marie-Louise Vaessen	Karen-Margrete Harup	Ingegärd Fredin	Irma Schumacher	Elisabeth Ahlgren	Fritze Carstensen
	DEN – 1:06.3	USA – 1:06.5	NED – 1:07.6	DEN – 1:08.1	SWE – 1:08.4	NED – 1:08.4	SWE – 1:08.8	DEN – 1:09.1
Men 100m Freestyle - World Record (55.4 Alan Ford USA) Olympic Record (57.5 Masaharu Taguchi JPN 1936)								
	Walter Ris	Alan Ford	Géza Kádas	Keith Carter	Alexandre Jany	Per-Olof Olsson	Zoltán Szilárd	Taha El Gamal
	USA – 57.3 o	USA – 57.8	HUN – 58.1	USA – 58.3	FRA – 58.3	SWE – 59.3	HUN – 59.6	EGY 1:00.5
Women 400m Freestyle – World Record (5:00.1 Ragnhild Hveger DEN) Olympic Record (5:26.4 Rie Mastenbroek NED 1936)								
	Ann Curtis	Karen-Margrete Harup	Catherine Gibson	Fernande Caroen	Brenda Helser	Piedade Silva Tavares	Fritze Carstensen	Nancy Lees
	USA – 5:17.8 o	DEN – 5:21.2	GBR – 5:22.5	BEL – 5:25.3	USA – 5:26.0	BRA – 5:29.4	DEN – 5:29.4	USA – 5:32.9
Men 400m Freestyle - World Record (4:35.2 Alexandre Jany FRA) Olympic Record (4:44.5 Jack Medica USA 1936)								
	William Smith	James McLane	John Marshall	Géza Kádas	György Mitró	Alexandre Jany	Jack Hale	Alfredo Yantorno
	USA – 4:41.0 o	USA – 4:43.4	AUS – 4:47.4	HUN – 4:49.4	HUN – 4:49.9	FRA – 4:51.4	GBR – 4:55.9	ARG – 4:58.7

w World Record   *o* Olympic Record   *p* Preliminary Heat   *dq* Disqualified   *e* Equal to World Record   *eo* Equal to Olympic Record
dns Did Not Start   *dnf* Did Not Finish   *ac* Also Competed   *r* Relay Lead-off Split   *E* Estimated

OLYMPIAD XIV – 1948 – LONDON, GREAT BRITAIN

1948 OLYMPIC SWIMMING FINALS

Men 1500m Freestyle - World Record (18:58.8 Tomikatsu Amano JPN) Olympic Record (19:12.4 Kusuo Kitamura JPN 1932)

Gold	Silver	Bronze	Fourth	Fifth	Sixth	Seventh	Eighth
James McLane	John Marshall	György Mitró	György Csordás	Marjan Stipetic	Forbes Norris	Donald Bland	William Heusner
USA – 19:18.5	AUS – 19:31.3	HUN – 19:43.2	HUN – 19:54.2	YUG – 20:10.7	USA – 20:18.8	GBR – 20:19.8	USA – 20:45.4

Women 100m Backstroke - World Record (1:10.9 Cornelia Kint NED) Olympic Record (1:16.6 Dina Nida Senff NED 1936)

Gold	Silver	Bronze	Fourth	Fifth	Sixth	Seventh	Eighth
Karen-Margrete Harup	Suzanne Zimmerman	Judith Davies	Ilona Novák	Hendrika van der Horst	Dirkje van Ekris	Muriel Mellon	Greta Galliard
DEN – 1:14.4 *o*	USA – 1:16.0	AUS – 1:16.7	HUN – 1:18.4	NED – 1:18.8	NED – 1:18.9	USA – 1:19.0	NED – 1:19.1

Men 100m Backstroke - World Record (1:04.0 Allen Stack USA) Olympic Record (1:05.9 Adolf Kiefer USA 1936)

Gold	Silver	Bronze	Fourth	Fifth	Sixth	Seventh	Eighth
Allen Stack	Robert Cowell	Georges Vallerey	Mario Chaves	Clemente Mejia Avila	Johannes Wild	W. John Brockway	Albert Kinnear
USA – 1:06.4	USA – 1:06.5	FRA – 1:07.8	ARG – 1:09.0	MEX – 1:09.0	RSA – 1:09.1	GBR – 1:09.2	GBR – 1:09.6

Women 200m Breaststroke - World Record (2:49.2 Petronella van Vliet NED) Olympic Record (3:01.9 H. Maehata JPN 1936)

Gold	Silver	Bronze	Fourth	Fifth	Sixth	Seventh	Eighth
Petronella van Vliet	Beatrice Lyons	Éva Novák	Éva Székely	Adriana de Groot	Elizabeth Church	Antonia Horn	Jytte Hansen
NED – 2:57.2	AUS – 2:57.7	HUN – 3:00.2	HUN – 3:02.5	NED – 3:02.6	GBR – 3:06.1	NED – 3:07.5	DEN – 3:08.1

Men 200m Breaststroke - World Record (2:30.0 Joseph Verdeur USA) Olympic Record (2:41.5 Tetsuo Hamuro JPN 1936)

Gold	Silver	Bronze	Fourth	Fifth	Sixth	Seventh	Eighth
Joseph Verdeur	Keith Carter	Robert Sohl	John Davies	Anton "Tone" Cerer	Willy Otto Jordan	Ahmed Kandil	Bjorn Bonte
USA – 2:39.3 *o*	USA – 2:40.2	USA – 2:43.9	AUS – 2:43.7	YUG – 2:46.1	BRA – 2:46.4	EGY – 2:47.5	NED – 2:47.6

1948 OLYMPIC SWIMMING FINALS

RELAY EVENTS

	Gold	Silver	Bronze	Fourth	Fifth	Sixth	Seventh	Eighth

Women 400m Freestyle Relay - World Record (4:27.6 DEN)   Olympic Record (4:36.0 NED 1936)

Gold	Silver	Bronze	Fourth	Fifth	Sixth	Seventh	Eighth
Marie Corridon, Thelma Kalama, Brenda Helser, Ann Curtis	Eva Riise, Karen-Margrete Harup, Greta Andersen, Fritze Carstensen, *p* – Elvi Carlsen Svendsen	Irma Schumacher, Margot Marsman, Marie-Louise Vaessen, Johanna Termeulen	Patricia Nielsen, Margaret Wellington, Lillian Preece, Catherine Gibson	Mária Littomeritzky, Judit Temes, Ilona Novák, Éva Székely	Eleonora Schmitt, Maria Leão da Costa Talita de, Alencar Rodrigues, Piedade Silva Tavares	Josette Arene, Gisele Vallerey, Colette Thomas, Ginette Jany, *p* – Marie Foucher-Cretau	Gisela Thidholm, Elisabeth Ahlgren, Marianne Lundquist, Inggeard Fredin
USA – 4:29.2 o	DEN – 4:29.6	NED – 4:31.6	GBR – 4:34.7	HUN – 4:44.8	BRA – 4:49.1	FRA – 4:49.8	SWE – dq

Men 800m Freestyle Relay - World and Olympic Record (8:51.5 JPN 1936)

Gold	Silver	Bronze	Fourth	Fifth	Sixth	Seventh	Eighth
Walter Ris, Wallace Wolf, William Smith, *p* – Robert Gibe, William Dudley, Edwin Gilbert, Eugene Rogers	Elemér Szathmáry, György Mitró, Imre Nyéki, Géza Kádas	Joseph Bernardo, Henri Padou, René Cornu, Alexandre Jany	Martin Lundén, Per-Olof Östrand, Olle Johansson, Per-Olof Olsson	Vanja Ilic, Ciril Pelhan, Ivan Puhar, Branko Vidovic	Horacio White, José Durañona, Juan Garay, Alfredo Yantorno, *p* – Antonio Canton	Ramon Bravo Prieto, Angel Maldonado Campos, Alfredo Apolonio Diaz Castillo, Alberto Isaac Ahumada	Sergio Alencar Rodrigues, Willy Jordan, Rof Kestener Egon, Aram Boghossian
USA – 8:46.0 w	HUN – 8:48.4	FRA – 9:08.0	SWE – 9:09.1	YUG – 9:14.0	ARG – 9:19.2	MEX – 9:20.2	BRA – 9:31.0

Chapter 13

Olympiad XV - 1952
Helsinki, Finland

helsinki is the smallest city ever to host the Olympic Games. Sixty-nine countries were represented by 4,925 competitors and a growing number of these athletes were women (518). The 1952 Games also witnessed the return of the Russians as the Soviet Union to Olympic competition after a forty-year absence.

The Hungarian women dominated the pool, winning four of the five events. Three different swimmers captured gold in the women's events.

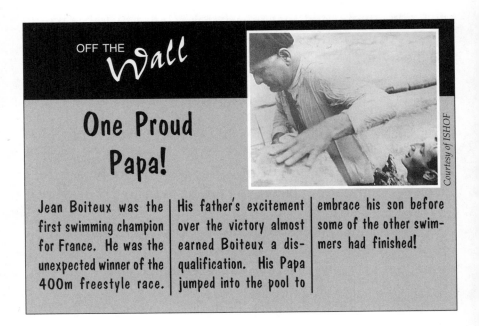

OFF THE *Wall*

Courtesy of ISHOF

One Proud Papa!

Jean Boiteux was the first swimming champion for France. He was the unexpected winner of the 400m freestyle race. His father's excitement over the victory almost earned Boiteux a disqualification. His Papa jumped into the pool to embrace his son before some of the other swimmers had finished!

SPLASH BACK

Oyakawa Cracks Keifer's Olympic Record

At the age of fifteen, American Yoshinobu "Yoshi" Oyakawa, was considered a late comer to competitive swimming. Only three years later in 1952, he would make Olympic history.

Yoshi broke Adolph Kiefer's Olympic 100m backstroke record set back in 1936, as he took gold in Helsinki. He was also a member of the 1956 U.S. Olympic Swim Team, a squad that included six fellow Hawaiian Islanders.

JOHN DAVIES
AUSTRALIA

Two-time Olympian John Davies of Australia represented the end of an era for butterfly breaststrokers at the 1952 Helsinki Games.

A subsequent rules change, beginning with the 1956 Olympic Games mandated that breaststroke/butterfly races would then be two separate events, and swimmers could no longer use the fly stroke in breaststroke competition.

With the rule change, it was thought that John Davies' gold medal performance and Olympic record for the 200m breaststroke (2:34.4), would be unreachable, since he used the faster butterfly stroke to set the record. However, three Olympiads later, at the 1964 Olympic Games, five of the 200m breaststroke finalists swam 2:31.1 or better, swimming the actual breaststroke.

With this rule change, official world record and Olympic record standards for the breaststroke events would be based on times attained using only the actual breaststroke.

Prior to the 1952 Olympics, John Davies swam for the University of Michigan. Matt Mann was his coach. Davies represented his native Australia at the Helsinki Games and ironically, the United States Olympic swim coach was Mann.

After the 1952 Olympic Games, Davies went on to complete his education in the United States. He obtained U.S. citizenship, practiced law in California and was later appointed a U.S. District judge.

FORD KONNO
UNITED STATES

Suffering from a serious sinus infection during the Olympic Trials, Ford Konno almost failed to qualify for the United States Olympic Team. A triple medalist in 1952, Konno took

Courtesy of ISHOF

gold in the 1500m freestyle, another with the 800m free relay squad, and a silver medal for the 400m freestyle event.

Konno returned to the Olympic Games in 1956 as a member of the silver medal winning 800m freestyle relay team. This two-time Olympian married teammate Evelyn Kawamoto, a double medalist at the Helsinki Games.

Ford Konno National AAU Outdoor Champion 1951.

ÉVA SZÉKELY
HUNGARY

Éva Székely's amazing career spanned three Olympiads. She was a member of the Hungarian team in 1948, 1952, and 1956. In 1936, when Hungarian Ferene Csik won the 100m freestyle and the national anthem was played, nine-year old Éva Székely decided to win a gold medal.

In 1952 Éva was the first, and last female to use the butterfly arm stroke to win a gold medal for the 200m breaststroke event. At the 1956 Olympic Games, she once again swam the 200m breaststroke event and won silver, this time using the breaststroke.

Growing up during World War II, Éva lived in a Swiss-run safe house in Budapest. At the age of 14 she was expelled from the local swimming team because she was Jewish, but she dreamed of becoming an Olympic Champion. To stay fit, each morning she would run up and down the stairs of her five-story apartment building 100 times.

Éva Székely 200m breaststroke champion.

Courtesy of ISHOF

Éva Székely married fellow Hungarian Dezso Gyarmarti. In Helsinki they won "his and her" gold medals. Gyarmarti, a water polo player, competed in five Olympiads, winning five Olympic medals.

Days before the Gyarmartis left to participate in the 1956 Olympic Games a revolt erupted in Hungary. They were unable to change their plans and had to leave their daughter Andrea behind. Worried sick about her daughter, Éva lost 12 pounds and had little sleep. Even with the uncertainty she managed to capture a silver medal. It was one of the few times she had been beaten in competition.

"There is one thing that cannot be taken away from anybody, one's inner security, which consists of faith, discipline, willpower, knowledge, humanity, and never accepting the finality of evil."
— *Éva Székely*

L A N E   L I N E S

"Temes Place in Time"

Judit Temes, a member of Hungary's gold medal relay team, also won a bronze medal for the 100m freestyle. Temes posted a time of 1:05.5 and a new Olympic record in the qualifying heat of the 100m freestyle, over a second faster than the subsequent winning time of 1:06.8. During the final of this event, not one judge had placed Temes in the medal count. However, a review of the official times placed Temes third and she was awarded the bronze medal.

KATALIN SZÖKE
HUNGARY

Introduced to swimming at the age of six months, Katalin Szöke was known as, "Kati, the World's First Waterproof Baby." She was actually able to tread water, unassisted, before the age of two!

In the 100m freestyle event of these 1952 Games, spectators saw the lead change three times in the last 10 meters. The first six finishers touched within two feet of each other in the final of this event. The race was so close it took the judges 10 minutes to declare Katalin the champion.

Szöke also anchored Hungary's powerful 400m freestyle relay team to victory, finishing five full seconds ahead of the silver medal Netherlands' relay squad. At the ripe old age of 16, "the waterproof baby" had earned two Olympic gold medals.

Valéria Gyenge
Hungary

Gold medal winner in the 400m freestyle.

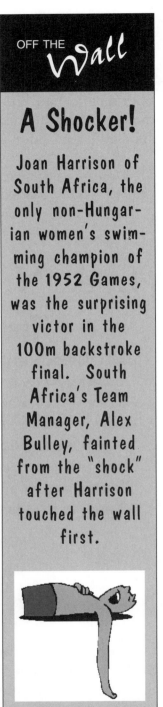

OFF THE *Wall*

A Shocker!

Joan Harrison of South Africa, the only non-Hungarian women's swimming champion of the 1952 Games, was the surprising victor in the 100m backstroke final. South Africa's Team Manager, Alex Bulley, fainted from the "shock" after Harrison touched the wall first.

1952 OLYMPIC SWIMMING FINALS

INDIVIDUAL EVENTS

Gold	Silver	Bronze	Fourth	Fifth	Sixth	Seventh	Eighth
Women 100m Freestyle - World Record (1:04.6 W. den Ouden NED) Olympic Record (1:05.9 Rie Mastenbroek NED 1936)							
Katalin Szöke	Johanna Termeulen	Judit Temes p - 1:05.5 o	Joan Harrison	Joan Alderson	Irma Heijting-Schulmacher	Marilee Stephan	Angela Barnwell
HUN – 1:06.8	NED – 1:07.0	HUN – 1:07.1	RSA – 1:07.1	USA – 1:07.1	NED – 1:07.3	USA – 1:08.0	GBR – 1:08.6
Men 100m Freestyle - World Record (55.4 Alan Ford USA) Olympic Record (57.3 Walter Ris USA 1948)							
Clarke Scholes p - 57.1 o	Hiroshi Suzuki	Göran Larsson	Toru Goto	Géza Kádas	Aldo Eminente	Rex Aubrey	Ronald Gora
USA – 57.4	JPN – 57.4	SWE – 58.2	JPN – 58.5	HUN – 58.6	AUS – 58.7	FRA – 58.7	USA – 58.8
Women 400m Freestyle – World Record (5:00.1 Ragnhild Hveger DEN) Olympic Record (5:17.8 Ann Curtis USA 1948)							
Valéria Gyenge	Éva Novák	Evelyn Kawamoto	Carolyn Green	Ragnhild Andersen-Hveger	Éva Székely	Anna Maria Schultz	Greta Andersen
HUN – 5:12.1 o	HUN – 5:13.7	USA – 5:14.6	USA – 5:16.5	DEN – 5:16.9	HUN - 5:17.9	ARG – 5:24.0	DEN – 5:27.0

w World Record   o Olympic Record   p Preliminary Heat   dq Disqualified   e Equal to World Record   eo Equal to Olympic Record
dns Did Not Start   dnf Did Not Finish   ac Also Competed   r Relay Lead-off Split   E Estimated

OLYMPIAD XV – 1952 – HELSINKI, FINLAND

1952 OLYMPIC SWIMMING FINALS

	Gold	Silver	Bronze	Fourth	Fifth	Sixth	Seventh	Eighth
Men 400m Freestyle - World Record (4:26.9 John Marshall AUS) Olympic Record (4:41.0 William Smith USA 1948)								
	Jean Boiteux FRA – 4:30.7 *o*	Ford Konno USA – 4:31.3	Per-Olof Östrand SWE – 4:35.2	Peter Duncan RSA – 4:37.9	John Wardrop GBR – 4:39.9	Wayne Moore USA – 4:40.1	James McLane USA – 4:40.3	Hironashin Furuhashi JPN – 4:42.1
Men 1500m Freestyle - World Record (18:19.0 Hironashin Furuhashi JPN) Olympic Record (19:12.4 K. Kitamura JPN 1932)								
	Ford Konno USA – 18:30.3 *o*	Shiro Hashizume JPN – 18:41.4	Tetsuo Okamoto BRA – 18:51.3	James McLane USA – 18:51.5	Joseph Bernardo FRA – 18:59.1	Yasuo Kitamura JPN – 19:00.4	Peter Duncan RSA – 19:12.1	John Marshall AUS – 19:53.4
Women 100m Backstroke - World Record (1:10.9 Cornelia Kint NED) Olympic Record (1:14.4 Karen M. Harup DEN 1948)								
	Joan Harrison RSA – 1:14.3	Geertje Wielema *p* – 1:13.8 *o* NED – 1:14.5	Jean Stewart NZE – 1:15.8	Johanna de Korte NED – 1:15.8	Barbara Stark USA – 1:16.2	Gertrud Herbruck GER – 1:18.0	Margaret McDowell GBR – 1:18.4	Hendrika van der Horst NED – *du*
Men 100m Backstroke - World Record (1:03.6 Allen Stack USA) Olympic Record (1:05.9 Adolf Kiefer USA 1936)								
	Yoshinobu Oyakawa USA – 1:05.4 *o*	Gilbert Bozon FRA – 1:06.2	Jack Taylor USA – 1:06.4	Allen Stack USA – 1:07.6	Pedro Galvao ARG – 1:07.7	Robert Wardrop GBR – 1:07.8	Boris Skanata YUG – 1:08.1	Nicolaas Meiring RSA – 1:08.3
Women 200m Breaststroke - World Record (2:48.5 Éva Novák HUN) Olympic Record (2:57.0 Petronella van Vliet NED 1948)								
	Éva Székely HUN – 2:51.7 *o*	Éva Novák HUN – 2:54.4	Helen "Elenor" Gordon GBR – 2:57.6	Klára Killermann HUN – 2:57.6	Jytte Hansen DEN – 2:57.8	Maria Havrysh SOV – 2:58.9	Ulla-Britt Eklund SWE – 3:01.8	Petronella Garritsen NED – 3:02.1
Men 200m Breaststroke - World Record (2:27.3 Herbert Klein GER) Olympic Record (2:39.3 Joseph Verdeur USA 1948)								
	John Davies AUS – 2:34.4 *o*	Bowen Stassforth USA – 2:34.7	Herbert Klein GER – 2:35.9	Nobuyasu Hirayama JPN – 2:37.4	Takayoshi Kajikawa JPN – 2:38.6	Jiro Nagasawa JPN – 2:39.1	Maurice Lusien FRA – 2:39.8	Ludevit Komadel CZE – 2:40.1

1952 OLYMPIC SWIMMING FINALS

RELAY EVENTS

	Gold	Silver	Bronze	Fourth	Fifth	Sixth	Seventh	Eighth

Women 400m Freestyle Relay - World Record (4:27.2 HUN) — Olympic Record (4:29.2 USA 1948)

	Gold	Silver	Bronze	Fourth	Fifth	Sixth	Seventh	Eighth
	Ilona Nová, Judit Temes, Éva Novák, Katalin Szöke, p – Mária Littomericzky	Marie-Louise Linssen (Vaessen), Koosje van Voorn, Johanna Termeulen, Irma Heijting-Schuhmacher	Jacqueline La Vine, Marilee Stepan, Joan Alderson, Evelyn Kawamoto	Rita Larsen, Mette Ove-Peterson, Greta Andersen, Ragnhild Andersen-Hveger	Phyllis Linton, Jean Botham, Angela Barnwell, Lillian Preece	Marianne Lundquist, Anita Andersson, Maud Berglund, Inegärd Fredin	Elisabeth Rechlin, Vera Schäferkordt, Kati Jansen, Gisela Jacobs (Arendt)	Gaby Tanguy, Maryse Morandini, Ginette Jany, Josette Arene
	HUN – 4:24.4 w	NED – 4:29.0	USA – 4:30.1	DEN – 4:36.2	GBR – 4:37.8	SWE – 4:39.0	GER – 4:40.3	FRA – 4:44.1

Men 800m Freestyle Relay - World Record (8:29.4 USA) — Olympic Record (8:46.0 USA 1948)

	Gold	Silver	Bronze	Fourth	Fifth	Sixth	Seventh	Eighth
	Wayne Moore, William Woolsey, Ford Konno, James McLane, p – Wallace Wolf, Donald Sheff, Frank Dooley, Burwell Jones	Hiroshi Suzuki, Yoshihiro Hamaguchi, Toru Goto, Teijiro Tanikawa	Joseph Bernardo, Aldo Eminente, Alexandre Jany, Jean Boiteux	Lars Svanteson, Göran Larsson, Per-Olof Östrand, Olle Johansson, p – Rolf Olander	László Gyöngyösi, György Csordás, Géza Kádas, Imre Nyéki, p – Gusztáv Kettesi	Frank Botham, Ronald Burns, Thomas Welsh, John Wardrop	Graham Johnston, Dennis Ford, John Durr, Peter Duncan	Federico Zwanck, Marcelo Trabucco, Pedro Galvao, Alfredo Yantorno
	USA – 8:31.1 o	JPN – 8:33.5	FRA – 8:45.9	SWE – 8:46.8	HUN – 8:52.6	GBR – 8:52.9	RSA – 8:55.1	ARG – 8:56.9

Chapter 14

Olympiad XVI was the first to be held in the Southern Hemisphere. Sixty-nine of the seventy-four invited countries were present.

For the first time, the butterfly stroke and the breaststroke were separated into two different events. Unfortunately there were differences in the interpretation of what was considered a "breaststroke," and it lead to six disqualifications.

The men and women from "down under" came out on top in the pool. It was the start of a new era in swimming...that of the "awesome Aussies."

LORRAINE CRAPP
AUSTRALIA

Lorraine Crapp of Australia was the first woman to break the five-minute barrier in the 400m freestyle event. She broke Ragnhild Hvegar's world record, set 16 years earlier (Hvegar's record was set in a 25m pool giving her the extra turn advantage).

Coach Frank Gutherie thought Lorraine too quick for her peers, so he had her train with the Australian Men's Team. In 1956 Crapp set four world records in one swim (200m, 220y, 400m & 440y freestyle). Incredibly, two months later she would repeat this accomplishment.

In 1955 Lorraine suffered a severe ear infection and it was feared that she would not recover her winning form. Recover she did! In 1956, during the training period prior to the Olympic Games, she broke 18 world records.

Lorraine went on to claim a total of four Olympic medals during the 1956 and 1960 Olympic Games.

Australian teammates (L-R) Lorraine Crapp, Sandra Morgan, Ilsa Konrads, and Dawn Fraser.

Courtesy of ISHOF

DAWN FRASER
AUSTRALIA

Dawn Fraser, the youngest of eight children, was enticed into her sport after she teased some swimmers at the local pool in Balmain, Australia. The coach, Harry Gallagher, challenged Fraser to swim against them and quickly saw her talent.

In 1956, Dawn broke Willy den Ouden's 20-year world record. She also became the first woman to break the one-minute barrier for the 100m freestyle and eventually lowered it to 58.9 seconds.

This record stood for close to eight years!

After winning the 100m freestyle final at the 1956 Games, Dawn borrowed a ladder from a TV crew and climbed into the stands to share tears of joy with her parents. It was a moment to savor and one that the family dedicated to the memory of Dawn's deceased brother. From this day forward, and for the next 15 years, Dawn Fraser would hold the 100m freestyle record.

Fraser wrote in her biography, "Below the Surface," that the night before her Olympic 100m freestyle swim in 1956 she had a nightmare. "The gun went off," she said, "but I had honey on my feet and it was hard to pull them away from the starting block. I finally fought free and dived high...it seemed a long time before I hit the water and the water wasn't water, it was spaghetti... Of course I fouled up the turn and took a few mouthfuls and I woke up gasping and fighting in a sea of spaghetti."

In 1964 tragedy struck. Dawn was in an auto accident that took the life of her mother. Her sister, also a passenger in the car, was knocked unconscious. Fraser suffered a chipped vertebra and spent six weeks in a plaster cast.

OFF THE *Wall*

"Not Suitable"

Dawn Fraser was nervous and tense before her races. Once at a meet in Sydney, she started to peel off her gym suit when an official put his hand up in front of her. "Don't lift that jacket any higher," he said, "You've forgotten your bathing suit." The young Aussie looked down to discover the official was right!

Nude Swimming

Astoundingly, Fraser worked her way back into Olympic

form just seven months later. At the age of 27, she qualified for her third Olympic Team, and was known as "Granny" to her teammates.

The high spirited Aussie was known to break rules as often as records. At the 1964 Games Fraser led a midnight raid to borrow a "souvenir flag" from the Emperor's Palace in Tokyo. Dawn was arrested but the charges were dropped and the Emperor graciously gave her the flag as a gift.

The Australian Swimming Union did not let Fraser off so lightly. She was initially given a ten-year suspension. Ironically, the decision came down just after Dawn had been named, "Australian of the Year." After four years her suspension was lifted. Dawn Fraser was later elected to the Parliament of New South Wales.

Olympic 1ST
What a Streak!

Dawn Fraser is one of the greatest swimmers the world has ever seen. She was the first swimmer of either sex to win the same event in three successive Olympiads (1956, 1960 & 1964). Her total Olympic winnings number four gold and four silver medals.

MASARU FURUKAWA
JAPAN

Masaru Furukawa of Japan was the eventual winner of the men's 200m breaststroke...and the least visible! His extraordinary technique kept him submerged for 75% of the race. A loophole in the breaststroke rules and Furukawa's incredible lung capacity gained him gold.

In a Tokyo meet on October 1, 1956, Furukawa broke world records, in the 200m, 200y, 100m and 100y breaststroke events in only two swims! He took only five breaths during the entire 100m / 100y breaststroke swim. However, soon after the 1956 Games, F.I.N.A. put an end to the "underwater era" and Furukawa's swimming career along with it.

SPLASH BACK

Grinham's Gold First for Britain Since Morton in '24!

Judy Grinham's win in the 100m backstroke, made her the first British swimmer to win a gold medal in 32 years. Not since Lucy Morton in 1924 had Great Britain held swimming gold. Grinham's world record breaking time (1:12.9) was ratified as the first long-course world record for the 100m backstroke.

JON MALCOLM HENRICKS
AUSTRALIA

Jon Henricks was the gold medal victor in the 100m freestyle event in 1956. It was his 56th straight win at that distance during a three-year period. The Olympic final made history, with all three medal winners, Henricks, John Devitt, and Gary Chapman breaking the Olympic record for an Australian sweep. Henricks won an additional gold medal anchoring Australia's 800m free relay team.

Jon Henricks is the first swimmer to "shave down" for competition, an innovation that is still adhered to universally by swimmers today. Henricks recapped how this ritual came about.

"Back in January of 1953 I'd been converted to sprints and seemed to have "plateau'd" at about 59.2 for 100m. In those days, it

was certainly good enough to place in the 100.

We lived on the water at Rhodes. Every week we'd watch the sailors preparing the hulls of the VJ's for racing. They took an inordinate time getting them smooth. My father said to me one day, "You know, son, you're as hairy as an old goat. Why don't we scrape you down like they do the hulls of a boat?

And so we did. At first I only shaved my chest, rationalizing that I needed my arms and legs to get power. But that first experiment got me down to 58.2 in the state champs. There was no doubt in my mind that the technique worked, so for the Aussie champs (I believe February 1953) we shaved chest, arms and legs. I equaled the Olympic record for meters in a 55y pool (22" longer) and from then on "shaving down" became my ritual." — J.M. Henricks

Henricks missed the 1952 Games due to ear trouble. On his way to Rome for the 1960 Olympics, he was one of many Olympic Australian Team members struck by an illness. Henricks was favored in Rome to win the 100m

OFF THE Wall

Vitamin C Trickery!

Harry Gallagher was one of Australia's finest coaches and was as well known for his sense of humor as his coaching ability. Jon Henricks shared this story:

"Coach Gallagher had noticed the Russians were recording our every move in training...filming everything. While in the lockers, Coach Gallagher called a quick meeting. We were to start the workout weary and bedraggled. Our times were to be 75% or less. Then he'd imperiously call us all to him on the deck. He would then surreptitiously give us each a 100mg vitamin C pill. We then did a series of 100% plus sprints, packed up and went home. After the swimming was over, Harry and I were invited to have dinner with the Russian coaches. They tried every trick to find out what it was we had ingested. We all had a great chuckle...never did let them know."

"Incidentally, the dedication those Russian coaches had to learning certainly paid off. Even after the break-up of the USSR, their swim program still is a threat," added Henricks.

freestyle, but was too sick to swim the final or the relay.

Henricks' 1956 Olympic winning time was later ratified as the first long-course world record and he also helped set four world record relay marks. Jon Henricks is an executive vice president for an industrial distribution company, resides in the United States, where he and his wife raised four children.

Courtesy of Jon Henricks

Sprinter Jon Henricks

SHELLY MANN
UNITED STATES

Stricken by polio at the age of six, Shelly Mann swam to strengthen her limbs. At the age of 12 she began swimming competitively, and soon grew to be one of the most versatile swimmers in the world.

She is recognized as the first great female four-stroke swimmer (individual medley). At one time Mann held world records in the 100m fly, 200m fly, 100m freestyle, 400m IM. She also won the U.S. National Championship in the backstroke.

In addition to her Olympic 100m butterfly win, she collected a silver medal as a member of the American relay squad and placed sixth in the 100m freestyle final. She was the only American woman to win a swimming title at the 1956 Olympic Games.

SPLASH BACK

Rose Wins Two!

In 1956, Murray Rose won two individual freestyle events in one Olympiad. The great Hawaiian swimmer Duke Kahanamoku was the last male swimmer to accomplish this feat back in 1924.

IAIN MURRAY ROSE
AUSTRALIA

Murray Rose was the first male swimmer in 32 years to win two individual freestyle events in one Olympiad. He was the youngest triple gold medalist in the history of the Olympic Games, at 17 years and 332 days.

Courtesy of ISHOF

Youngest triple gold medalist in Olympic history.

Rose returned to the Games in 1960 and made history once again by becoming the first male ever to successfully defend the Olympic 400m swim title, a distinction he still owns. Rose collected a total of four gold, one silver, and one bronze medal during his Olympic career.

Rose was unable to return to Australia in 1964 for their National Championships, unaware that they were to serve as the Olympic Trials. He was not awarded a berth on the Olympic team.

Sentiment was high in favor of allowing Rose to compete. In August of that year he had broken the world record in the 1500m freestyle event at the American National Championships. Unfortunately, the Australian Swimming Union ruled against Rose and upheld the decision they had handed down.

Murray Rose's swimming career included nine years as a world record holder. During his reign Rose held world records for 1650y, 1500m, 880y, 800m, 440y, 400m, and 200m freestyle events.

SCORE
BOARD
Deja Vu
1956 Melbourne

400M FREESTYLE			1500M FREESTYLE
Murray Rose	(AUS)	Gold	Murray Rose
Tsuyoshi Yamanaka	(JPN)	Silver	Tsuyoshi Yamanaka
George Breen	(USA)	Bronze	George Breen

LANE LINES

Saving His Best for Last?

George Breen of the United States broke the world record in a qualifying round of the 1500m freestyle, but placed third in the final, swimming close to six seconds slower than his preliminary heat.

David Theile- Australia

medal count 3

1956 – Melbourne
100m Backstroke - Gold
Olympic Record

1960 – Rome
100m Backstroke – Gold
Olympic Record
400m Medley Relay – Silver

Between Olympiads, Theile attended medical school and later became a surgeon.

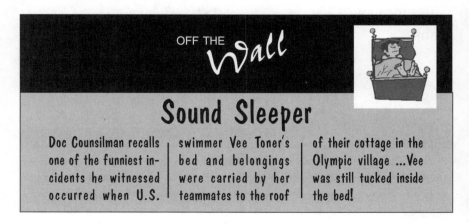

OFF THE **Wall**

Sound Sleeper

Doc Counsilman recalls one of the funniest incidents he witnessed occurred when U.S. swimmer Vee Toner's bed and belongings were carried by her teammates to the roof of their cottage in the Olympic village ...Vee was still tucked inside the bed!

WILLIAM YORZYK
UNITED STATES

With the addition of the butterfly event to the 1956 Olympic program, William "Bill" Yorzyk of Northampton, Massachusetts became the first Olympic Champion of the 200m butterfly. He was the only male from the United States Swim Team to win gold at these Games.

Yorzyk's swimming career amazingly began as a freshman at Springfield College in Massachusetts. It was here that he met Coach Charles "Red" Sylvia, who immediately recognized Yorzyk's talent and helped him develop to his full potential. Yorzyk was the first to swim the fly using two kicks to "one arm cycle," in competition.

Despite his late start, Bill set eleven world records and captured five National butterfly championships.

Yorzyk later graduated from the University of Toronto and became an anesthesiologist. Dr. Yorzyk served as an associate physician to the 1964 Olympic Team.

Courtesy of ISHOF

Yorzyk on the fly.

SPLASH BACK

Gallagher Matches "Big Bill's Feat of '24 !

At the 1924 Olympic Games Americans Ethel Lackie and Johnny Weissmuller were both coached to victory in the 100m freestyle event by William Bachrach. "Big Bill" was the first person to coach both the men's and women's champion in this event at the same Olympiad. Thirty-two years later, Harry Gallagher coached both Australian swimmers Dawn Fraser and Jon Henricks to gold in the 100m free.

1956 OLYMPIC SWIMMING FINALS

Gold	Silver	Bronze	Fourth	Fifth	Sixth	Seventh	Eighth

INDIVIDUAL EVENTS

Women 100m Freestyle - World Record (1:02.4 Lorraine Crapp AUS)   Olympic Record (1:05.5 Judit Temes HUN 1952)

Gold	Silver	Bronze	Fourth	Fifth	Sixth	Seventh	Eighth
Dawn Fraser	Lorraine Crapp	Faith Leech	Joan Rosazza	Virginia Grant	Shelley Mann	Marrion Roe	Natalie Myburgh
AUS – 1:02.0 w	AUS – 1:02.3	AUS – 1:05.1	USA – 1:05.2	CAN – 1:05.4	USA – 1:05.6	NZE – 1:05.6	RSA – 1:05.8

Men 100m Freestyle - World Record (54.8 Richard Cleveland USA)   Olympic Record (57.1 Clarke Scholes USA 1952)

Gold	Silver	Bronze	Fourth	Fifth	Sixth	Seventh	Eighth
Jon Henricks	John Devitt	Gary Chapman	Logan Reid Patterson	Richard Hanley	William Woolsey	Atsushi Tani	Aldo Eminente
AUS – 55.4 o	AUS – 55.8	AUS – 56.7	USA – 57.2	USA – 57.6	USA – 57.6	JPN – 58.0	FRA – 58.1

Women 400m Freestyle – World Record (4:47.2 Lorraine Crapp AUS)   Olympic Record (5:12.1 Valéria Gyenge HUN 1952)

Gold	Silver	Bronze	Fourth	Fifth	Sixth	Seventh	Eighth
Lorraine Crapp	Dawn Fraser	Sylvia Ruuska	Marley Shriver	Rypszima Szekely	Sandra Morgan	Heda Frost	Valéria Gyenge
AUS – 4:54.6 o	AUS – 5:02.5	USA – 5:07.1	USA – 5:12.9	HUN – 5:14.2	AUS – 5:14.3	FRA – 5:15.4	HUN – 5:21.0

w World Record   o Olympic Record   p Preliminary Heat   dq Disqualified   e Equal to World Record   eo Equal to Olympic Record
dns Did Not Start   dnf Did Not Finish   ac Also competed   r Relay Lead-off Split   E Estimated

OLYMPIAD XVI – 1956 – MELBOURNE, AUSTRALIA

1956 OLYMPIC SWIMMING FINALS

	Gold	Silver	Bronze	Fourth	Fifth	Sixth	Seventh	Eighth
Men 400m Freestyle - World Record (4:26.7 Ford Konno USA) Olympic Record (4:30.7 Jean Boiteux FRA 1952)	Murray Rose	Tsuyoshi Yamanaka	George Breen	Kevin O'Halloran	Hans Zierold	Garry Winram	Koji Nonoshita	Angelo Romani
	AUS – 4:27.3 o	JPN – 4:30.4	USA – 4:32.5	AUS – 4:32.9	GDR – 4:34.6	AUS – 4:34.9	JPN – 4:38.2	ITA – 4:41.7
Men 1500m Freestyle - World Record (17:59.5 Murray Rose AUS) Olympic Record (18:30.3 Ford Kono USA 1952)	Murray Rose	Tsuyoshi Yamanaka	George Breen	Murray Garretty	William Slater	Jean Boitteux	Yukiyoshi Aoki	Garry Winram
	AUS – 17:58.9	JPN – 18:00.3	p – 17:52.9 USA – 18:08.2	AUS – 18:26.5	CAN – 18:38.1	FRA – 18:38.3	JPN – 18:38.3	AUS – 19:06.2
Women 100m Backstroke - World Record (1:10.9 Cornelia Kint NED) Olympic Record (1:13.8 G. Wielema NED 1952)	Judith Grinham	Carin Cone	Margaret Edwards	Helga Schmidt	Maureen Murphy	Julie Hoyle	Sara Barber	Gerganyia Beckitt
	GBR – 1:12.9 o	USA – 1:12.9	GBR – 1:13.1	GER – 1:13.4	USA – 1:14.1	GBR – 1:14.3	CAN – 1:14.3	AUS – 1:14.7
Men 100m Backstroke - World Record (1:02.1 Gilbert Bozon FRA) Olympic Record (1:05.4 Yoshinobu Oyakawa USA 1952)	David Theile	John Monckton	Frank McKinney	Robert Christophe	John Hayres	Graham Sykes	Albert Wiggins	Yoshinobu Oyakawa
	AUS – 1:02.2 o	AUS – 1:03.2	USA – 1:04.5	FRA – 1:04.9	AUS – 1:05.0	GBR – 1:05.6	USA – 1:05.8	USA – 1:06.9

1956 OLYMPIC SWIMMING FINALS

Gold	Silver	Bronze	Fourth	Fifth	Sixth	Seventh	Eighth
Women 200m Breaststroke - World Record (**2:46.4 Adelaide den Haan NED) Olympic Record (2:51.7 É. Székely HUN 1952)							
Ursula Happe	Éva Székely	Eva-Maria ten Elsen	Vinka Jericevic	Klára Killermann	Helen "Elenor" Gordon	Mary Sears	Christine Gosden
GER **2:53.1 o	HUN – 2:54.8	GDR – 2:55.1	YUG – 2:55.8	HUN – 2:56.1	GBR – 2:56.1	USA – 2:57.2	GBR – 2:59.2
Men 200m Breaststroke - World Record (**2:31.0 Masaru Furukawa JPN) Olympic Record (2:34.4 John Davies AUS 1952)							
Masaru Furukawa	Masahiro Yoshimura	Kharis Yunichev	Terry Gathercole	Ihor Zasyeda	Knud Gleie	Manuel Sanguily	Hughes Broussard
JPN **2:34.7 o	JPN – 2:36.7	SOV – 2:36.8	AUS – 2:38.7	SOV – 2:39.0	DEN – 2:40.0	CUB – 2:42.0	FRA - dq
Women 100m Butterfly - World Record (1:10.5 Aartje Voorbij NED)				1896-1952 – Event Not Held On Olympic Program			
Shelly Mann	Nancy Ramey	Mary Sears	Maria Littomeritzky	Beverly Bainbridge	Jutta Langenau	Elizabeth Whittall	Sara Barber
USA – 1:11.0 o	USA – 1:11.9	USA – 1:14.4	HUN – 1:14.9	AUS – 1:15.2	GDR – 1:17.4	CAN – 1:17.9	CAN – 1:18.4
Men 200m Butterfly - World Record (2:16.7 William Yorzyk USA)				1896-1952 -Event Not Held On Olympic Program			
William Yorzyk	György Tumpek	Takashi Ishimoto	Jack Nelson	John Marshall	Eulalio Rios Aleman	Brian Wilkinson	Aleandru Popescu
USA – 2:19.3 o	HUN – 2:23.8	JPN – 2:23.9	USA – 2:26.6	AUS – 2:27.2	MEX – 2:27.3	AUS – 2:29.7	ROM – 2:31.0

Record based on the butterfly stroke **not being used during the breaststroke event.
Beginning with this Olympiad the breaststroke and butterfly strokes were swum as two separate events.

1956 OLYMPIC SWIMMING FINALS

RELAY EVENTS

Women 400m Freestyle Relay - World Record (4:19.7 AUS)   Olympic Record (4:24.4 HUN 1952)

Gold	Silver	Bronze	Fourth	Fifth	Sixth	Seventh	Eighth
Dawn Fraser, Faith Leech, Sandra Morgan, *p* – Lorraine Crapp, *p* – Margaret Gibson	Sylvia Ruuska, Shelly Mann, Nancy Simons, Joan Rosazza, *p* – Betty Brey, Kathryn Knapp, Marley Shriver	Jeanette Myburgh, Susan Roberts, Natalie Myburgh, Moira Abernathy	Ingrid Künzel, Hertha Hasse, Kathi Jansen, Birgit Klomp	Helen Stewart, Gladys Priestley, Sara Barber, Virginia Grant	Anita Hellström, Birgitta Wängberg, Anna Larsson, Kate Jobson	Mária Littomeritzky, Katalin Szöke, Judit Temes, Valeria Gyenge	Frances Hogben, Judith Grinham, Margaret Girvan, Fearne Ewart
AUS – 4:17.1 w	USA – 4:19.2	RSA – 4:25.7	GER – 4:26.1	CAN – 4:28.3	SWE – 4:30.0	HUN – 4:31.1	GBR – 4:35.8

Men 800m Freestyle Relay - World Record (8:24.5 SOV)   Olympic Record (8:31.1 USA 1952)

Gold	Silver	Bronze	Fourth	Fifth	Sixth	Seventh	Eighth
Kevin O'Halloran, John Devitt, Murray Rose, Jon Henricks, *p* – Gary Chapman, Graham Hamilton, Murray Garretty	Richard Hanley, George Breen, William Woolsey, Ford Kono, *p* – Perry Jecku, Richard Tanabe	Vitaly Sorokin, Vladimir Strushanov, Gennady Nikolayev, Boris Nikitin	Manabu Koga, Atsushi Tani, Koji Nonoshita, Tsuyoshi Yamanaka	Hans Köhler, Hans-Joachim Reich, Hans Zierold, Horst Bleeker	Ken. Williams, Ronald Roberts, Neil McKecknie, John Wardrop	Frederico Dennerlein, Paolo Galletti, Guido Elmi, Anthony Romani	William Steuart, Anthony Briscoe, Dennis Ford, Peter Duncan
AUS – 8:23.6 w	USA – 8:31.5	SOV – 8:34.7	JPN – 8:36.6	GER/GDR 8:43.4	GBR – 8:45.2	ITA – 8:46.2	RSA – 8:49.5

Chapter 15

Olympiad XVII - 1960
Rome, Italy

in 1960 the Olympics entered our living rooms for the first time with worldwide coverage of the Games. The competition was as hot as the temperatures in Rome.

"Underwater stroking," banned in 1957, accounted for the times of the 1960 men's breaststroke final being over six seconds slower than the previous Games.

The Australian Men's Swim Team continued to rule the water despite many members suffering from what came to be called "Roman Tummy." The Aussie women's domination ended, with the exception of Dawn Fraser and her second consecutive gold medal swim in the 100m freestyle.

The United States' Olympic Women's Swim Team, referred to as the "Water Babies," consisted of 14 swimmers ranging in age from 13 to 18. Not since 1932 had the American women done so well.

Olympic 1ST
Golden Medley

The 4X100m medley relay format made it's first appearance in Olympic swimming competition at the 1960 Games, in both the men's and women's program.

The United States' Men's and Women's Swim Teams swept both the freestyle and medley relay races in world record time.

THE DEVITT – LARSON DECISION

Perhaps the most controversial call in Olympic history came during the Men's 100m freestyle final in Rome. Australian John Devitt and Lance Larson of the United States both came thundering to the wall in an explosive finish.

(left)
Lance
Larson
(bottom)
John
Devitt

To many it appeared that Larson had touched out Devitt. In fact, Devitt offered his congratulations to Larson before climbing out of the pool. To the astonishment of both competitors, Devitt was announced the winner.

Photos courtesy of ISHOF

It was revealed that of the three first place judges, two picked Devitt as the winner. However, two of the three second-place judges had also picked Devitt for second place! This tally gave each of the two swimmers three first place votes, as well as three second-place votes.

To confuse the issue even further, a check of the two teams of timers was conducted. Each of the three timers on Devitt clocked him at an identical time of 55.2. Larson was timed at 55.0, 55.1 and 55.1. This proved that Larson's swim was in fact faster than Devitts' official first place finish.

Film of the race was reviewed and it appeared that Larson had, in fact, touched before Devitt. It was also revealed that the unofficial judging machine, which was manually operated, clearly indicated the Larson had touched first.

The solution to this embarrassment was the changing of Lance Larson's time to match Devitt's 55.2. Despite the overwhelming evidence in Larson's favor, the decision stood. John Devitt was awarded the gold medal and Lance Larson the silver.

Ironically, both Larson and Devitt co-held the Olympic record at the 55.2 time. Protests were filed on Larson's behalf for years to no avail. He is destined to remain an "unofficial Olympic Champion."

GEORGE BREEN
UNITED STATES

George Breen failed to make the football team at Cortland State and so began his swim career. Under "Doc" Counsilman's tutelage Breen went on to collect a total of four Olympic medals between the 1956 and 1960 Games.

At the 1956 AAU Indoor Championship at Yale, Breen set a long course record in the 1500m freestyle, lowering his personal best by 13.1 seconds. The second place swimmer came in one minute and 18 seconds behind him. No one in the history of these championships had ever finished that far ahead of the second place finisher.

At the 1956 Olympic Games George Breen set a world record in the 1500m freestyle event, smashing the 1500m record he had set at Yale by another 13 seconds. Unfortunately this record came during a preliminary race and Breen "peaked too early," placing third in the Olympic final. The gold medalist in that race, Murray Rose, had a winning time that was six seconds slower than George's new world record.

LYNN BURKE
UNITED STATES

Lynn Burke's victory in the 100m backstroke at the 1960 Olympic Games was the United States' first win in this event since 1932. In July of 1960, Burke broke Cornelia Kint's 100m backstroke time (1:10.9) set back in 1939. Burke proceeded to break her own world record twice at the Olympic Trials held the following month (1:09.2).

Courtesy of ISHOF

100m Backstroke medalists: S. Tanaka (JPN), L. Burke (U.S.A.), N. Steward (GBR).

Burke and her best friend, fellow Olympian Chris Von Saltza, trained together under world renowned Coach George Haines. They lived together for a time at Von Saltza's home while training for the upcoming Olympic Games. Lynn Burke and Chris Von Saltza even won gold together, as members of the 400m medley relay team.

L A N E   L I N E S

Early Bird Gets the Gold

Anita Lonsbrough of Great Britain found that she needed to get up several hours prior to a morning race to be prepared. In Rome she set her clock for 4 a.m. to be physically and mentally ready for her 10:00 a.m. heat. Lonsbrough went on to out swim the German duo of Wiltrud Urselmann and Barbara Gobel for gold in the 200m breaststroke final.

OFF THE *Wall*

Farrell Olympic Bound

American freestyle sprinter Jeff Farrell was considered the man to beat in the 100m freestyle event in Rome. Then the unthinkable happened. Six days before the U.S. Olympic Trials, Farrell had to be rushed to a hospital for an emergency appendectomy.

Before his surgery Farrell's doctor advised him that it would be six weeks before he could swim again. Two days after surgery, however, this courageous athlete was back in the water; he had been given permission to use the hospital pool. For the next four days Farrell battled constant pain but continued working with his swimming coach, Bob Kiphuth, in his bid to gain a berth on the U.S. Olympic Team.

Refusing a special dispensation, Jeff competed at the Trials wrapped tightly in adhesive bandages. Most assumed the recent surgery had taken its toll. Farrell however, recalls his 100m free final at the Olympic Trials differently:

"The reason I did not qualify for an individual event was that, believe it or not, despite the bandage around my waist, I was overconfident going into the finals of the 100 freestyle (I was fastest in prelims and 2nd fastest in semifinals). I had been the fastest in the world in the 100 for the previous year, and I really should have made it. But, overconfident, I lost my concentration and swam into the lane line about 15 or 20 meters from the end. I was third, missing second by one-tenth of a second, and they only took two in each individual event that year."

Farrell's fourth place finish in the 200m free final qualified him for a much-deserved place on the U.S. Olympic Team, as a member of the relay squad. The crowd showed its support by giving Jeff a well-deserved standing ovation.

Farrell was back to world class form by the time the Americans arrived in Rome. He anchored both the 4X100m medley and the 4X200m free relay teams to world record times. Jeff Farrell was a champion long before he won gold in Rome.

JOHN KONRADS
AUSTRALIA

John Konrads was stricken with childhood polio and began swimming to combat the effects of the disease. He continued swimming long after his recovery and became one of the world's premier distance swimmers.

Konrads was the world record holder in both the 400m and 1500m freestyle events entering the 1960 Olympic Games. The 17 year-old Konrads captured gold in the 1500m freestyle event, bronze in the 400m, and yet another bronze with the 800m free relay team. Ilsa Konrads, John's sister, captured a silver medal as a member of the 400m free relay squad at these same Games.

Frank McKinney - U.S.A.

1956 – Melbourne
100m Backstroke – Bronze

1960 – Rome
100m Backstroke – Silver
400m Medley Relay - Gold

WILLIAM MULLIKEN
UNITED STATES

At the 1960 Olympic Games Bill Mulliken was initially going to room with diver Sam Hall. As they were settling into their room at the Olympic Village, Coach Gus Stager came in. Stager said to Sammy, "Well, we're going to room all you guys who have a chance to win a gold medal in singles, so Sammy, you come with me, and Bill, you wait here and I'll send you another roommate."

Mulliken surprised everyone, including his coach! In the semi-finals of the 200m breast, he set an Olympic record with a time that was over three seconds faster than his previous best. In the 200m breaststroke final Mulliken captured gold and had a "room for one" at the top of the podium.

Coach Stager would later credit Bill's unexpected victory

with motivating the rest of the team in their bid to unseat the heavily favored Australians. The American men rallied and swam to gold in both the freestyle and medley relays.

Mulliken would later become very active in Masters swimming. In 1986, at the age of 46, he swam against Yoshihiko Osaki, the silver medalist in Rome. Despite finishing second, Mulliken actually swam faster than he had the first time he placed at Nationals 27 years earlier.

SCORE
B O A R D

Murray Rose and Tsuyoshi Yamanaka both competed in the 400m freestyle event at the 1956 and 1960 Olympic Games. Not only did they finish first and second in both Olympiads respectively, but the identical amount of distance separated them as well.

MIKE TROY
UNITED STATES

Courtesy of ISHOF

Mike Troy on the fly.

Olympian butterflyer Mike Troy had "PAIN" painted in foot high, black letters on the wall of his fraternity room. They were there to remind him, as the Olympic Trials approached, to "swim until it hurts."

Coached by James "Doc" Counsilman at Indiana University, the morning practice sessions were early and exhausting.

"Lots of guys sleep in swimsuits so they can stay in bed longer. Sometimes they go three days without taking them off." –M..Troy

The pain paid off and Troy became a part of Olympic history. His win in the 200m butterfly set a new world record. This versatile swimmer struck gold again, swimming the third leg of the world record breaking 800m freestyle team.

Mike Troy went on to become a naval officer and was decorated for bravery while serving in Vietnam.

CHRIS VON SALTZA
UNITED STATES

When Chris Von Saltza was eleven years old she was introduced to Coach George Haines of the Santa Clara Swim Club. Because he was busy with another swimmer at the moment, Haines asked Chris to kick a few lengths of the pool until he could get back to her. One hundred and forty-four laps later, Coach Haines finally noticed Chris.

That story captures the essence of Chris Von Saltza's work ethic, an ethic that led her to Rome and four Olympic medals (gold- 400m free, gold-

Chris Von Saltza off the blocks.

Courtesy of ISHOF

400m free relay, gold-400m medley relay, silver-100m free).

A charismatic sixteen year-old, Chris could be seen carrying her lucky stuffed frog throughout the 1960 Games. Von Saltza's accomplishments ignited an interest in competitive swimming in the United States. A product of the AAU age-group swimming program, she was one of its first international champions.

Von Saltza retired from competitive swimming in 1961. She went on to Stanford and majored in Asian History. Chris Von Saltza later participated in a program, sponsored by the State Department, working as a coach/consultant teaching competitive swimming in South Korea, Hong Kong, and various other Asian countries.

OFF THE *Wall*

Fan to the Rescue

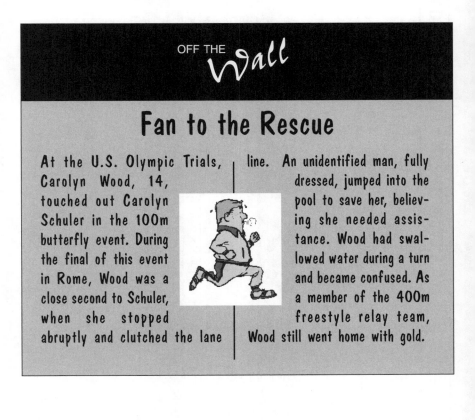

At the U.S. Olympic Trials, Carolyn Wood, 14, touched out Carolyn Schuler in the 100m butterfly event. During the final of this event in Rome, Wood was a close second to Schuler, when she stopped abruptly and clutched the lane line. An unidentified man, fully dressed, jumped into the pool to save her, believing she needed assistance. Wood had swallowed water during a turn and became confused. As a member of the 400m freestyle relay team, Wood still went home with gold.

1960 OLYMPIC SWIMMING FINALS

| Gold | Silver | Bronze | Fourth | Fifth | Sixth | Seventh | Eighth |

INDIVIDUAL EVENTS

Women 100m Freestyle - World Record (1:00.2 110y Dawn Fraser Aus)   Olympic Record (1:02.0 Dawn Fraser Aus 1956)

Gold	Silver	Bronze	Fourth	Fifth	Sixth	Seventh	Eighth
Dawn Fraser	Christine Von Saltza	Natalie Steward	Carolyn Wood	Csilla Dobai-Madarasz	Erica Terpstra	Cockie Gastelaars	Marie Stewart
AUS – 1:01.2 o	USA – 1:02.8	GBR – 1:03.1	USA – 1:03.4	HUN – 1:03.6	NED – 1:04.3	NED – 1:04.7	CAN – 1:05.5

Men 100m Freestyle - World Record (54.6 John Devitt AUS)   Olympic Record (55.4 Jon Henricks AUS 1956)

Gold	Silver	Bronze	Fourth	Fifth	Sixth	Seventh	Eighth
John Devitt	Lance Larson	Manuel Dos Santos	R. Bruce Hunter	Gyula Dobai	Richard Pound	Aubrey Burer	Per-Ola Lindberg
AUS – 55.2 o	USA – 55.2 o	BRA – 55.4	USA – 55.6	HUN – 56.3	CAN – 56.3	RSA – 56.3	SWE – 57.1

Women 400m Freestyle - World Record (4:44.5 Christine Von Saltza USA) Olympic Record (4:54.6 Lorraine Crapp AUS 1956)

Gold	Silver	Bronze	Fourth	Fifth	Sixth	Seventh	Eighth
Christine Von Saltza	Jane Cederqvist	Catharina Lagerberg	Ilsa Konrads	Dawn Fraser	A. Nancy Rae	Cornelia Schimmel	Bibbi Segerstrom
USA – 4:50.6 o	SWE – 4:53.9	NED – 4:56.9	AUS – 4:57.9	AUS – 4:58.5	GBR – 4:59.7	NED – 5:02.3	SWE – 5:02.4

w World Record   o Olympic Record   p Preliminary Heat   dq Disqualified   e Equal to World Record   eo Equal to Olympic Record
dns Did Not Start   dnf Did Not Finish   ac Also Competed   r Relay Lead-off Split   E Estimated

OLYMPIAD XVII – 1960 – ROME, ITALY

1960 OLYMPIC SWIMMING FINALS

Gold	Silver	Bronze	Fourth	Fifth	Sixth	Seventh	Eighth
Men 400m Freestyle - World Record (4:15.9 440y John Konrads AUS)					Olympic Record (4:27.3 Murray Rose AUS 1956)		
Murray Rose	Tsuyoshi Yamanaka	John Konrads	Ian Black	Alan Somers	Murray McLachlan	Eugene Lenz	Makoto Fukui
AUS – 4:18.3 o	JPN – 4:21.4	AUS – 4:21.8	GBR – 4:21.8	USA – 4:22.0	RSA – 4:26.3	USA – 4:26.8	JPN – 4:29.6
Men 1500m Freestyle - World Record (17:11.0 John Konrads AUS)					Olympic Record (17.52.9 George Breen USA 1956)		
John Konrads	Murray Rose	George Breen	Tsuyoshi Yamanaka	József Katona	Murray McLachlan	Alan Somers	Richard Campion
AUS – 17:19.6 o	AUS – 17:21.7	USA – 17:30.6	JPN – 17:34.7	HUN – 17:43.7	RSA – 17:44.9	USA – 18:02.8	GBR – 18:22.7
Women 100m Backstroke - World Record (1:09.2 Lynn Burke USA)					Olympic Record (1:12.9 Judith Grinham GBR 1956)		
Lynn Burke	Natalie Steward	Satoko Tanaka	Laura Ranwell	Rosy Piacentini	Sylvia Lewis	Maria van Velsen	Nadine Delache
USA – 1:09.3 o	GBR – 1:10.8	JPN – 1:11.4	RSA – 1:11.4	FRA – 1:11.4	GBR – 1:11.8	NED – 1:12.1	FRA – 1:12.4
Men 100m Backstroke - World Record (1:01.5 110y John Monckton AUS)					Olympic Record (1:02.2 David Theile AUS 1956)		
David Theile	Frank McKinney	Robert Bennett	Robert Christophe	Leonid Barbier	Wolfgang Wagner	John Monckton	Veiko Siimar
AUS – 1:01.9 o	USA – 1:02.1	USA – 1:02.3	FRA – 1:03.2	SOV – 1:03.5	GDR – 1:03.5	AUS – 1:04.1	SOV – 1:04.6

1960 OLYMPIC SWIMMING FINALS

	Gold	Silver	Bronze	Fourth	Fifth	Sixth	Seventh	Eighth

Women 200m Breaststroke - World Record (2:50.2 Wiltrud Urselmann GER)Olympic Record (2:53.1 Ursula Happe GER 1956)

Gold	Silver	Bronze	Fourth	Fifth	Sixth	Seventh	Eighth
Anita Lonsbrough	Wiltrud Urselmann	Barbara Göbel	Adelaide den Haan	Margareta Kok	Anne Warner	Patty Kempner	Dorrit Kristensen
GBR – 2:49.5 w	GER – 2:50.0	GDR – 2:53.6	NED – 2:54.4	NED – 2:54.6	USA – 2:55.4	USA – 2:55.5	DEN – 2:55.7

Men 200m Breaststroke – World Record (2:36.5 Terry Gathercole AUS) Olympic Record (2:34.7 Masaru Furukawa JPN 1956)

Gold	Silver	Bronze	Fourth	Fifth	Sixth	Seventh	Eighth
William Mulliken	Yoshihiko Osaki	Wieger Mensonides	Egon Henninger	Roberto Lazzari	Terry Gathercole	Andrzej Klopotowski	Paul Hait
USA – 2:37.4	JPN – 2:38.0	NED – 2:39.7	GDR – 2:40.1	ITA – 2:40.1	AUS – 2:40.2	POL – 2:41.2	USA – 2:41.4

Women 100m Butterfly - World Record (1:09.1 Nancy Ramey USA) Olympic Record (1:11.0 Shelly Mann USA 1956)

Gold	Silver	Bronze	Fourth	Fifth	Sixth	Seventh	Eighth
Carolyn Schuler	Marianne Heemskerk	Janice Andrew	Sheila Watt	Aarije Voorbij	Zinaida Belovetskaya	Kristina Larsson	Carolyn Wood
USA – 1:09.5 o	NED – 1:10.4	AUS – 1:12.2	GBR – 1:13.3	NED – 1:13.3	SOV – 1:13.3	SWE – 1:13.6	USA – duf

Men 200m Butterfly - World Record (2:13.2 Michael Troy USA) Olympic Record (2:19.3 William Yorzyk USA 1956)

Gold	Silver	Bronze	Fourth	Fifth	Sixth	Seventh	Eighth
Michael Troy	Neville Hayes	J. David Gillanders	Federico Dennerlein	Haruo Yoshimuta	Kevin Berry	Valentin Kuzmin	Kenzo Izutsu
USA – 2:12.8 w	AUS – 2:14.6	USA – 2:15.3	ITA – 2:16.0	JPN – 2:18.3	AUS – 2:18.5	SOV – 2:18.9	JPN – 2:19.4

1960 OLYMPIC SWIMMING FINALS

RELAY EVENTS

Women 400m Medley Relay - World Record (4:44.6 USA) — 1896-1956 – Event Not Held On Olympic Program

Gold	Silver	Bronze	Fourth	Fifth	Sixth	Seventh	Eighth
Lynn Burke. Patty Kempner. Carolyn Schuler. Christine Von Saltza *p – Anne Warner. Carolyn Wood. Joan Spillane*	Marilyn Wilson. Rosemary Lassig. Janice Andrew. Dawn Fraser *p – Amber Gergay Beckett. Ilsa Konrads*	Ingrid Schmidt. Ursula Küper. Bärbel Fuhrmann. Ursel Brunner	Maria van Velsen. Adelaide den Haan. Marianne Heemskerk. Erica Terpstra *p – Catherina Lagerberg*	Sylvia Lewis. Anita Lonsbrough. Sheila Watt. Natalie Steward *p – Jean Oldroyd*	Magdolna Dávid. Klára Bartos-Killermann. Márta Egerváry. Csilla Dobai-Madarász	Satoko Tanaka. Yoshiko Takamatsu. Shizue Miyabe. Yoshiko Sato	Larissa Viktorova. Lyudmila Korobova. Zinaida Belovskaya. Marina Shamal *p – Valentina Poznyak*
USA – 4:41.1 w	AUS – 4:45.9	GDR/GER – 4:47.6	NED – 4:47.6	GBR – 4:47.6	HUN – 4:53.7	JPN – 4:56.4	SOV – 4:58.1

Men 400m Medley Relay - World Record (4:09.2 USA) — 1896-1956 – Event Not Held On Olympic Program

Gold	Silver	Bronze	Fourth	Fifth	Sixth	Seventh	Eighth
Frank McKinney, Paul Hait, Lance Larson, F.Jeff Farrell *p – Robert Bennett, David Gillanders, Stephen Clark*	David Theile, Terry Gathercole, Neville Hayes, Geoffrey Shipton *p – Julian Carroll, William Burton, Kevin Berry*	Kazuo Tomita, Koichi Hirakida, Yoshihiko Osaki, Keigo Shimizu *p – Kazuo Watanabe, Katsuki Ishikara*	Robert Wheaton, Steve Rabinovitch, Cameron Grout, Richard Pound	Leonid Barbier, Leonid Kolesnikov, Grigory Kiselyov, Igor Lushkovski	Guiseppe Avellone, Roberto Lazzari, Federico Dennerlein, Bruno Bianchi	Graham Sykes, Christopher Walkden, Ian Black, Stanley Clarke	Johannes Jiskoot, Wieger Mensonides, Gerrit Korteweg, Ronald Kroon
USA – 4:05.4 w	AUS – 4:12.0	JPN – 4:12.2	CAN – 4:16.8	SOV – 4:16.8	ITA – 4:17.2	GBR – 4:17.6	NED – 4:18.2

1960 OLYMPIC SWIMMING FINALS

Women 400m Freestyle Relay - World Record (4:16.2 440y AUS)   Olympic Record (4:17.1 AUS 1956)

Gold	Silver	Bronze	Fourth	Fifth	Sixth	Seventh	Eighth
Joan Spillane, Shirley Stobs, Carolyn Wood, Christine Von Saltza, p – Donna De Varona, Susan Doerr, Sylvia Ruuska, Molly Botkin	Dawn Fraser, Ilsa Konrads, Lorraine Crapp, Alva Colquhoun, p – Sandra Morgan, Ruth Everuss	Christel Steffin, Heidi Pechstein, Gisela Weiss, Ursula Brunner	Anna Temesvári, Mária Frank, Katalin Boros, Csilla Dobai-Madarász	Natalie Steward, Beryl Noakes, Judy Samuel, Christine Harris	Inger Thorngren, Karin Larsson, Kristina Larsson, Birte Segerström	Paola Saini, Annamaria Cecchi, Rosanna Contardo, Maria Christina Pacifici, p - Daniela Beneck	Irina Liakhovskaya, Ulvi Voog, Galina Sosnova, Marina Shamal
USA – 4:08.9 w	AUS – 4:11.3	GDR/GER 4:19.7	HUN – 4:21.2	GBR – 4:24.6	SWE – 4:25.1	ITA – 4:26.8	SOV – 4:29.0

Men 800m Freestyle Relay - World Record (8:16.6 880y AUS)   Olympic Record (8:23.6 AUS - 1956)

Gold	Silver	Bronze	Fourth	Fifth	Sixth	Seventh	Eighth
George Harrison, Richard Blick, Michael Troy, Jeff Farrell, p – William Darnton, Thomas Winters, Stephen Clark	Makoto Fukui, Hiroshi Ishii, Tsuyoshi Yamanaka, Tatsuo Fujimoto	David Dickson, John Devitt, Murray Rose, John Konrads, p - John Rigby, Allan Wood	Hamilton Milton, John Martin-Dye, Richard Campion, Ian Black	Ilkka Suvanto, Kari Haavisto, Stig-Olof Grenner, Harri Käyhko	Sven-Göran Johansson, Lars-Erik Bengtsson, Bengt Nordvall, Per-Ola Lindberg, Almsted Bengt	Frank Wiegand, Gerhard Hetz, Hans Zierold, Hans Klein	Igor Lushkovski, Gennady Nikolayev, Vitaly Sorokin, Boris Nikitin, p - Sergei Tovstoplet
USA – 8:10.2 w	JPN – 8:13.2	AUS – 8:13.8	GBR – 8:28.1	FIN – 8:29.7	SWE – 8:31.0	GER/GDR 8:31.8	SOV – 8:32.2

Chapter 16

Olympiad XVIII - 1964
Tokyo, Japan

In 1964 the Olympics were held in Asia for the first time. The Japanese spared no expense, and even the continual downpour of rain could not dampen the enthusiasm of the spectators attending.

At the opening ceremonies the teams entered the stadium in a very choreographed, orderly fashion, strictly following the planned program. The closing ceremony was a different story. The athletes entered the stadium interspersed with one another, portraying the spirit of unity.

The announcer tried to bring order to this moving spectacle by requesting that they march in rows of eight. Most of the athletes continued onward, arm-in-arm ignoring the announcer. The Japanese Team, however, formed a formal line at the end.

Of a possible 18 gold medals awarded for men's and women's swimming, the United States Olympic Team went home with 13. They were nothing short of phenomenal.

Olympic 1ST

Relays Added to Event List

A new event was added to the Olympic swim program; the 400m individual medley, for both men and women. A third relay event, the 4X100m free, was also added to the men's competition.

These "water babies" were a direct result of the American age group swim programs' coming of age. These programs developed the potential of thousands of children and teenagers across the country. The average age of the U.S. Women's Swim Team in 1964 was slightly over 16 years.

"This is the greatest moment in American swimming history. We'd better enjoy it now, because I don't see how the United States can ever again reach such a position of dominance."

— *"Doc" Counsilman*

LANE LINES

Broken Records

Not one Olympic swimming record survived these Games. Records broken in one heat were toppled in the next, then shattered in the finals.

KEVIN BERRY
AUSTRALIA

Two-time Olympian Kevin Berry was only fifteen years old when he represented Australia in Rome. He finished a very respectable sixth in the 200m butterfly event.

When not training, this hard working teenager from Marrickville, Sydney, was employed as a dishwasher at a local steakhouse. Just prior to the 1964 Tokyo Games, Australia's

Olympic Team was given a reception at this establishment. Berry worked that morning, attended the party, and then returned to the kitchen to wash the dishes.

In 1964 Kevin Berry made his second Olympic appearance. As the current world record holder of the 200m fly, Berry was the heavy favorite to win gold in Tokyo. Triumph he did, breaking his own world mark (2:06.6). He was also a member of Australia's bronze medal winning medley relay team.

STEVE CLARK
UNITED STATES

Courtesy of ISHOF

4X100m free relay team of Steve Clark, Mike Austin, Gary Ilman and Don Schollander.

Steve Clark represented the U.S. at both the 1960 and 1964 Olympic Games. An untimely bout of tendonitis of the shoulder at the 1964 Olympic Trials kept him from qualifying for an individual event. Fortunately for the U.S. Olympic Team, he qualified for the relays. His condition had subsided by the time he reached Tokyo. Steve was an essential member of all three relay teams winning gold with each.

Clark recalled his first day of practice at the Santa Clara Swim Club at the age of eight, "My parents were late to pick me up and I was so scared and crying...I almost quit then and there."

A short course racer known for his quick, precision turns, Clark was the first to swim under 21.0 seconds for 50 yards. Clark also equaled the world record for 100m (52.9) in Tokyo, swimming the first leg of the 400m freestyle relay and earning himself a much deserved berth on the 400m medley relay team.

"I engaged in self-hypnosis, before it became popular, to try to channel my emotions into something positive," Clark stated when asked if he practiced some pre-event ritual.

Swimming for Yale, Clark earned five individual NCAA titles. After retiring from swimming, Clark went on to Harvard Law School. He later wrote a book entitled, *Competitive Swimming As I See It*. Steve Clark continues to compete in Masters Swimming.

SCORE
BOARD

During the men's 100m freestyle event a controversy erupted over the awarding of the bronze medal. Both Han-Joachim Klein of Germany and Gary Ilman of the United States clocked in at the same time. The judges were split as to who touched first.

The electronic timers were consulted, even though they were not used officially. Ilman and Klein had stopped the timing device at the exact 100th of a second, but Klein finished 1/1000th of a second faster. The judges consulted with one another over a half-hour, before awarding Klein the bronze medal.

DONNA DEVARONA
UNITED STATES

Donna deVarona started her Olympic career at the early age of 13. She was the youngest American on the 1960 Olympic Team. During her swimming career she collected 37 individual national titles, and held world records in eight long course events. In Tokyo the "Queen of Swimming" won two gold medals.

Courtesy of ISHOF

Donna deVarona at finish of 1964 400m IM final.

Donna set her first world record weeks before the Rome Games. Had the individual medley been included on the Olympic program in 1960, she would have likely become the youngest Olympic swimming champion.

This accomplished athlete was the most photographed female athlete of her time. She was on the cover of Life, The Saturday Evening Post, Time, and Sports Illustrated... twice!

After Tokyo, Donna collected endless awards and titles, including America's Outstanding Woman Athlete. In 1965 deVarona became the first woman commentator for sports broadcasting on network television. Her career included working for Wide World of Sports, as well as covering the 1968, 1972, 1976 and the 1984 Olympic Games for ABC television.

Donna deVarona has had a tremendous influence on women's sports. She is a founding member and past president of the Women's Sports Foundation and has worked as a consultant to the U.S. Senate in the preparing of the Amateur Sports Act.

LANE LINES

Queen of Swimming

DeVarona was the most versatile swimmer of her time. Not only did she own the individual medley, at one time or another, she held the world's fastest times in three strokes; the butterfly, back and freestyle.

VIRGINIA "GINNY" DUENKEL
UNITED STATES

Courtesy of ISHOF

400m USA Sweep - Ginny Duenkel (ctr) flanked by M. Ramenofsky and T. Stickles

Ginny's first international championship was at the 1964 Olympic Games. Her surprising win in the 400m freestyle came the day after capturing the bronze in the 100m backstroke event. Duenkel's best events, the 1500m freestyle and the 200m backstroke, were not offered on the women's 1964 Olympic program, yet she managed to come home with two Olympic medals.

SPLASH BACK

Forty Years Between Sweeps!

400m U.S.A. SWEEP

1924			1964	
M. Norelius	6:02.2ω	Gold	O. Duenkel	4:43.3o
H. Wainwright	6:03.8	Silver	M. Ramenofsky	4:44.6
G. Ederle	6:04.8	Bronze	T. Stickles	4:47.2

CATHY FERGUSON
UNITED STATES

The 100m backstroke event in Tokyo brought together six women who at one time held world records in the backstroke in various distances. Among them was 16 year old Cathy Ferguson, the 200m world record holder. The first three finishers, Ferguson, Christine Caron of France and Duenkel toppled the world record in this heated final.

Cathy prevailed smashing teammate Ginny Duenkel's 100m backstroke world mark and earned a berth on the U.S. medley relay team, where she captured a second gold medal.

Ferguson roomed at the Olympic Village with fellow backstroker Ginny Duenkel, who captured the bronze in the 100m event. When asked about rooming with a rival, Cathy

OFF THE Wall

"A Stitch in Time"

Richard Roth's gold medal winning performance in the 400m individual medley was probably one of the most heroic efforts by any athlete during the 1964 Olympic Games.

Roth, the current world record holder in this event, suffered an appendicitis attack and was told he needed immediate surgery. His response, "No! I'm not missing the Olympic final no matter what happens." He packed his side with ice that night.

Not only did Roth win, but he set a new world and Olympic record for the 400 IM. His world record would stand for four years. Roth later said, "I forgot my hot appendix during the race."

After receiving his Olympic medal Roth returned to the hospital and had his appendix removed. His appendix now floats in a jar and can be viewed at the International Olympic Hall of Fame. Roth retired in his swimming prime at the age of 19.

responded, "But that is the essence of the Olympic Games, to be able to separate when it's time to work and when it's time to play. We understood this, and sometimes I think our countries would be in a lot better shape if they were run by athletes."

Jed Graef - United States

Jed Graef won his first major title at the 1964 Olympic Games. This 6'6" Princeton grad led the American sweep of the 200m backstroke final in world record time (2:10.3), followed by team-mates Gary Dilley and Bob Bennett.

IAN O'BRIEN
AUSTRALIA

Ian O'Brien of Australia was the surprise victor in the 200m breaststroke in 1964. O'Brien pulled ahead in the last 5 meters of the final to triumph over Georgy Prokopenko of Russia and American Chet Jastremski to set a new world record (2:27.8).

O'Brien also collected a bronze medal as a member of Australia's 400m medley relay team in Tokyo. Ian arrived in Mexico City in 1968 to defend his Olympic 200m breaststroke title, finishing fourth. During his swim career he won nine Australian breaststroke championships and set four world marks.

GALINA PROZUMENSHCHYKOVA
SOVIET UNION

Galina Prozumenshchykova was the only European to win a gold medal in swimming at the Tokyo Games. Her win in the 200m breast-

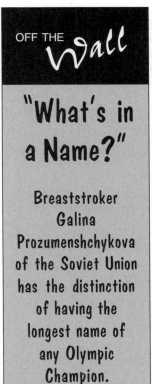

"What's in a Name?"

Breaststroker
Galina
Prozumenshchykova
of the Soviet Union
has the distinction
of having the
longest name of
any Olympic
Champion.

stroke in 1964 was the Soviet Union's first Olympic swimming gold medal.

Prozumenshchykova was a member of the U.S.S.R.'s 1968 Olympic Team. A gold medal hopeful, Galina had to fight off the effects of the high altitude in Mexico City. She managed a silver and bronze performance in the breaststroke events. After the 200m race Galina collapsed and had to be carried to the dressing room by a small and some would say heroic, Mexican.

Eight years after winning her first Olympic medal, Prozumenshchykova, now married and known as Galina Stepanova, arrived in Munich for her third Olympic Games. This timeless Olympic Champion again swam the 100m and 200m breaststroke, winning a silver and bronze medal respectively.

Courtesy of ISHOF

Galina Prozumenshchykova 200m breaststroke champion.

DON SCHOLLANDER
UNITED STATES

Don Schollander's love of the water likely came from his mother Martha, an avid swimmer, who worked in the old Tarzan movies with Johnny Weissmuller, as a stunt double for actress Maureen O'Sullivan.

Schollander is a product of age group swimming. At the age of 11 he found himself at the bottom of his age group, after having been at the top and winning races in the 10 and under category. Feeling discouraged and contemplating quitting, his father advised him, "You can quit swimming if you want to, but it will be when you're at the top of your age group, not at the bottom."

Schollander was the master of "psyching-out" his opponents. While on the blocks he would say such things as, "I feel great" or "Boy, I'm going to have a good time." He would offer comments to other swimmers, "I was watching your start. It's really interesting. I noticed that you start kicking before you get in the water. Doesn't that slow you down?"

Schollander held 22 world records, as well as 37 American marks. In 1963, he was the first man to break the two-minute barrier for the 200m freestyle, an event not offered at the 1964 Games. After the 1964 Olympics the awards were

Olympic 1ST

Four Gold Medals

Don Schollander, at the age of 18, became the first swimmer to win four gold medals at one Olympiad.

numerous, including being voted the 1964 Sullivan Award winner as the Amateur Athlete of the Year.

After the Tokyo Games, Schollander began his freshman year at Yale. He returned to the Mexico Games to win yet more medals. He won a silver in the 200m freestyle, last seen as an event in the 1900 Olympic Games (1904 had a 200y event) and won his final Olympic gold as a member of the 4X200m freestyle relay team.

Americans Don Schollander and Sharon Stouder top medal winners make Olympic history.

Photos courtesy of ISHOF

After the 1968 Olympic Games, Don Schollander announced his retirement in no uncertain terms. He stated, "I'm finished with the water - in fact, I may not take a bath or a shower for another two years."

SHARON STOUDER
UNITED STATES

At the age of eight Sharon Stouder competed in her first swim meet, winning two "firsts" and setting two age group records. Stouder, at 12, swam to victory in 20 national age group events. At the age of 15 she was off to Japan to make Olympic history.

In Tokyo, Stouder won three gold medals and one silver. During the 100m free final, Dawn Fraser took gold and Sharon silver, to be the first and second women, respectively,

SPLASH BACK

"Rie-peat"

Sharon Stouder's feat of 3 gold medals and 1 silver medal matched Holland's Hendrika "Rie" Mastenbroek's 1936 performance.

to break the one minute barrier.

Sharon's world record time of 1:04.7 in the 100m butterfly would remain an Olympic record for eight years. The gold winning relay teams, of which Stouder was a member, each set new world marks.

After the 1964 Olympic Games, Sharon Stouder was named, "World Woman Swimmer of the Year," by ABC Television, Swimming World and Sports Illustrated. She went on to graduate from Stanford University and completed her graduate work in Santa Barbara, at the University of California.

ROBERT WINDLE
AUSTRALIA

Bob Windle represented Australia at the 1960, 1964 and 1968 Olympic Games. Primarily a distance swimmer, his two world records, ironically, were set in the 200m and 220y distances.

At the 1960 Olympic Games, Windle served as a relay alternate. He returned to the Olympic Games in 1964 as Australia's brightest hope for a medal in the 1500m freestyle event. He was not expected to capture the title,

Betty on the Lookout!

The segregated dormitories in Japan had guards posted every 100 feet to prevent the men from entering the woman's dormitory. This served as a challenge to many of the spirited Olympians. American women's chaperone Betty Philcox lost 30 pounds trying to keep track of her swimmers' whereabouts!

because his pre-Olympic times did not rival those of the other finalists.

During the 1500m final in Tokyo, Windle was 12 meters ahead at the 750-meter mark. He held on to his lead and set a new Olympic record (17:01.), beating the second place finisher, American John Nelson, by 1.3 seconds. Windle's Australian teammate, Allan Wood, took the bronze medal. Windle anchored Australia's bronze medal winning 400m freestyle relay team, as well.

Robert Windle represented his country for his third and final Olympic Games in Mexico City. He swam in both the 800m and 400m freestyle relays, winning a silver and bronze medal. Bob Windle collected four Olympic medals during his swimming career and eleven Australian Championships.

1964 OLYMPIC SWIMMING FINALS

Gold	Silver	Bronze	Fourth	Fifth	Sixth	Seventh	Eighth

INDIVIDUAL EVENTS

Women 100m Freestyle - World Record (58.9 Dawn Fraser AUS) Olympic Record (1:01.2 Dawn Fraser AUS 1960)

Gold	Silver	Bronze	Fourth	Fifth	Sixth	Seventh	Eighth
Dawn Fraser	Sharon Stouder	Kathleen Ellis	Erica Terpstra	Marion Lay	Csilla Dobai-Madarász	Ann Hagberg	Lynette Bell
AUS – 59.5 o	USA – 59.9	USA – 1:00.8	NED – 1:01.8	CAN – 1:02.2	HUN – 1:02.4	SWE – 1:02.5	AUS – 1:02.7

Men 100m Freestyle - World Record (52.9 Alain Gottvalles FRA) Olympic Record (55.2 J. Devitt AUS/L. Larson USA 1960)

Gold	Silver	Bronze	Fourth	Fifth	Sixth	Seventh	Eighth
Donald Schollander	Robert McGregor	Hans-Joachim Klein	Gary Ilman	Alain Gottvalles	Michael Austin	Gyula Dobai	Uwe Jacobsen
USA – 53.4 o	GBR – 53.5	GER – 54.0	USA – 54.0	FRA – 54.2	USA – 54.5	HUN – 54.9	GER – 56.1

Women 400m Freestyle - World Record (4:39.5 M. Ramenofsky USA) Olympic Record (4:50.6 Christine Von Saltza USA 1960)

Gold	Silver	Bronze	Fourth	Fifth	Sixth	Seventh	Eighth
Virginia Duenkel	Marilyn Ramenofsky	Terri Stickles	Jane Hughes	Elizabeth Long	Kim Herford	Gun Lilja	
USA – 4:43.3 o	USA – 4:44.6	USA – 4:47.2	CAN – 4:50.9	GBR – 4:52.0	AUS – 4:52.9	SWE – 4:53.0	

Men 400m Freestyle - World Record (4:12.7 Donald Schollander USA) Olympic Record (4:18.3 Murray Rose AUS 1960)

Gold	Silver	Bronze	Fourth	Fifth	Sixth	Seventh	Eighth
Donald Schollander	Frank Wiegand	Allan Wood	Roy Saari	John Nelson	Tsuyoshi Yamanaka	Russell Phegan	Semyon Belits-Geiman
USA – 4:12.2 w	GDR – 4:14.9	AUS – 4:15.1	USA – 4:16.7	USA – 4:16.9	JPN – 4:19.1	AUS – 4:20.2	SOV – 4:21.4

w World Record o Olympic Record p Preliminary Heat dq Disqualified e Equal to World Record eo Equal to Olympic Record
dns Did Not Start dnf Did Not Finish ac Also Competed r Relay Lead-off Split E Estimated

OLYMPIAD XVIII – 1964 – TOKYO, JAPAN

1964 OLYMPIC SWIMMING FINALS

	Gold	Silver	Bronze	Fourth	Fifth	Sixth	Seventh	Eighth
Men 1500m Freestyle - World Record (16:58.7 Roy Saari USA)						Olympic Record (17:19.6 John Konrads AUS 1960)		
	Robert Windle	John Nelson	Allan Wood	William Farley	Russell Phegan	Sueaki Sasaki	Roy Saari	József Katona
	AUS – 17:01.7 o	USA – 17:03.0	AUS – 17:07.7	USA – 17:18.2	AUS – 17:22.4	JPN – 17:25.3	USA – 17:29.2	HUN – 17:30.8
Women 100m Backstroke - World Record (1:08.3 Virginia Duenkel USA)						Olympic Record (1:09.3 Lynn Burke USA 1960)		
	Cathy Ferguson	Christine Caron	Virginia Duenkel	Satoko Tanaka	Nina Harmar	Linda Ludgrove	Eileen Weir	Jill Norfolk
	USA – 1:07.7 w	FRA – 1:07.9	USA – 1:08.0	JPN – 1:08.6	USA – 1:09.4	GBR – 1:09.5	CAN – 1:09.8	GBR – 1:11.2
Men 200m Backstroke - World Record (2:10.9 Thomas Stock USA)					1904-1960 - Event Not Held On Olympic Program			
	Jed Graef	Gary Dilley	Robert Bennett	Shigeo Fukushima	Ernst-Joachim Küppers	Viktor Mazanov	Ralph Hutton	Peter Reynolds
	USA – 2:10.3 w	USA – 2:10.5	USA – 2:13.1	JPN – 2:13.2	GER – 2:15.7	SOV – 2:15.9	CAN – 2:15.9	AUS – 2:16.6
Women 200m Breaststroke - World Record (2:45.4 Prozumenshchykova SOV)					Olympic Record (2:49.5 Lonsbrough GBR 1960)			
	Galina Prozumenshchy-kova	Claudia Kolb	Svetlana Babanina	Stella Mitchell	Jill Slattery	Bärbel Grimmer	Klena Bimolt	Ursula Küper
	SOV – 2:46.4 o	USA – 2:47.6	SOV – 2:48.6	GBR – 2:49.0	GBR – 2:49.6	GDR – 2:51.0	NED – 2:51.3	GDR – 2:53.9
Men 200m Breaststroke – World Record (2:28.2 Chester Jastremski USA)					Olympic Record (2:37.2 William Mulliken USA 1960)			
	Ian O'Brien	Heorhy Prokopenko	Chester Jastremski	Aleksandr Tutakayev	Egon Henninger	Osamu Tsurumine	Wayne Anderson	Vladimir Kosinsky
	AUS – 2:27.8 w	SOV– 2:28.2	USA – 2:29.6	SOV – 2:31.0	GDR – 2:31.1	JPN – 2:33.6	USA – 2:35.0	SOV – 2:38.1

1964 OLYMPIC SWIMMING FINALS

	Gold	Silver	Bronze	Fourth	Fifth	Sixth	Seventh	Eighth
Women 100m Butterfly - World Record (1:05.1 (110y) Ada Kok NED) Olympic Record (1:09.5 Carolyn Schuler USA 1960)								
	Sharon Stouder	Ada Kok	Kathleen Ellis	Ella Pyrhönen	Donna De Varona	Heike Hustede	Eiko Takahashi	Mary Stewart
	USA – 1:04.7 w	NED – 1:05.6	USA – 1:06.0	FIN – 1:07.3	USA – 1:08.0	GER – 1:08.5	JPN – 1:09.1	CAN – 1:10.0
Men 200m Butterfly - World Record (2:06.9 Kevin Berry AUS) Olympic Record (2:12.8 Michael Troy 1960)								
	Kevin Berry	Carl Robie	Fred Schmidt	Philip Riker	Valentin Kuzmin	Yoshinori Kadonaga	Brett Hill	Daniel Sherry
	AUS – 2:06.6 w	USA – 2:07.5	USA – 2:09.3	USA – 2:11.0	SOV – 2:11.3	JPN – 2:12.6	AUS – 2:12.8	CAN – 2:14.6
Women 400m Individual Medley - World Record (5:14.9 De Varona USA) 1896-1960 - Event Not Held On Olympic Program								
	Donna De Varona	Sharon Finneran	Martha Randall	Veronika Holletz	Linda McGill	Elisabeth Heukels	Anita Lonsbrough	Márta Egerváry
	USA – 5:18.7 o	USA – 5:24.1	USA – 5:24.2	GDR – 5:25.6	AUS – 5:28.4	NED – 5:30.3	GBR – 5:30.5	HUN – 5:38.4
Men 400m Individual Medley - World Record (4:48.6 Richard Roth USA) 1896-1960 - Event Not Held On Olympic Program								
	Richard Roth	Roy Saari	Gerhard Hetz	Carl Robie	John Gilchrist	Johannes Jiskoot	György Kosztolánczy	Terry Buck
	USA – 4:45.4 w	USA – 4:47.1	GER – 4:51.0	USA – 4:51.4	CAN – 4:57.6	NED – 5:01.9	HUN – 5:01.9	AUS – 5:03.0

1964 OLYMPIC SWIMMING FINALS

RELAY EVENTS

Women 400m Medley Relay - World Record (4:34.6 USA) — Olympic Record (4:41.1 USA 1960)

Gold	Silver	Bronze	Fourth	Fifth	Sixth	Seventh	Eighth
Cathy Ferguson, Cynthia Goyette, Sharon Stouder, Kathleen Ellis, *p* - Nina Harmar, Judith Reeder, Susan Pitt, Pokey Watson	Kornelia Winkel, Klena Bimolt, Ada Kok, Erica Terpstra, *p* - Aartje Lasterie	Tatyana Savelyeva, Svetlana Babanina, Tetyana Devyatova, Natalya Ustinova	Satoko Tanaka, Noriko Yamamoto, Eiko Takahashi, Michiko Kihara	Jill Norfolk, Stella Mitchell, Mary Anne Cotterill, Elizabeth Long, *p* - Linda Ludgrove	Eileen Weir, Marion Lay, Mary Stewart, Helen Kennedy	Ingrid Schmidt, Bärbel Grimmer, Heike Hustede, Martina Grunert	Mária Balla, Zsuzsa Kovacs, Márta Egerváry, Csilla Dobai-Madarász
USA – 4:33.9 w	NED - 4:37.0	SOV – 4:39.2	JPN – 4:42.0	GBR – 4:45.8	CAN – 4:49.9	GDR/GER - *dq*	HUN - *dq*

Men 400m Medley Relay - World Record (4:00.1 USA) — Olympic Record (4:05.4 USA 1960)

Gold	Silver	Bronze	Fourth	Fifth	Sixth	Seventh	Eighth
Harold T. Mann, William Craig, Fred Schmidt, Stephen Clark, *p* - Richard McGeagh, Virgi Luken, Walter Richardson, Robert Bennett	Ernst-Joachim Küppers, Egon Henninger, Horst-Günther Gregor, Hans-Joachim Klein	Peter Reynolds, Ian O'Brien, Kevin Berry, David Dickson, *p* - Peter Tonkin	Viktor Mazanov, Heorhy Prokopenko, Valentin Kuzmin, Vladimir Schuvalov *p* - Aleksandr Tutakayev, V. Semchenkov	Shigeo Fukushima, Kenji Ishikawa, Isao Nakajima, Yukiaki Okabe	József Csikány, Ferenc Lenkei, József Gurrich, Gyula Dobai	Chiaffredo Rora, Gian Corrado Gross, Giampiero Fossati, Pietro Boscaini	Geoffrey Thwaites, Neil Nicholson, Brian Jenkins, Robert McGregor
USA - 3:58.4	GDR/GER 4:01.6	AUS - 4:02.3	SOV - 4:04.2	JPN - 4:06.6	HUN - 4:08.5	ITA - 4:10.3	GBR - 4:11.4

1964 OLYMPIC SWIMMING FINALS

Women 400m Freestyle Relay - World Record (4:07.6 USA) — Olympic Record (4:08.9 USA 1960)

Gold	Silver	Bronze	Fourth	Fifth	Sixth	Seventh	Eighth
Sharon Stouder, Donna De Varona, Pokey Watson, Kathleen Ellis, *p - Jeanne Hallock, Ericka Bricker, Lynne Allsup, Patience Sherman*	Robyn Thorn, Janice Murphy, Lynette Bell, Dawn Fraser, *p - Jan Turner*	Paulina van der Wildt, Catharina Beumer, Wilhelmina van Weerdenburg, Erica Terpstra	Judit Turóczy, Éva Erdélyi, Katalin Takács, Csilla Dobai-Madarász, *p - Mária Frank*	Ann-Charlott Lilja, Katrin Andersson-Ulla Järfvelt, Ann-Christine Hagberg	Marina Grunert, Traudi Beierlin, Rita Schumacher, Heidi Pechstein	Mary Stewart, Patricia Pacurici, Helen Kennedy, Marion Lay	Paola Saini, Maria Christina Pacifici, Mara Sacchi, Daniela Beneck
USA – 4:03.8 w	AUS – 4:06.9	NED – 4:12.0	HUN – 4:12.1	SWE – 4:14.0	GDR/GER 4:15.0	CAN – 4:15.9	ITA – 4:17.2

Men 400m Freestyle Relay - World Record (3:36.1 USA) — 1896-1960 - Event Not Held On Olympic Program

Gold	Silver	Bronze	Fourth	Fifth	Sixth	Seventh	Eighth
Stephen Clark, Michael Austin, Gary Ilman, Don Schollander, *p - Lary Schulhof*	Horst Löffler, Frank Wiegand, Uwe Jacobsen, Hans-Joachim Klein	David Dickson, Peter Doak, John Ryan, Robert Windle	Kunihiro Iwasaki, Tadaharu Goto, Tatsuo Fujimoto, Yukiaki Okabe, *p - Katsuki Ishihara*	Bengt-Olof Nordvall, E. Lester Eriksson, Jan Lundin, Per-Ola Lindberg	Viktor Mazanov, Vladimir Shuvalov, Viktor Semchenkov, Yuri Sumtsov, *p - Vladimir Berezin*	Robert Lord, John Martin-Dye, Peter Kendrew, Robert McGregor	Alain Gottvalles, Gerard Gropaiz, Pierre Canavese, Jean Curtillet, *p - Robert Christophe*
USA – 3:32.2 w	GDR/GER 3:37.2	AUS – 3:39.1	JPN – 3:40.5	SWE – 3:40.7	SOV – 3:42.1	GBR – 3:42.6	FRA - dq

1964 OLYMPIC SWIMMING FINALS

	Gold	Silver	Bronze	Fourth	Fifth	Sixth	Seventh	Eighth
Men 800m Freestyle Relay - World Record (8:01.8 USA)						Olympic Record (8:10.2 USA 1960)		
	Stephen Clark, Roy Saari, Gary Ilman, Don Schollander, *p* - W.illiam Mettler, David Lyons, Michael Wall, Robert Townsend	Horst-Günther Gregor, Gerhard Hetz, Frank Wiegand, Hans-Joachim Klein	Makoto Fukui, Kunihiro Iwasaki, Toshio Shoji, Yukiaki Okabe	David Dickson, Allan Wood, Peter Doak, Robert Windle *p* - John Konrads, John Ryan	Mats Svensson, E. Lester Eriksson, Hans Rosendahl, Jan Lundin	Jean-Pascal Curtillet, Pierre Canavese, Francis Luyce, Alain Gottvalles	Samyon Belits-Geiman, Vladimir Berezin, Aleksandr Paramonov, Yevgeny Novikov	Sergio De Gregorio, Bruno Bianchi, Giovanni Orlando, Pietro Bascaini
	USA – 7:52.1 *w* GDR/GER 7:59.3		JPN – 8:03.8	AUS – 8:05.5	SWE – 8:08.0	FRA – 8:08.7	SOV – 8:15.1	ITA – 8:18.1

Chapter 17

Olympiad XIX - 1968
Mexico City, Mexico

In the year 1968 the Olympic Games were held on Latin American soil for the first time. An altitude of almost 7,500 feet above sea level added a new dimension to Olympic competition.

The high altitude affected events that required continuous effort for over three minutes. Some of the events in Mexico compared to results that dated as far back as the 1948 Olympics.

There were other obstacles in Mexico. Stomach problems plagued many of the athletes, hindering their performances. Swimmers complained of a slow pool because the water was kept just far enough below the gutters to create everything but white caps as the swimmers competed.

American swimmer Ken Walsh described the competition pool in these words; "It's murder in there. You make a turn and suddenly you're going bump, bump, bump, over the waves, almost enough to make you sea sick."

The Olympic swimming program was expanded extensively to include the 200m freestyle, 100m breaststroke, 200m IM, and 100m butterfly in the men's program. The men's 100m backstroke also returned, having been discontinued in Tokyo. The 200m IM, 200m freestyle, 800m freestyle, 200m backstroke, 100m breaststroke, and 200m butterfly were added to the women's events.

In Mexico City, the combined total for the men and women's swimming events was 29. The United States Olympic Swim Team captured 21 gold, 14 silver, and 16 bronze medals.

OFF THE *Wall*

"Faint Memory"

John Ferris of the United States, the 200 IM bronze medalist, still wobbly and weak from the effects of altitude, valiantly attempted to maintain his stance on the award platform during the playing of the National Anthem. Midway through, Ferris whispered to teammate Charlie Hickcox, "Look out, here I go," and fainted. Hickcox held Ferris up as the Anthem finished, but finally had to let him slip down as oxygen was administered.

Courtesy of ISHOF

CATIE BALL
UNITED STATES

Catie Ball held all four world records for the breaststroke in 1968. She was the overwhelming favorite going into Mexico City.

Early in the week, Ball raced as a member of the winning medley relay team. Then she suffered an athlete's worst nightmare. She was struck down with a viral infection so severe it shattered her Olympic dreams. She took fifth in the 100m breaststroke and was unable to compete in the preliminary heats for the 200m event.

Sick and weak, Catie Ball lost 10 pounds during the course of the Olympic Games. An untimely illness had likely cost this accomplished swimmer her chance for Olympic greatness.

LANE LINES

American Carl Robie

Carl Robie was one of the few to participate in both the 1964 and 1968 Olympic Games. In Tokyo, Robie was favored to capture the 200m butterfly title, but placed second.

Mexico City was a different story. Robie, now in law school and considered past his prime by many, limited his competition to the 200m fly. Carl Robie led the race from the 100m mark to win Olympic gold.

DJURDJICA BJEDOV
YUGOSLAVIA

Djurdjica Bjedov was initially selected for the Yugoslavian Olympic Team to form a medley relay squad to compete in Mexico City. This medley relay team was disqualified in an early heat, but Bjedov became a part of Olympic lore.

Bjedov qualified fifth for the 100m breaststroke final, swimming in lane two. Not only did she touch out Galina Prozumenshchykova by a tenth of a second to take gold; she captured the silver medal in the 200m event.

Djurdjica Bjedov's win in the 100m breaststroke was Yugoslavia's first and only Olympic swimming championship.

SPLASH BACK

Champion Again

Like Mike Burton, Great Britain's Henry "Happy" Taylor captured the 1500m freestyle event in two consecutive Games, but Taylor's wins were only two years apart. (Intercalated Games of 1906 and the 1908 Olympic Games)

MICHAEL BURTON
UNITED STATES

Michael Burton was a long distance swimming specialist who was known as "Mr. Machine." He was fortunate to be competing much less setting records. At the age of 13, while riding on the handlebars of a friend's bike, an oncoming truck struck him. Mike was lucky to be alive but it was believed that sports were not in his future.

About one year after the accident Mike started swimming for Coach Sherman Chavoor of the Arden Hills Swim Club in California. Mike's swimming was intended to be therapy for his injured leg.

Burton became the first American swimmer to win the Olympic 1500m freestyle event twice (1968 and 1972). At the 1968 Games, he also won the 400m freestyle championship. This win was made more remarkable by the fact that he had collapsed from nausea in an elevator the day before the preliminary heats.

While swimming for U.C.L.A Burton held four NCAA titles and he set world records in the 800m and 1500m freestyle events. In the 1972 Munich Games, Burton, then 25, set a new world record (15:52.58), during the 1500m free final and collected his third Olympic gold medal.

Upon retirement from swim competition Michael Burton went on to coach and later founded the Des Moines, Iowa Acquatic Club.

SCORE
B O A R D

Men's Olympic Double Distance Winners

Year	Swimmer	400m tm	Cntry	1500m tm
1968	M. Burton	4:09.0*o*	USA	16:38.9*o*
1956	M. Rose	4:27.3*o*	AUS	17:58.9
1920	N. Ross	5:26.8	USA	22:23.2
1912	G. Hodgson	5:24.4*o*	CAN	22:00.0*w*
1908	H. Taylor	5:36.8	GBR	22:48.4*w*

CHARLES HICKCOX
UNITED STATES

When Charles Hickcox was thirteen years old, he and his sister Mary Sue were interested in joining the swim club in Phoenix. The coach took one look at the two of them and declared, "I'll take the girl, but that boy is too skinny. Get lost kid."

Hickcox did anything but. After a successful age group career, he went on to swim for "Doc" Counsilman at Indiana. He was a driving force in winning Counsilman his first NCAA title.

Counsilman spoke of Hickcox, "He was so good, but so raw. His turns were agonizing. I thought he'd kill himself going into the wall. But he worked, I'll tell you..."

Charles Hickcox went on to become a versatile swimmer whose specialty was the backstroke. Along with his three gold medals

Courtesy of ISHOF

400m medley relay (L-R) K. Walsh, D. Russell, D. McKenzie and C. Hickcox.

(medley relay, 200m and 400m IM), he also picked up a fourth medal as the second place finisher in the 100m backstroke event at the 1968 Olympic Games. After graduating from Indiana he retired from swimming.

Donald McKenzie

USA

100m breaststroke
Gold

400m medley relay
Gold

medal
2 *count*

Lynette McClements

Australia

100m butterfly
Gold

400m medley relay
Silver

ADA KOK
HOLLAND

At thirteen Ada Kok of Amsterdam was already training with the National Dutch Swimming Team. This Dutch teenager grew to to be over six feet tall.

Over the years Kok practiced some interesting pre-race rituals. She always took a dressing room with the number five in it and always draped a white towel over her right shoulder as she marched in for her race.

Courtesy of ISHOF

Prior to the 1964 Tokyo Games, Ada, the world record holder in the 100m butterfly and an experienced international competitor, was heavily favored to win gold.

Olympic Champion Ada Kok

Kok won silver in the 100m butterfly and medley relay events at the 1964 Games. During that medley relay Kok out swam Sharon Stouder, who had beaten her earlier in the 100m fly final. In the end the stronger American team prevailed.

At Mexico City, Kok again aspired to win the Olympic Title that had eluded her in Tokyo. In her first event, the 100m butterfly, she placed fourth.

With the addition of the 200m fly to the Olympic program, Ada had one last opportunity to win a long overdue Olympic title. Kok found herself in second behind East German Helga Linder at the 100m mark (1.4 seconds behind). A determined Kok fought back valiantly and took her Olympic crown by a margin of one tenth of a second.

Ada Kok was diagnosed with a blood disease in 1984. This courageous Olympian battled back as she did in the pool and conquered this adversity as well. She currently works as a sports promotion consultant for SPEEDO International.

L A N E   L I N E S

Peaking at the Olympics

Jan Henne of the United States was the 100m freestyle champion at the 1968 Olympic Games despite not having ever won a national freestyle event in her own country. She collected a second gold medal swimming the anchor of the 400m freestyle relay team, a silver for the 200m freestyle, and a bronze for the 200m IM.

CLAUDIA KOLB
UNITED STATES

Claudia Kolb of Santa Clara, California, is the third oldest of Barbara and Bill Kolb's ten children. She competed in her first Olympics in Tokyo, at 14 years of age. Seeded only fifth in the 200m breaststroke final, she was in fourth place after 175 meters. Suddenly Kolb put on a burst of speed in the final 10 meters, splitting the mighty Russian duo of Galina Prozumenshchykova and Svetlana Babanina, to seize the silver.

By 1966, Kolb, a member of George Haines' Santa Clara Swim Club, had already set a world record in the 100m breaststroke. However, she shifted gears and set her sights on the individual medley events.

By August of that year, Kolb was the first world record holder of the 200m individual medley. During a thirteen month span, Kolb broke the world record in the 400m IM four times.

As the 1968 Olympics approached, Claudia was the current record holder in both events and heavily favored to win gold. She easily won the 200m IM event by 4.1 seconds, followed by U.S. teammates Sue Pedersen and Jan Henne in an American sweep. Kolb won her final in the 400m IM by a 20 meter margin, 13.7 seconds ahead of the second place finisher. Not since 1928 had a woman swimmer won her Olympic final so decisively.

Courtesy of ISHOF

Santa Clara teammates Mark Spitz and Claudia Kolb.

When asked who was most instrumental in her success, Kolb responded, "No question, my coach George Haines. He not only developed me, but had enormous confidence in my ability and toughness. He made me want to work hard everyday. I always looked forward to practice."

By the end of Kolb's career she had attained 25 U.S. National titles and set 23 world records. Claudia's most prized win was not as a swimmer but as a coach. In 1980 she coached Stanford University's Women's Swim Team to a thrilling AIAN National Championship over Texas by a mere six points.

Claudia Kolb resides with her family in Spokane, Washington where she is the Athletic Director at Saint Georges's School.

ROLAND MATTHES
EAST GERMANY

Roland Matthes was a phenomenal and seemingly tireless backstroker. He competed in the 1968, 1972 and 1976 Olympiads. His Olympic medals totaled four gold, two silver, and two bronze medals.

Matthes remained untouchable in the backstroke for seven years of international competition. During his swimming career he held 19 world records, the first of which he accomplished at the age of sixteen.

Courtesy of ISHOF

Matthes would stroke eight to ten times less per 50 meters than his competitors. A lean six foot, two inches, and known for his powerful kick, the American swimmers referred to him as "Rolling Mattress."

Olympian Mike Troy had this to say about the soft-spoken Matthes, "He's so nice, it's too bad he's so fast."

Roland Matthes with one of his eight Olympic medals.

In 1978, Matthes married fellow Olympian and superstar, Kornelia Ender and later had a daughter, Francesca.

DEBBIE MEYER
UNITED STATES

On Christmas Day 1964, 12 year-old Debbie Meyer received a stopwatch from her Father that was simply inscribed; "Mexico City, 1968." "I did not even know what the Olympics were!", said Meyer.

Soon after that Christmas, Meyer's family left the East Coast and moved to Sacramento, California. She started swimming competitively in 1965 for Coach Sherman Chavoor of the Arden Hills Swim Club.

Chavoor was considered a taskmaster. He believed in punctuality, obedience and most of all endurance. Any swimmer who arrived late, it was rumored, would be punished by pulling weeds for one hour!

Meyer set world records in the 200m, 400m and 800m freestyle at the U.S. Olympic Trials. The 200m

Olympic 1st

Debbie Meyer, at 16, was the first swimmer to win three gold medals for individual events during one Olympiad. What makes this accomplishment even more astounding is that Meyer's events were the longer freestyle distances where the effects of the high altitude were even more pronounced.

and 800m freestyle were new events to the Olympic program. She went on to become the first champion of these events.

Meyer's only complaint concerning her Olympic experience was that the United States Olympic Team's uniforms were so "icky" that athletes from the other countries would not trade with her.

Debbie Meyer triple freestyle winner.

Courtesy of ISHOF

Meyer had decided before the Olympic Games started that if she won one gold medal she would give it to her parents. Should she capture a second gold it would go to her coach, Sherman Chavoor. If she could win a third, it would be hers alone. Debbie Meyer fulfilled her ultimate dream.

Debbie Meyer was the first woman to break the 18-minute barrier in the 1500m freestyle. Meyer eventually lowered her 1500m time to 17:19.9. This event was not offered on the Olympic program for women.

During a period of approximately 25 months, Meyer would set 20 world record marks at various distances in freestyle and relay events. Prior to the Olympic Games, TASS, the Soviet

SPLASH BACK
If it was Only an Event.....

American Debbie Meyer's 1500m freestyle world record of 17:19.9 would have beaten Murray Rose's 1956 Olympic time by 39 seconds. Note the 1500m freestyle event is still not an event on the women's Olympic program as of 1996.

News agency, named Debbie Woman Athlete of the Year. After the Olympics, she received the Sullivan Award as the amateur athlete of the year.

Debbie Meyer resides in Folsom, California with her family. She is the owner and operator of the Debbie Meyer Swim School and conducts swim clinics across the country.

FELIPE MÚÑOZ MEXICO

Ten days of competition had passed and Mexico, the host country, had yet to win a gold medal in any event. Seventeen year-old Felipe "Pepe" Múñoz, stepped up to the blocks and changed all that.

Competing in the 200m breaststroke final was the favored Vladimir Kosinsky (Sov), the record holder for the event. Midway through the final Múñoz was in fourth behind the mighty threesome of Kosinky, Egon Henninger (GDR), and Brian Job (USA). Felipe made his move. As he came off the wall for his final

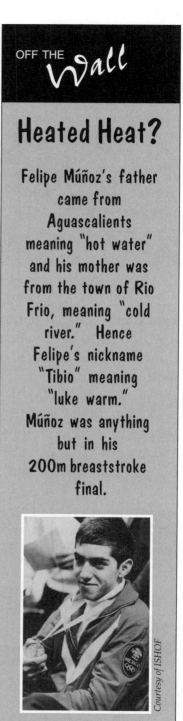

Heated Heat?

Felipe Múñoz's father came from Aguascalients meaning "hot water" and his mother was from the town of Rio Frio, meaning "cold river." Hence Felipe's nickname "Tibio" meaning "luke warm." Múñoz was anything but in his 200m breaststroke final.

Courtesy of ISHOF

50 meters, he was only inches out of second place. The Mexican fans went crazy, cheering Pepe on through this heated race.

At the final 25 meters, Múñoz caught Kosinsky and with only a few meters to go, plunged ahead to win. Without a chance to catch his breath, Pepe was snatched from the pool and carried around the arena as his fellow countrymen rejoiced in his victory. Felipe "Pepe" Múñoz was instantly proclaimed a national hero.

LILLIAN "POKEY" WATSON
UNITED STATES

"Pokey" Watson, a Santa Clara Club swimmer, was the youngest competitor on the U.S. Olympic Team in 1964. She won gold as a member of the 400m freestyle team.

Watson, in 1966, held the world record for one year, in the 200m freestyle event. She won three national outdoor

Courtesy of ISHOF

1968 200m backstroke finish (bottom to top) K. Hall (USA), Pokey Watson (U.S.A.), and E. Tanner (CAN).

freestyle championships during her swimming career. This accomplished freestyler swam the 200m backstroke at the 1968 Olympic Games, an event in which she had never won a national outdoor title. Watson not only won the Olympic 200m backstroke title, but did so decisively.

MICHAEL WENDEN
AUSTRALIA

Australian sprinter Michael Wenden prepared himself for the 1968 Olympics by swimming simulated races in training, a practice not common among sprinters at that time. This "Swimming Machine" was in prime condition by the time he reached the Mexico Games.

Wenden, who captured gold in the 200m freestyle, may be best remembered as the man who beat Don Schollander. Schollander was undefeated in this event for the previous five years. The eighteen year old Wenden also captured (in world record time) the 100m freestyle crown, a silver in the 800m freestyle and a bronze for the 400m freestyle relays.

OFF THE *Wall*

"Suit Salute"

In 1974, "The Swimming Machine," Michael Wenden, competed in the Commonwealth Games where he dominated the competition. While still in his robe, he modestly removed his swimsuit and threw it into the crowd to symbolize his departure from swimming. It was caught by a 12 year old boy!

SHARON WICHMAN
UNITED STATES

Sharon Wichman began year round swimming at the age of twelve. Four years later she won a gold medal in the 200m breaststroke event accomplishing what no other American female swimmer had previously done in Olympic competition.

In Mexico City, teammate Catie Ball, the current world record holder of the 200m breaststroke, was favored to win. Like so many of the athletes, Catie was struck hard by the stomach ailments of Mexico. Sharon Wichman stepped in and not only won gold, but did so setting a new Olympic record.

Wichman liked the close races and her most memorable Olympic moment was her 200m breaststroke final with defending champion Galina Prozumenshchykova. Wichman recalls,

"... finishing the race and turning around to see the big board's red light on my lane, signifying I had won and realizing the dream I had had for four years playing over and over in my mind and that I had worked so hard to make come true, had actually come true. I also couldn't wait to hug the Russian girl for such a good close race and pushing each other to be the best we could be."

THE 100M BACKSTROKE FINAL

As the 1968 Olympics approached, the current world record holder of the 100m backstroke was the South African, Karen Muir. Because of the racial policies of their country, South Africans had been banned from participation in the Games since 1964. The woman to beat therefore, could not be present.

These circumstances made Canadian Elaine Tanner the favorite. Tanner proceeded to set Olympic records in the heats prior to

LANE LINES

A Change in Strategies

Mark Spitz and Doug Russell of the United States had raced each other numerous times in the 100m butterfly event and each time Spitz won. During these races, Russell always led early but Spitz would finish strongly to take the win. Ironically in Mexico City, these two swimmers both decided to change their strategy for the final. Spitz took it out fast, but Russell still strong came from behind to beat Spitz for the first time.

the final. She was Canada's brightest hope for gold and the pressure on her was tremendous.

American backstroker, Kaye Hall swam against Tanner several times previously and lost to her, including the semifinals the previous day. The final however was a different story. Hall and Tanner swam dead even for the first 50 meters, but at the turn Hall forged ahead and kept that lead beating Tanner by one–half second.

Tanner who posted her best time during this race, later spoke of the pressure, "Usually, before a race, you're concentrating on strategy, the other swimmers, the race. But at Mexico City, all I could think about was the twenty million people who are expecting me to win."

Elaine Tanner, who was nicknamed Canada's "Mighty Mouse," collected a silver medal for each of the backstroke events and a bronze medal swimming the third leg of Canada's 400m freestyle relay team.

Kaye Hall, in addition to her 100m back title, collected a silver medal in the 200m backstroke final and a gold medal as a member of the United States 400m medley relay team.

1968 OLYMPIC SWIMMING FINALS

INDIVIDUAL EVENTS

Gold	Silver	Bronze	Fourth	Fifth	Sixth	Seventh	Eighth

Women 100m Freestyle - World Record (58.9 Dawn Fraser AUS)   Olympic Record (59.5 Dawn Fraser AUS 1964)

Gold	Silver	Bronze	Fourth	Fifth	Sixth	Seventh	Eighth
Jan Henne	Susan Pedersen	Linda Gustavson	Marion Lay	Martina Grunert	Alexandra Jackson	Mirjana Segrt	Judit Turoczy
USA – 1:00.0	USA – 1:00.3	USA – 1:00.3	CAN – 1:00.5	GDR – 1:01.0	GBR – 1:01.0	YUG – 1:01.5	HUN – 1:01.6

Men 100m Freestyle - World Record (52.6 K. Walsh USA/ Z.Zorn USA)   Olympic Record (53.4 Don Schollander USA 1964)

Gold	Silver	Bronze	Fourth	Fifth	Sixth	Seventh	Eighth
Michael Wenden	Kenneth Walsh	Mark Spitz	Robert McGregor	Leonid Ilyichov	Georgi Kulikov	Luis Nicolao	Zachary Zorn
AUS – 52.2 w	USA – 52.8	USA – 53.0	GBR – 53.5	SOV – 53.8	SOV – 53.9	ARG – 53.9	USA – 53.9

Women 200m Freestyle - World Record (2:06.7 Deborah Meyer USA)   1896-1964 - Event Not Held On Olympic Program

Gold	Silver	Bronze	Fourth	Fifth	Sixth	Seventh	Eighth
Deborah Meyer	Jan Henne	Jane Barkman	Gabriele Wetzko	Mirjana Segrt	Claude Mandonnaud	Lynette Bell	Olga Kozicova
USA – 2:10.5 o	USA – 2:11.0	USA – 2:11.2	GDR – 2:12.3	YUG – 2:13.3	FRA – 2:14.9	AUS – 2:15.1	CZE – 2:16.0

Men 200m Freestyle - World Record (1:54.3 Don Schollander USA)   1906-196 - Event Not Held On Olympic Program

Gold	Silver	Bronze	Fourth	Fifth	Sixth	Seventh	Eighth
Michael Wenden	Donald Schollander	John Nelson	Ralph Hutton	Alain Mosconi	Robert Windle	Semyon Belits-Geiman	Stephen Rerych
AUS – 1:55.2 o	1:55.8 – USA	USA – 1:58.1	CAN – 1:58.6	FRA – 1:59.1	AUS – 2:00.9	SOV – 2:01.5	USA – dns

w World Record   *o* Olympic Record   *p* Preliminary Heat   *dq* Disqualified   *e* Equal to World Record   *eo* Equal to Olympic Record
dns Did Not Start   *dnf* Did Not Finish   *ac* Also Competed   *r* Relay Lead-off Split   *E* Estimated

OLYMPIAD XIX – 1968 – MEXICO CITY, MEXICO

1968 OLYMPIC SWIMMING FINALS

	Gold	Silver	Bronze	Fourth	Fifth	Sixth	Seventh	Eighth
Women 400m Freestyle - World Record (4:24.5 Deborah Meyer USA) Olympic Record (4:43.3 Virginia Duenkel USA 1964)								
	Debbie Meyer	Linda Gustavson	Karen Moras	Pamela Kruse	Maria Teresa Ramirez	Gabriele Wetzko	Angela Coughlan	Ingrid Morris
	USA – 4:31.8 o	USA – 4:35.5	AUS – 4:37.0	USA – 4:37.2	MEX – 4:40.2	GDR – 4:42.2	CAN – 4:51.9	SWE – 4:53.8
Men 400m Freestyle - World Record (4:06.5 Ralph Hutton CAN) Olympic Record (4:12.2 Don Schollander USA 1964)								
	Michael Burton	Ralph Hutton	Alain Mosconi	Gregory Brough	John Nelson		Hans-Joachim Fassnacht	Brent Berk
	USA – 4:09.0 o	CAN – 4:11.7	FRA – 4:13.3	AUS – 4:15.9	USA – 4:16.7	USA – 4:17.2	GER – 4:18.1	USA – 4:26.0
Women 800m Freestyle - World Record (9:10.4 Deborah Meyer USA) 1896-1964 - Event Not Held On Olympic Program								
	Deborah Meyer	Pamela Kruse	Maria Teresa Ramirez	Karen Moras	Patricia Caretto	Angela Coughlan	Denise Langford	Laura Vaca
	USA – 9:24.0 o	USA – 9:35.7	MEX – 9:38.5	AUS – 9:38.6	USA – 9:51.3	CAN – 9:56.4	AUS – 9:56.7	MEX – 10:02.5
Men 1500m Freestyle - World Record (16:08.5 Michael Burton USA) Olympic Record (17:01.7 Robert Windle AUS 1964)								
	Michael Burton	John Kinsella	Gregory Brough	Graham White	Ralph Hutton	Guillermo Echevarria	Juan Alanis	John Nelson
	USA – 16:38.9 o	USA – 16:57.3	AUS – 17:04.7	AUS – 17:08.0	CAN – 17:15.6	MEX – 17:36.4	MEX – 17:46.6	USA – 18:05.1
Women 100m Backstroke - World Record (1:06.4 Karen Muir RSA) Olympic Record (1:07.7 Cathy Ferguson USA 1964)								
	Kaye Hall	Elaine Tanner	Jane Swagerty	Kendis Moore	Andrea Gyarmati	Lynette Watson	Sylvie Canet	Glenda Stirling
	USA – 1:06.2 w	CAN – 1:06.7	USA – 1:08.1	USA – 1:08.3	HUN – 1:09.1	AUS – 1:09.1	FRA – 1:09.3	NZE – 1:10.6

1968 OLYMPIC SWIMMING FINALS

Gold	Silver	Bronze	Fourth	Fifth	Sixth	Seventh	Eighth
Men 100m Backstroke – World Record (58.4 Roland Matthes GDR)					**1964 - Event Not Held On Olympic Program**		
Roland Matthes	Charles Hickcox	Ronald Mills	Larry Barbiere	James Shaw	Bob Schoutsen	Reinhard Blechert	Franco Del Campo
GDR – 58.7 o	USA – 1:00.2	USA – 1:00.5	USA – 1:01.1	CAN – 1:01.4	NED – 1:01.8	GER – 1:01.9	ITA – 1:02.0
Women 200m Backstroke – World Record (2:23.8 Karen Muir RSA)					**1896-1964 - Event Not Held On Olympic Program**		
Lillian "Pokey" Watson	Elaine Tanner	Kaye Hall	Lynette Watson	Wendy Burrell	Zdenka Gasparac	Maria Corominas	Bendicte Duprez
USA – 2:24.8 o	CAN – 2:27.4	USA – 2:28.9	AUS – 2:29.5	GBR – 2:32.3	YUG – 2:33.9	ESP – 2:33.5	FRA – 2:36.6
Men 200m Backstroke – World Record (2:07.5 Roland Matthes GDR)					Olympic Record (2:10.3 Jed Graef USA 1964)		
Roland Matthes	Mitchell Ivey	Jack Horsley	Gary Hall	Santiago Esteva	Leonid Dobrosskokin	Joachim Rother	Franco Del Campo
GDR – 2:09.6 o	USA – 2:10.6	USA – 2:10.9	USA – 2:12.6	ESP – 2:12.9	SOV – 2:15.4	GDR – 2:15.8	ITA – 2:16.5
Women 100m Breaststroke – World Record (1:14.2 Catie Ball USA)					**1896-1964 – Event Not Held On Olympic Program**		
Djurdjica Bjedov	Galina Prozumen-shchykova	Sharon Wichman	Uta Frommater	Catie Ball	Kyoe Nakagawa	Svetlana Babanina	Ana Norbis
YUG – 1:15.8 o	SOV – 1:15.9	USA – 1:16.1	GER – 1:16.2	USA – 1:16.7	JPN – 1:17.0	SOV – 1:17.2	URU – 1:17.3
Men 100m Breaststroke - World Record (1:06.2 Nikolai Pankin RUS)					**1896-1964 – Event Not Held On Olympic Program**		
Donald McKenzie	Vladimir Kosinsky	Nikolai Pankin	José Sylvio Fiolo	Yevhen Mykhaylov	Ian O'Brien	Alberto Forelli	Egon Henninger
USA – 1:07.7 o	SOV – 1:08.0	SOV – 1:08.0	BRA – 1:08.1	SOV – 1:08.4	AUS – 1:08.6	ARG – 1:08.7	GDR – 1:09.7

1968 OLYMPIC SWIMMING FINALS

	Gold	Silver	Bronze	Fourth	Fifth	Sixth	Seventh	Eighth

Women 200m Breaststroke - World Record (2:38.5 Catie Ball USA) Olympic Record (2:46.4 Prozumenshchykova SOV 1964)

	Gold	Silver	Bronze	Fourth	Fifth	Sixth	Seventh	Eighth
	Sharon Wichman	Djurdjica Bjedov	Galina Prozumenshchykova	Alla Grebennikova	Cathy Jamison	Svetlana Babanina	Chieno Shibata	Ana Norbis
	USA – 2:44.4 o	YUG – 2:46.4	SOV – 2:47.0	SOV – 2:47.1	USA – 2:48.4	SOV – 2:48.4	JPN – 2:51.5	URU – 2:51.9

Men 200m Breaststroke - World Record (2:27.4 Vladimir Kosinsky RUS) Olympic Record (2:27.8 Ian O'Brien AUS 1964)

	Gold	Silver	Bronze	Fourth	Fifth	Sixth	Seventh	Eighth
	Felipe Muñoz	Vladimir Kosinsky	Brian Job	Nikolai Pankin	Yevhen Mykhaylov	Egon Henninger	Philip Long	Osamu Tsurumine
	MEX – 2:28.7	SOV – 2:29.2	USA – 2:29.9	SOV – 2:30.3	SOV – 2:32.8	GDR – 2:33.2	USA – 2:33.6	JPN – 2:34.9

Women 100m Butterfly - World Record (1:04.5 Ada Kok NED) Olympic Record (1:04.7 Sharon Stouder USA 1964)

	Gold	Silver	Bronze	Fourth	Fifth	Sixth	Seventh	Eighth
	Lynette McClements	Ellie Daniel	Susan Shields	Ada Kok	Andrea Gyarmati	Heike Hustede	Toni Hewitt	Helga Lindner
	AUS – 1:05.5	USA – 1:05.8	USA – 1:06.2	NED – 1:06.2	HUN – 1:06.8	GER – 1:06.9	USA – 1:07.5	GDR – 1:07.6

Men 100m Butterfly - World Record (55.6 Mark Spitz USA) 1896-1964 - Event Not Held On Olympic Program

	Gold	Silver	Bronze	Fourth	Fifth	Sixth	Seventh	Eighth
	Douglas Russell	Mark Spitz	Ross Wales	Volodymyr Nemshilov	Satoshi Maruya	Yuri Suzdaltsev	Lutz Stoklasa	Robert Cusack
	USA – 55.9	USA – 56.4	USA – 57.2	SOV – 58.1	JPN – 58.6	SOV – 58.8	GER – 58.9	AUS – 59.8

Women 200m Butterfly - World Record (2:21.0 220y Ada Kok NED) 1896-1964 - Event Not Held On Olympic Program

	Gold	Silver	Bronze	Fourth	Fifth	Sixth	Seventh	Eighth
	Ada Kok	Helga Lindner	Ellie Daniel	Toni Hewitt	Heike Hustede	Diane Giebel	Margaret Auton	Yasuko Fujii
	NED – 2:24.7 o	GDR – 2:24.8	USA – 2:25.9	USA – 2:26.2	GER – 2:27.9	USA – 2:31.7	GBR – 2:33.2	JPN – 2:34.3

1968 OLYMPIC SWIMMING FINALS

Gold	Silver	Bronze	Fourth	Fifth	Sixth	Seventh	Eighth

Men 200m Butterfly - World Record (2:05.7 Mark Spitz USA)   Olympic Record (2:06.6 Kevin Berry AUS 1964)

Gold	Silver	Bronze	Fourth	Fifth	Sixth	Seventh	Eighth
Carl Robie	Martin Woodroffe	John Ferris	Valentin Kuzmin	Peter Feil	Folkert Meeuw	Viktor Sharygin	Mark Spitz
USA – 2:08.7	GBR – 2:09.0	USA – 2:09.3	SOV – 2:10.6	SWE – 2:10.9	GER – 2:11.5	SOV – 2:11.9	USA – 2:13.5

Women 200m Individual Medley - World Record (2:23.5 C. Kolb USA)   1896-1964 - Event Not Held On Olympic Program

Gold	Silver	Bronze	Fourth	Fifth	Sixth	Seventh	Eighth
Claudia Kolb	Susan Pedersen	Jan Henne	Sabine Steinbach	Yoshimi Nishigawa	Marianne Seydel	Larissa Zakharova	Shelagh Ratcliff
USA – 2:24.7 o	USA – 2:28.8	USA – 2:31.4	GDR – 2:31.4	JPN – 2:33.7	GDR – 2:33.7	SOV – 2:37.0	GBR - dq

Men 200m Individual Medley - World Record (2:10.6 C. Hickcox USA)   1896-1964 - Event Not Held On Olympic Program

Gold	Silver	Bronze	Fourth	Fifth	Sixth	Seventh	Eighth
Charles Hickcox	Gregory Buckingham	John Ferris	Juan Bello	George Smith	John Gilchrist	Michael Holthaus	Péter Lázár
USA – 212.0 o	USA – 2:13.0	USA – 2:13.3	PER – 2:13.7	CAN – 2:15.9	CAN – 2:16.6	GER – 2:16.8	HUN – 2:18.3

Women 400m Individual Medley - World Record (5:04.7 Claudia Kolb USA)   Olympic Record (5:18.7 D. De Varona USA 1964)

Gold	Silver	Bronze	Fourth	Fifth	Sixth	Seventh	Eighth
Claudia Kolb	Lynn Vidali	Sabine Steinbach	Susan Pedersen	Shelagh Ratcliffe	Marianne Seydel	Tui Shipston	Laura Vaca
USA – 5:08.5 o	USA – 5:22.2	GDR – 5:25.3	USA - 5:25.8	GBR – 5:30.5	GDR – 5:32.0	NZE – 5:34.6	MEX – 5:35.7

Men 400m Individual Medley - World Record (4:39.0 C. Hickcox USA)   Olympic Record (4:45.4 Richard Roth USA 1964)

Gold	Silver	Bronze	Fourth	Fifth	Sixth	Seventh	Eighth
Charles Hickcox	Gary Hall	Michael Holthaus	Gregory Buckingham	John Gilchrist	Reinhard Merkel	Andrei Dunayev	Rafael Hernandez
USA – 4:48.4	USA – 4:48.7	GER – 4:51.4	USA – 4:51.4	CAN – 4:56.7	GER – 4:59.8	SOV – 5:00.3	MEX – 5:04.3

1968 OLYMPIC SWIMMING FINALS

RELAY EVENTS

Gold	Silver	Bronze	Fourth	Fifth	Sixth	Seventh	Eighth

Women 400m Medley Relay - World Record (4:28.1 USA)   Olympic Record (4:33.9 USA 1964)

Gold	Silver	Bronze	Fourth	Fifth	Sixth	Seventh	Eighth
USA – 4:28.3 o	AUS – 4:30.0	GER – 4:36.4	SOV – 4:37.0	GDR – 4:38.0	GBR – 4:38.3	NED – 4:38.7	HUN – 4:42.9
Kaye Hall, Catie Ball, Ellie Daniel, Susan Pedersen, p - Jane Swagerty, Suzy Jones, Susan Shields, Jan Henne	Lynnette Watson, Judy Playfair, Lynette McClements, Janet Steinbeck, p - Lynette Bell	Angelika Kraus, Uta Frommater, Heike Hustede, Heidemarie Reineck	Tinatin Lekveishvili, Alla Grebennikova, Tetyana Devyatova, Lidiya Hrebets, p - Larissa Zakharova	Martina Grunert, Eva Whittke, Helga Lindner, Uta Schmuck	Wendy Burrell, Dorothy Harrison, Margaret Auton, Alexandra Jackson	JacobjeButer, Klena Bimolt, Ada Kok, Petronella Bos	Mária Lantos, Edit Kovács, Andrea Gyarmati, Judit Turóczy

Men 400m Medley Relay - World Record (3:56.5 GDR)   Olympic Record (3:58.4 USA 1964)

Gold	Silver	Bronze	Fourth	Fifth	Sixth	Seventh	Eighth
USA – 3:54.9 w	GDR – 3:57.5	SOV – 4:00.7	AUS – 4:00.8	JPN – 4:01.8	GER – 4:05.4	CAN – 4:07.3	ESP – 4:08.8
Charles Hickcox, Donald McKenzie, Douglas Russell, Kenneth Walsh, p - Ronald Mills, Chester Jastremski, Carl Robie, Don Schollander	Roland Matthes, Egon Henninger, Horst-Günther Gregor, Frank Wiegand	Yuri Hromak, Vladimir Kossinsky, Volodymyr Nemshilov, Leonid Ilyichev, p - Viktor Mazano, Nikolai Pankin, Yuri Suzdatsev, Sergei Gusev	Karl Byrom, Ian O'Brien, Robert Cusack, Michael Wenden	Yasuo Tanaka, Nobutaka Taguchi, Satoshi Maruya, Kunihiro Iwasaki	Reinhard Blechert, Gregor Betz, Lutz Stoklasa, Wolfgang Kremer	James Shaw, William Mahony, Toomas Arusoo, John Gilchrist	Santiago Esteva, José Duran, Arturo Lan,g José Chicoy

1968 OLYMPIC SWIMMING FINALS

Women 400m Freestyle Relay - World Record (4:01.1 USA)   Olympic Record (4:03.8 USA 1964)

Gold	Silver	Bronze	Fourth	Fifth	Sixth	Seventh	Eighth
Jane Barkman, Linda Gustavson, Susan Pedersen, Jan Henne	Gabriele Wetzko, Roswitha Krause, Uta Schmuck, Martina Grunert *p* - Gabriele Perthes	Angela Coughlan, Marilyn Corson, Elaine Tanner, Marion Lay	Janet Steinbeck, Susan Eddy, Lynette Watson, Lynette Bell *p* - Julie McDonald	Edit Kovács, Magdolna Patoh, Andréa Gyarmati, Judit Turóczy	Shigeko Kawanishi, Yoshimi Nishigawa, Yasuko Fujii, Miwako Kobayashi *p* - Yumiko Ono	Shelagh Ratcliffe, Fiona Kellock, Susan Williams, Alexandra Jackson	Marie Kersaudy, Simone Hanner, Daniele Dorleans, Claude Mandonnaud
USA – 4:02.5 *u*	GDR – 4:05.7	CAN – 4:07.2	AUS – 4:08.7	HUN – 4:11.0	JPN – 4:13.6	GBR – 4:18.0	FRA - *dq*

Men 400m Freestyle Relay - World Record (3:32.5 USA)   Olympic Record (3:32.2 USA 1964)

Gold	Silver	Bronze	Fourth	Fifth	Sixth	Seventh	Eighth
Zachary Zorn, Stephen Rerych, Mark Spitz, Kenneth Walsh *p* - William Johnson, David Johnson, Michael Wall, Don Schollander	Semyon Belits-Geiman, Viktor Mazanov, Georgi Kulikov, Leonid Ilyichev *p* - Sergei Gusev	Gregory Rogers, Robert Windle, Robert Cusack, Michael Wenden	Michael Turner, David Hembrow, Robert McGregor, Anthony Jarvis	Frank Wiegand, Udo Poser, Horst-Günther Gregor, Lothar Gericke	Wolfgang Kremer, Olaf von Schilling, Peter Schorning, Hans Fassnacht	Glen Finch, George Smith, Ralph Hutton, John Gilchrist	Kunihiro Iwasaki, Masayuki Ohsawa, Satoru Nakano, Teruhiko Kitani
USA – 3:31.7 *w*	SOV – 3:34.2	AUS – 3:34.7	GBR – 3:38.4	GDR – 3:38.8	GER – 3:39.0	CAN – 3:39.2	JPN – 3:41.5

1968 OLYMPIC SWIMMING FINALS

Men 800m Freestyle Relay - World and Olympic Record (7:52.1 USA 1964)

Gold	Silver	Bronze	Fourth	Fifth	Sixth	Seventh	Eighth
John Nelson, Stephen Rerych, Mark Spitz, Donald Schollander, p - William Johnson, David Johnson, Andrew Strenk, Michael Wall	Gregory Rogers, Graham White, Robert Windle, Michael Wenden	Vladimir Bure, Semyon Belits-Geiman, Georgi Kulikov, Leonid Ilyichev	George Smith, Ronald Jacks, John Gilchrist, Ralph Hutton	Michel Rousseau, Gerard Letast, Francis Luyce, Alain Mosconi	Hans Fassnacht, Olaf von Schilling, Volkert Meeuw, Wolfgang Kremer	Frank Weigand, Horst-Günter Gregor, Alfred Müller, Jochen Herbst	Hans Ljungberg, Karl Larson, Sven Ferm, Erik Eriksson
USA – 7:52.33	AUS – 7:53.77	SOV – 8:01.66	CAN – 8:03.22	FRA – 8:03.77	GER – 8:04.33	GDR – 8:06.00	SWE – 8:12.11

Chapter 18

Olympiad XX - 1972
Munich, Germany

The Munich Games were billed as the "Games of Joy." Sadly they turned into the "Games of Terror."

The Olympic Games had grown and gained such popularity world wide that the television audience now numbered one billion. There were four thousand media personnel alone, attending these Games.

It may well be due to this phenomenal media blitz that the Black Septembrist's, an extreme and violent Palestinian terrorist group, chose the Olympic Games to draw worldwide attention to their political agenda.

Just before dawn on September 5, 1972, eight terrorists slipped into the Olympic Village. Their faces were masked and they were armed with machine guns as well as hand grenades concealed in athletic equipment bags. The seige would end with the death of eleven Israeli athletes, five of the terrorists and one German police officer.

There was considerable controversy over the decision to continue these Games in light of this horrendous tragedy. The majority of the athletes agreed that the Games should go on, fearing that if they did not continue, the future of the Olympic movement would be at risk.

On September 6th, a memorial service was held at the Olympic Stadium. The flags flew at half-mast with 80,000 in attendance mourning the fallen athletes. The Games resumed.

The swimming events had been completed prior to September 5, and the Olympic pool had seen its own share of history made. Thirty world and 84 Olympic records were broken or equaled in Munich.

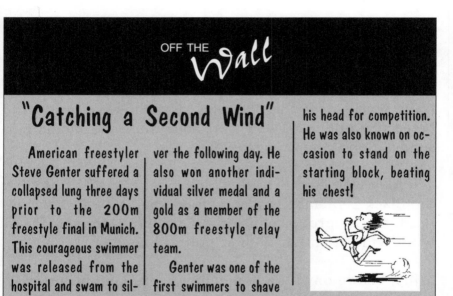

OFF THE *Wall*

"Catching a Second Wind"

American freestyler Steve Genter suffered a collapsed lung three days prior to the 200m freestyle final in Munich. This courageous swimmer was released from the hospital and swam to silver the following day. He also won another individual silver medal and a gold as a member of the 800m freestyle relay team.

Genter was one of the first swimmers to shave his head for competition. He was also known on occasion to stand on the starting block, beating his chest!

Catherine Carr *Keena Rothhammer*

USA *USA*

medal count
2

100m Breaststroke
Gold

400m Medley Relay
Gold

800m Freestyle
Gold

200m Freestyle
Bronze

MELISSA BELOTE
UNITED STATES

Courtesy of ISHOF

The young Melissa Belote.

Melissa Belote loved swimming but hated getting water in her eyes. The backstroke was the perfect solution.

Belote had been a surprise contender at the U.S. Olympic Trials, yet she went on to take two individual gold medals in both backstroke events in Munich. Belote broke the Olympic record during the 100m final and earned a berth on the U.S. medley relay team that went on to capture gold.

She broke her own record in the 200m backstroke twice, once in the preliminary heat and again during the final. With that win Belote earned her third gold medal of these Games. U.S. teammate, Susie Atwood had been favored in both backstroke events going into the Games. This took the pressure off Belote, and allowed her to relax, which she attributes to her winning performance.

Mike Stamm - U.S.A.

medal
count
3

400m Medley Relay – Gold
100m Backstroke – Silver
200m Backstroke - Silver

RICK DE MONT
UNITED STATES

Courtesy of ISHOF

Rick De Mont, a sixteen-year-old Californian, became the youngest male swimmer ever to win the 400m Olympic freestyle. A feat accomplished by the narrowest margin possible . . . one-hundreth of a second!

When Rick qualified for the U.S. Olympic Team he submitted all the necessary forms listing his medi-

Age Group champion Rick DeMont

cations. Protocol called for each country's team physicians to determine the components of a medication. They were then to cross-reference the components against the IOC (International Olympic Committee) list of banned substances. If one of the components found was on the list, the doctors were to find a substitute drug that was sanctioned by the IOC, for the athlete's use.

The U.S. Team doctors failed to thoroughly review DeMont's forms and never checked the components of his medication for a banned substance. The doctors instead advised the athletes not to use any drugs 48 hours prior to a race unless they first cleared it with the medical staff.

DeMont, who had taken asthma medication since the age of four, woke up the night before the 400m final wheezing and took a tablet of his asthma medication for relief. He was unaware that this tablet contained ephedrine, an IOC banned substance (the trace of ephedrine used in DeMont's asthma medication would not have enhanced his Olympic performance).

There was no indication of a problem at the award ceremonies and two days later he easily qualified for the 1500m freestyle event. Then the unthinkable happened. DeMont was stripped of his 400m freestyle gold medal, for failing the drug test he was given after his race.

To make matters worse, the drug test failure prevented DeMont's swimming of the 1500m event, of which he was the current world record holder. In the end, it was the U.S. Team Doctors who had failed. They took the accomplishment of a lifetime away from this young Olympian.

In 1973, DeMont won the 400m freestyle at the World Championships in a new world record time of 3:58.18. He was the first man to break the four-minute barrier for the 400m freestyle event and was named World Swimmer of the Year.

DeMont's gold medal was recently found in the archives of the IOC's museum. Rick's response, "Now if I could just get it back. I'm tired of being known as the gold medal loser." The IOC has yer to overturn their original decision. Rick DeMont continues his quest to regain his lost gold medal.

SCORE
BOARD

Men's 400m IM

Gold*	Gunnar Larsson	SWE	4:31.98	o
Silver	Tim McKee	USA	4:31.98	o
Bronze	András Hargitay	HUN	4:32.70	

*Officials determined Larsson had won by two-thousandths of a second.

It was argued that pool walls and lanes could vary slightly making it unfair to measure time to the thousandth of a second. A rules change resulted and times are now taken to hundredths of a second.

SHANE GOULD
AUSTRALIA

During the 1972 Olympics, 15-year-old phenomenon Shane Gould swam 12 races in eight days. She won five individual medals; three gold, one silver and a bronze. She was the first female swimmer to accomplish such a feat.

Courtesy of ISHOF

Shane Gould flys to the finish.

The American's, in an attempt to boost morale, privately wore T-shirts that read, "All that glitters is not Gould."

Between July of 1971 and January of 1972, Shane set world records in all five internationally recognized freestyle distances (100m, 200m, 400m, 800m and the 1500m). She also held a world record in the 200m individual medley.

On January 8, 1972, Shane Gould broke the oldest record on the books. It was a 16 year-old record set by fellow Australian Dawn Fraser, in the 100m freestyle (58.5).

In all, Gould set eleven world records in her short career. Tired of the all-consuming discipline of competitive swimming, Shane Gould retired just one year after the Munich Games, at the age of 16.

LANE LINES

"Aussie Gold Rush"

Gail Neall captured gold, setting a world record and surpassing her pre-Olympic personal best time in the 400m IM by seven seconds!

Eighteen-year-old Beverly Whitfield, came from last place to win the 200m breaststroke final. As she exited the pool she exclaimed, "For once I kept my cool. This is the greatest feeling in the world."

JERRY HEIDENREICH
UNITED STATES

Courtesy of ISHOF

Heidenreich psyching up for the 100m free final.

Heidenreich missed making the 1968 Olympic squad by only two tenths of a second. At that point he knew his chances were excellent for making the 1972 U.S. Olympic Team. He would be twenty-two and have completed college. The timing could not be better.

Heidenreich not only made the 1972 Olympic Team, he collected four Olympic medals. Spitz touched Jerry out by a mere half stroke in the 100m freestyle. In addition to the silver medal, the versatile Heidenreich also captured a bronze medal for the 100m butterfly. Swimming the third leg of the 400m free relay and anchor for the 400m medley relay, Heidenreich won two gold medals to add to his Olympic collection.

Heidenreich's pre-race rituals included a hot bath, listening to loud music with a great beat, and eating whatever he felt like having before competing! He liked to tie his swimsuit while up on the blocks, "to make the other guys wonder if theirs was tied tight enough."

When asked his favorite age group story Jerry remembered, "Dying our relay members' hair white at the big meet in the summer. We were ten, eleven and twelve years old, and the older girls, fifteen through seventeen, would bleach it for us. Sometimes it would be orange or turn green when we dove in the pool. One of the girls to dye my hair was Kitten Quick, sister of Richard Quick."

Jerry Heidenreich continues his contribution to the sport of swimming as an instructor and coach. He is the founder of the children's swim school, Aquatic Academy, in Dallas, Texas, and the proud father of a son, Austin.

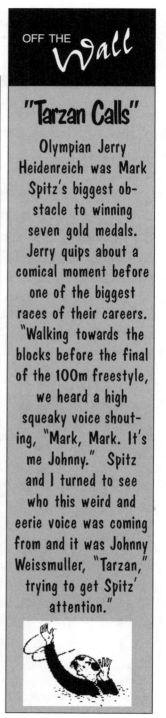

OFF THE **Wall**

"Tarzan Calls"

Olympian Jerry Heidenreich was Mark Spitz's biggest obstacle to winning seven gold medals. Jerry quips about a comical moment before one of the biggest races of their careers. "Walking towards the blocks before the final of the 100m freestyle, we heard a high squeaky voice shouting, "Mark, Mark. It's me Johnny." Spitz and I turned to see who this weird and eerie voice was coming from and it was Johnny Weissmuller, "Tarzan," trying to get Spitz' attention."

"To live the dream, you must first dream it. Learn to perform at an optimum level, not maximum. Embrace your competitors, they are what keep you getting better. Remember the most important thing (and fun) is in the journey, not the final destination."- J. Heidenreich

GUNNAR LARSSON
SWEDEN

Gunnar Larsson, 21, was the gold medal winner in both the 400m and the 200m individual medley at the 1972 Games. The 400m race would go down as one of the closest in Olympic history and would result in an international rule change.

Both Larsson and American Tim McKee were clocked at 4:31.98. The timing device was dismantled and upon inspection it was found that Larsson had touched two-thousandths of a second ahead of McKee.

This decision led to a change in the international swim-

SCORE
B O A R D
Men's 200m IM

Gold	Gunnar Larsson	SWE	2:07.17*w*
Silver	Tim McKee	USA	2:08.37
Bronze	Steven Furniss	USA	2:08.45
4th Place	Gary Hall	USA	2:08.49

First (4) finishers topple the world record of 2:09.3 set by Gunnar Larsson!

ming rules. Times and places would now be decided in hundredths of a second due to the possibility that lane lengths could vary slightly. Had this rule been in place at the 1972 Olympics, both Larsson and McKee would have been awarded gold medals.

KAREN MOE
UNITED STATES

Karen Moe swam under the tutelage of Coach George Haines of the Santa Clara Swim Club. She broke her first world record in 1970 at the age of seventeen. It was then she realized that the Olympics were a possibility for her. Karen made the 1972 Olympic Team

Courtesy of ISHOF

Moe takes questions from the media.

and realized her dream, swimming to victory in the 200m butterfly.

Before a race, Moe would stand behind the blocks shaking out her arms

OFF THE *Wall*

Slo-Moe-tion

Karen Moe was chosen by **SPEEDO** to model the "new suits," at the 1976 training camp. She recalled, "They had just designed the crossback suit. I was to change behind a screen and show off to the waiting team. Well, I had no idea what the suit was supposed to look like! I kept putting my legs through the wrong holes and I had the worst time getting it on. Meanwhile the team was hooting and hollering!"

and moving about. She explained, "I always was afraid that if I stopped moving my fear would paralyze me and I wouldn't be able to move at all."

Karen Moe Thorton is currently the assistant athletic director for the University of California in Berkeley. To Olympic hopefuls she advises, "Even as you strive for excellence in your sport, keep balance in your life by paying attention to family, friends, school and other interests."

SANDRA NEILSON
UNITED STATES

In Munich, Sandra Neilson handed Shane Gould her first loss in two years. She and teammate Shirley Babashoff swam to gold and silver, respectively, in the 100m freestyle.

Neilson was a member of the historic 400m free relay squad that broke the four-minute barrier in August of 1972, (3:58.11). Twelve days later, the East German Team tied that world record. The American women knew what they faced going into these Olympic Games. During the 400m freestyle final, Neilson led off the relay, gaining a lead of a quarter of a second over the East German, Gabriele Wetzko.

Neilson's relay teammates, Jennifer Kemp, Jane Barkman and anchor Shirley Babashoff, each met the challenge and were able to defeat the East Germans, establishing another world record in the process.

Sandra Neilson anchored the winning 400m medley relay as well. That team also set a new world record and brought Neilson's personal take to three gold medals.

Neilson came out of retirement and returned to Senior swimming, clocking more than a second under her 1972 Olympic winning time of 58.9. At age 32, Neilson was the first woman over 30 to final, with a 6th place, in Olympic Trials, just missing a berth on the USA team with a time that would've finaled at the Seoul Olympics.

SPLASH BACK

A family Business

Andrea Gyarmati won a silver medal in the 100m backstroke and a bronze in the 100m fly in Munich. A two-time Olympian, she is the daughter of Olympic swimmer Eva Szekely (1952 & 1956) and Olympian Dezso Gyarmati (1948, 1952, 1956, 1960 & 1964) who competed in water polo for Hungary.

MARK SPITZ
UNITED STATES

Abendzeitung, a Munich newspaper, dubbed Mark Spitz, "Mark der Hai," which translated to "Mark the Shark." During the course of his swimming career Spitz set 33 world

Courtesy of ISHOF

The underwater form of Mark Spitz

records, only seven of these as a member of a relay team. His specialties ranged from the 100m and 200m freestyles to the 100m and 200m butterfly.

This prolific medal winner won a total of nine gold, one silver and one bronze during the 1968 and 1972 Olympic Games. Prior to his 1972 feat, Spitz was named the 1971 Sullivan award recipient as the nation's outstanding amateur athlete.

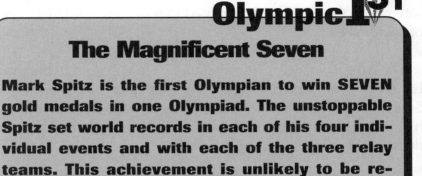

Olympic 1ST

The Magnificent Seven

Mark Spitz is the first Olympian to win SEVEN gold medals in one Olympiad. The unstoppable Spitz set world records in each of his four individual events and with each of the three relay teams. This achievement is unlikely to be repeated in Olympic swimming history.

Much has been written of Spitz's *disappointing* 1968 Olympic performance in Mexico. However, he came home with an individual silver, a bronze, and two gold medals as a member of two U.S.A. relay teams.

Growing up, Spitz' Father, Arnold, often reminded his son, "Swimming isn't everything, winning is." It would appear these are words Mark swam by.

Midway to winning his seven gold medals, Spitz could not allow himself to relax. He said, "This isn't fun, not yet at least. It's tremendous–the pressure of not losing. I'd rather win six out of six, or even four out of four, than six out of seven. It's reached a point where my self-esteem comes into it. I just don't want to lose."

The 100m freestyle event was the one race in which Spitz was considered vulnerable. Rumors began spreading that Spitz might withdraw from the event. Spitz's coach, Sherm Chavoor, went to speak to his swimmer, telling him he would be perceived as a chicken if he withdrew. Whatever reservations Spitz may have had were gone.

In the final, Spitz, who had finished behind Heidenreich in the preliminary heats, changed his strategy. He went out full force from the onset and managed to reach the wall just ahead of Heidenreich.

The Americans were heavily favored to win gold in the medley relay event and their performance disappointed no one. Spitz took his seventh gold. Knowing they had just witnessed history, his relay teammates hoisted Spitz onto their shoulders, honoring his accomplishments.

After his historic performance Spitz said, "Day in and day out, swimming is 90% physical. You've got to do the physical work in training, and don't need much mental. But in a big meet like this, it's 90% mental and 10% physical. Your body is ready and now it becomes mind versus matter."

Mark Spitz retired from swimming immediately following the Munich Games, having achieved the ultimate Olympic dream of seven gold medals in one Olympiad.

LANE LINES

"Powerful Medley"

The United States 400m medley relay team was made up of powerhouses Mike Stamm, Tom Bruce, Jerry Heidenreich (who had won silver in each of their specialties) and gold medalist Mark Spitz. Small wonder they annihilated the existing world record and finished almost four seconds ahead of the second place East German Team.

LANE LINES

"Flying Through Records"

Mayumi Aoki of Japan entered the Munich Games as the world record holder of the 100m butterfly event. During a preliminary heat, Hungarian Andrea Gyarmati broke Aoki's mark. At the 50 meter mark of the finals, Aoki was in seventh place, but flew through the last 50 meters for the win and a new world record. Roswitha Beier of East Germany captured the silver medal, also eclipsing the previous world record.

NOBUTAKA TAGUCHI
JAPAN

Nobutaka Taguchi's win in the 100m breaststroke distinguished him as Japan's first Olympic swimming champion since 1956.

Courtesy of ISHOF

Nobutaka Taguchi celebrates Japan's first Olympic swimming victory in 26 years.

The 100m breaststroke world record was broken three times during the Munich competition. During a preliminary round, American John Hencken lowered the record to (1:05.68). Taguchi then proceeded to break Hencken's mark in the next heat and again during the final (1:04.94.).

Nobutaka Taguchi also won a bronze medal in the 200m breaststroke event and represented Japan again at the 1976 Montreal Games.

1972 OLYMPIC SWIMMING FINALS

INDIVIDUAL EVENTS

Gold	Silver	Bronze	Fourth	Fifth	Sixth	Seventh	Eighth

Women 100m Freestyle - World Record (58.5 Shane Gould AUS) — Olympic Record (59.5 Dawn Fraser AUS 1964)

Gold	Silver	Bronze	Fourth	Fifth	Sixth	Seventh	Eighth
Sandra Neilson	Shirley Babashoff	Shane Gould	Gabriele Wetzko	Heidemarie Reineck	Andrea Eife	Magdolna Patoh	Enith Brigitha
USA - 58.59 o	USA - 59.02	AUS - 59.06	GDR - 59.21	GER - 59.73	GDR - 59.91	HUN - 1:00.02	NED - 1:00.09

Men 100m Freestyle - World Record (51.47 Mark Spitz USA) — Olympic Record (52.2 Michael Wenden AUS)

Gold	Silver	Bronze	Fourth	Fifth	Sixth	Seventh	Eighth
Mark Spitz	Jerry Heidenreich	Vladimir Bure	John Murphy	Michael Wenden	Igor Grivennikov	Michel Rousseau	Klaus Steinbach
USA - 51.22 w	USA - 51.65	SOV - 51.77	USA 52.08	AUS - 52.41	SOV - 52.44	FRA - 52.90	GER - 52.92

Women 200m Freestyle - World Record (2:05.21 Shirley Babashoff USA) — Olympic Record (2:10.5 Debbie Meyer USA 1968)

Gold	Silver	Bronze	Fourth	Fifth	Sixth	Seventh	Eighth
Shane Gould	Shirley Babashoff	Keena Rothhammer	Ann Marshall	Andrea Eife	Hansje Bunschoten	Anke Rijnders	Karin Tuelling
AUS - 2:03.56 w	USA - 2:04.33	USA - 2:04.92	USA - 2:05.45	GDR - 2:06.27	NED - 2:08.40	NED - 2:09.41	GDR - 2:11.70

Men 200m Freestyle - World Record (1:53.5 Mark Spitz USA) — Olympic Record (1:55.2 Michael Wenden AUS 1968)

Gold	Silver	Bronze	Fourth	Fifth	Sixth	Seventh	Eighth
Mark Spitz	Steven Genter	Werner Lampe	Michael Wenden	Frederick Tyler	Klaus Steinbach	Vladimir Bure	Ralph Hutton
USA -1:52.78 w	USA - 1:53.73	GER – 1:53.99	AUS – 1:54.40	USA – 1:54.96	GER – 1:55.65	SOV - 1:57.24	CAN – 1:57.56

w **World Record**   *o* **Olympic Record**   *p* **Preliminary Heat**   *dq* **Disqualified**   *e* **Equal to World Record**   *eo* **Equal to Olympic Record**
dns **Did Not Start**   *dnf* **Did Not Finish**   *ac* **Also Competed**   *r* **Relay Lead-off Split**   *E* **Estimated**

OLYMPIAD XX – 1972 – MUNICH, GERMANY

1972 OLYMPIC SWIMMING FINALS

Gold	Silver	Bronze	Fourth	Fifth	Sixth	Seventh	Eighth

Women 400m Freestyle - World Record (4:21.2 Shane Gould AUS)   Olympic Record (4:31.8 Debbie Meyer USA 1968)

Gold	Silver	Bronze	Fourth	Fifth	Sixth	Seventh	Eighth
Shane Gould	Novella Calligaris	Gudrun Wegner	Shirley Babashoff	Jenny Wylie	Keena Rothhammer	Hansje Bunschoten	Anke Rijnders
AUS – 4:19.04w	ITA – 4:22.44	GDR – 4:23.11	USA – 4:23.59	USA – 4:24.07	USA – 4:24.22	NED – 4:29.70	NED – 4:31.51

Men 400m Freestyle - World Record (4:00.11 Kurt Krumpholz)   Olympic Record (4:09.0 Mike Burton USA 1968)

Gold	Silver	Bronze	Fourth	Fifth	Sixth	Seventh	Eighth
Bradford Cooper	Steven Genter	Tom McBreen	Graham Windeatt	Brian Brinkley	Bengt Gingsjö	Werner Lampe	Rick DeMont
AUS -4:00.27 o	USA – 4:01.94	USA – 4:02.64	AUS – 4:02.93	GBR – 4:06.69	SWE – 4:06.75	GER – 4:06.97	* USA - dq

Women 800m Freestyle - World Record (8:53.83 Jo Harshberger USA)   Olympic Record (9:24.0 Debbie Meyer USA 1968)

Gold	Silver	Bronze	Fourth	Fifth	Sixth	Seventh	Eighth
Keena Rothhammer	Shane Gould	Novella Calligaris	Ann Simmons	Gudrun Wegner	Jo Harshberger	Hansje Bunschoten	Narelle Moras
USA – 8:53.68 w	AUS – 8:56.39	ITA – 8:57.46	USA – 8:57.62	GDR – 8:58.89	USA – 9:01.21	NED – 9:16.69	AUS – 9:19.06

Men 1500m Freestyle - World Record (15:52.91 Rick DeMont USA)   Olympic Record (16:38.9 Mike Burton USA 1968)

Gold	Silver	Bronze	Fourth	Fifth	Sixth	Seventh	Eighth
Mike Burton	Graham Windeatt	Douglas Northway	Bengt Gingsjö	Graham White	Mark Treffers	Bradford Cooper	Guillermo Garcia
USA-15:52.58 w	AUS-15:58.48	USA-16:09.25	SWE-16:16.01	AUS-16:17.22	NZE-16:18.84	AUS-16:30.49	MEX-16:36.03

Women 100m Backstroke - World Record (1:05.6 Karen Muir RSA)   Olympic Record (1:06.2 Kaye Hall USA 1968)

Gold	Silver	Bronze	Fourth	Fifth	Sixth	Seventh	Eighth
Melissa Belote	Andrea Gyarmati	Susan Atwood	Karen Moe	Wendy Cook	Enith Brigitha	Christine Herbst	Silke Pielen
USA-1:05.78 o	HUN – 1:06.26	USA – 1:06.34	USA – 1:06.69	CAN – 1:06.70	NED – 1:06.82	GDR – 1:07.27	GER – 1:07.36

Men 100m Backstroke – World Record (56.3 Roland Matthes GDR)   Olympic Record (58.7 Roland Matthes GDR 1968)

Gold	Silver	Bronze	Fourth	Fifth	Sixth	Seventh	Eighth
Roland Matthes	Michael Stamm	John Murphy	Mitchell Ivey	Igor Grivennikov	Lutz Wanja	Jürgen Kriger	Tadashi Honda
GDR – 56.58 o	USA – 57.70	USA – 58.35	USA – 58.48	SOV – 59.50	GDR – 59.80	GDR – 59.93	JPN – 1:00.41

* Awarded the gold medal but was later disqualified (See Rick DeMont Profile)

1972 OLYMPIC SWIMMING FINALS

	Gold	Silver	Bronze	Fourth	Fifth	Sixth	Seventh	Eighth
Women 200m Backstroke - World Record (2:20.64 Melissa Belote USA) Olympic Record (2:24.8 Pokey Watson USA 1968)	Melissa Belote USA – 2:19.19 n	Susan Atwood USA – 2:20.38	Donna Gurr CAN – 2:23.22	Annegret Kober GER – 2:23.35	Christine Herbst GDR – 2:23.44	Enith Brigitha NED – 2:23.70	Deborah Palmer AUS – 2:24.65	Leslie Cliff CAN – 2:25.80
Men 200m Backstroke - World Record (2:02.8 Roland Matthes GDR) Olympic Record (2:09.6 Roland Matthes GDR 1968)	Roland Matthes GDR – 2:02.82 e	Michael Stamm USA – 2:04.09	Mitchell Ivey USA – 2:04.33	Bradford Cooper AUS – 2:06.59	Tim McKee USA – 2:07.29	Lothar Noack GDR – 2:08.67	Zoltán Verrasztó HUN – 2:10.09	Jean-Paul Berjeaud FRA – 2:11.77
Women 100m Breaststroke - World Record (1:14.2 Catie Ball USA) Olympic Record (1:15.8 Djurdjica Bjedov YUG 1968)	Catherine Carr USA – 1:13.58 w	G. Prozumen-shchikova SOV – 1:14.99	Beverley Whitfield AUS – 1:15.73	Agnes Kiss-Kaczander HUN – 1:16.26	Judy Melick USA – 1:17.16	Verena Eberle GER – 1:17.16	Britt-Marie Smedh SWE – 1:17.19	Dorothy Harrison GBR – 1:17.49
Men 100m Breaststroke - World Record (1:05.8 Nikolai Pankin SOV) Olympic Record (1:07.7 Donald McKenzie USA 1968)	Nobutaka Taguchi JPN – 1:04.94 w	Thomas Bruce USA – 1:05.43	John Hencken USA – 1:05.61	Mark Chatfield USA – 1:06.01	Walter Kusch GER – 1:06.23	José Sylvio Fiolo BRA – 1:06.24	Nikolai Pankin SOV – 1:06.36	David Wilkie GBR – 1:06.52
Women 200m Breaststroke - World Record (2:38.5 Catie Ball USA) Olympic Record (2:44.4 Sharon Wichman USA 1968)	Beverley Whitfield AUS – 2:41.71 o	Dana Schoenfield USA – 2:42.05	Galina Prozumen-sheykova SOV – 2:42.36	Claudia Clevenger USA – 2:42.88	Petra Nows GER – 2:43.41	Agnes Kiss-Kaczander HUN – 2:43.41	Lyudmila Porubaiko SOV – 2:44.48	Eva Kiss HUN – 2:45.12

1972 OLYMPIC SWIMMING FINALS

Gold	Silver	Bronze	Fourth	Fifth	Sixth	Seventh	Eighth
Men 200m Breaststroke – World Record (2:22.79 John Hencken USA) Olympic Record (2:27.8 Ian O'Brien AUS 1964)							
John Hencken	David Wilkie	Nobutaka Taguchi	Richard Colella	Felipe Múñoz	Walter Kusch	Igor Cherdakov	Klaus Katzur
USA –2:21.55 w	GBR – 2:23.67	JPN – 2:23.88	USA – 2:24.28	MEX – 2:26.44	GER – 2:26.55	SOV – 2:27.15	GDR – 2:27.44
Women 100m Butterfly - World Record (1:03.9 Mayumi Aoki JPN) Olympic Record (1:04.7 Sharon Stouder USA 1964)							
Mayumi Aoki	Roswitha Beier	Andrea Gyarmati	Deena Deardurff	Dana Shrader	Ellie Daniel	Gudrun Beckmann	Noriko Asano
JPN – 1:03.34 w	GDR – 1:03.61	HUN – 1:03.73	USA – 1:03.95	USA – 1:03.98	USA – 1:04.08	GER – 1:04.15.	JPN – 1:04.25
Men 100m Butterfly - World Record (54.56 Mark Spitz USA) Olympic Record (55.9 Douglas Russell USA 1968)							
Mark Spitz	Bruce Robertson	Jerry Heidenreich	Roland Matthes	David Edgar	Byron MacDonald	Hartmut Flöckner	Neil Rogers
USA – 54.27 w	CAN – 55.56	USA – 55.74	GDR – 55.87	USA – 56.11	CAN – 57.27	GDR – 57.40	AUS – 57.90
Women 200m Butterfly - World Record (2:16.62 Karen Moe USA) Olympic Record (2:24.7 Ada Kok NED 1968)							
Karen Moe	Lynn Colella	Ellie Daniel	Rosemarie Kother	Noriko Asano	Helga Lindner	Gail Neall	Mayumi Aoki
USA – 2:15.57 w	USA – 2:16.34	USA – 2:16.74	GDR – 2:17.11	JPN – 2:19.50	GDR – 2:20.47	AUS – 2:21.88	JPN – 2:22.84
Men 200m Butterfly - World Record (2:01.53 Mark Spitz USA) Olympic Record (2:06.6 Kevin Berry AUS 1964)							
Mark Spitz	Gary Hall	Robin Backhaus	Jorgé Delgado Panchama	Hans Fassnacht	András Hargitay	Hartmut Flöckner	Folkert Meeuw
USA – 2:00.70 w	USA – 2:02.86	USA – 2:03.23	ECU – 2:04.60	GER – 2:04.69	HUN – 2:04.69	GDR – 2:05.34	GER – 2:05.57
Women 200m Individual Medley - World Record (2:23.5 Claudia Kolb USA) Olympic Record (2:24.7 Claudia Kolb USA 1968)							
Shane Gould	Kornelia Ender	Lynn Vidali	Jennifer Bartz	Leslie Cliff	Evelyn Stolze	Yoshimi Nishigawa	Carolyn Woods
AUS– 2:23.07 w	GDR – 2:23.59	USA – 2:24.06	USA – 2:24.55	CAN – 2:24.83	GDR – 2:25.90	JPN – 2:26.35	USA – 2:27.42

1972 OLYMPIC SWIMMING FINALS

	Gold	Silver	Bronze	Fourth	Fifth	Sixth	Seventh	Eighth
Men 200m Individual Medley - World Record (2:09.3 G. Larsson SWE/G. Hall USA) Olympic Record (2:12.0 C.Hickcox 1968)	Gunnar Larsson	Tim McKee	Steve Furniss	Gary Hall	András Hargitay	Mikhail Suharev	Juan Bello	Hans Ljungberg
	SWE – 2:07.17 w	USA – 2:08.37	USA – 2:08.45	HUN – 2:08.49	HUN – 2:09.66	SOV – 2:11.78	PER – 2:11.87	SWE – 2:13.56
Women 400m Individual Medley - World Record (5:04.7 Claudia Kolb USA) Olympic Record (5:08.5 Claudia Kolb USA 1968)	Gail Neall	Leslie Cliff	Novella Calligaris	Jennifer Bartz	Evelyn Stolze	Mary Montgomery	Lynn Vidali	Nina Petrova
	AUS – 5:02.97 w	CAN – 5:03.57	ITA – 5:03.99	USA – 5:05.56	GDR – 5:06.80	USA – 5:09.98	USA – 5:13.06	SOV – 5:15.68
Men 400m Individual Medley - World Record (4:30.81 Gary Hall USA) Olympic Record (4:45.4 Richard Roth USA 1964)	Gunnar Larsson	Tim McKee	András Hargitay	Steven Furniss	Gary Hall	Bengt Gingsjö	Graham Windeatt	Wolfram Sperling
	SWE – 4:31.98 o	USA – 4:31.98o	HUN – 4:32.70	USA – 4:35.44	USA – 4:37.38	SWE – 4:37.96	AUS – 4:40.39	GDR – 4:40.66

1972 OLYMPIC SWIMMING FINALS

RELAY EVENTS

Women 400m Medley Relay - World Record (4:25.34 USA)
Olympic Record (4:28.3 USA 1968)

Gold	Silver	Bronze	Fourth	Fifth	Sixth	Seventh	Eighth
Melissa Belote, Catherine Carr, Deena Deardurff, Sandra Neilson *p* - Susan Atwood, Judith Melick, Dana Shrader, Shirley Babashoff	Christine Herbst, Renate Vogel, Roswitha Beier, Kornelia Ender *p* - Gabriele Wetzko	Silke Pielen, Verena Eberle, Gudrun Beckmann, Heidemarie Reineck *p* - Annegret Kober, Edeltraud Koch, Jutta Weber	Tinatin Lekveishvili, Galina Prozumenshchykova, Stepanova Iryna Ustymenko, Tatyana Zolotnickaia	Enith Brigitha, Alie te Riet, Anke Rijnders, Hansje Bunschoten, *p* - Frieke Buys	Suzuko Matsumura, Yoko Yamamoto, Mayumi Aoki, Yoshimi Nishigawa	Wendy Cook, Sylvia Dockerill, Marylin Corson, Leslie Cliff	Diana Olsson, Brit-Marie Smedh, Eva Wikner, Anita Zarnowiecki
USA– 4:20.75 *w*	GDR – 4:24.91	GER – 4:26.46	SOV – 4:27.81	NED – 4:29.99	JPN – 4:31.56	CAN – 4:31.56	SWE – 4:32.61

Men 400m Medley Relay - World Record (3:50.4 USA)
Olympic Record (3:54.9 USA 1968)

Gold	Silver	Bronze	Fourth	Fifth	Sixth	Seventh	Eighth
Michael Stamm, Thomas Bruce, Mark Spitz, Jerry Heidenreich *p* - Mitchell Ivey, John Hencken, Gary Hall, David Fairbank	Roland Matthes, Klaus Katzur, Hartmut Flöckner, Lutz Unger	Eric Fish, William Mahony, Bruce Robertson, Robert Kasting *p* - William Kennedy	Igor Grivennikov, Nikolai Pankin, Viktor Sharygin, Vladimir Bure *p* - Viktor Stulikov, Viktor Aboimov	Romulo Duncan Arantes, José Sylvio Fiolo, Sergio Waismann, José Roberto Diñiz-Aranha	Tadashi Honda, Nobutaka Taguchi, Yasuhiro Komazaki, Jiro Sasaki	Colin Cunningham, David Wilkie, John Mills, Malcolm Windeatt	László Cseh, Sándor Szabó, István Szentirmay, Attila Császári *p* - András Hargitay
USA– 3:48.16 *w*	GDR – 3:52.12	CAN – 3:52.26	SOV - 3:53.26	BRA - 3:57.89	JPN – 3:58.23	GBR – 3:58.82	HUN – 3:59.07

1972 OLYMPIC SWIMMING FINALS

Women 400m Freestyle Relay - World Record (3:58.11 USA)

Olympic Record (4:02.5 USA 1968)

Gold	Silver	Bronze	Fourth	Fifth	Sixth	Seventh	Eighth
USA – 3:55.19 w	GDR – 3:55.55	GER – 3:57.93	HUN – 4:00.39	NED – 4:01.49	SWE – 4:02.69	CAN – 4:03.83	AUS – 4:04.82
Sandra Neilson,	Gabriele Wetzko,	Jutta Weber,	Andrea Gyarmati,	Enith Brigitha,	Anita Zamowiecki,	Wendy Cook,	Deborah Palmer,
Jennifer Kemp,	Andrea Eife,	Heidemarie Reineck,	Judit Turóczy,	Anke Rijnders,	Judy Wright,	Leanne Francis,	
Jane Barkman,	Elke Schmisch,	Gudrun Beckmann,	Edit Kovács,	Hansje Bunschoten,	Eva Andersson,	Mary-Beth Booth,	Sharon Booth,
Shirley Babashoff,	Kornelia Ender,	Angela Steinbach	Magdolna Patoh	Josien Elzerman	Diana Olsson,	Rondeau, Leslie	Shane Gould,
p - Kim Peyton,	p - Sylvia Eichner				Irwi Johansson	Cliff	p - Debra Cain
Lynn Skrifvars,							
Anne Marshall							

Men 400m Freestyle Relay - World Record (3:28.8 USA)

Olympic Record (3:31.7 USA 1968)

Gold	Silver	Bronze	Fourth	Fifth	Sixth	Seventh	Eighth
USA– 3:26.42 w	SOV – 3:29.72	GDR – 3:32.42	BRA - 3:33.14	CAN - 3:33.20	GER – 3:33.90	FRA - 3:34.13	ESP - 3:38.21
David Edgar,	Vladimir Bure,	Roland Matthes,	Ruy Aquino	Bruce	Klaus Steinbach,	Gilles Vigne,	Jorge Comas,
John Murphy,	Viktor Mazanov,	Wilfried	Oliveira, Paulo	Robertson, Brian	Werner Lampe,	Alain Mosconi,	Antonio
Jerry	Viktor	Hartung, Peter	Zanetti, Paulo	Phillips,	Rainer Jacob,	Alain Hermitte,	Culebras,
Heidenreich,	Aboimov, Igor	Bruch, Lutz	Becskehazy,	Timothy Bach,	Hans Fassnacht,	Michel	Enrique Melo,
Mark Spitz,	Grivennikov	Unger	José Diaz-	Robert Kasting	p - Gerhard	Rousseau	José Pujol
p - David	p - Georgy	p - Udo Poser	Aranha		Schiller, Hans-		
Fairbank, Gary	Kulikov				Günter Vosseler,		
Conelly					Kersten Meier		

1972 OLYMPIC SWIMMING FINALS

Gold	Silver	Bronze	Fourth	Fifth	Sixth	Seventh	Eighth

Men 800m Freestyle Relay - World Record (7:43.3 USA) Olympic Record (7:52.1 USA 1964)

Gold	Silver	Bronze	Fourth	Fifth	Sixth	Seventh	Eighth
John Kinsella, Frederick Tyler, Steven Genter, Mark Spitz, p - Gary Conelly, Thomas McBreen, Michael Burton	Klaus Steinbach, Werner Lampe, Hans-Günter Vosseler, Hans-Joachim Fassnacht, p - Gerhard Schiller, Folkert Meeuw	Igor Grivennikov, Viktor Mazanov, Georgi Kulikov, Vladimir Bure, p - Viktor Aboimov, Aleksandr Samsonov	Bengt Gingsjö, Hans Ljungberg, Anders Bellbring, Gunnar Larsson	Michael Wenden, Graham Windeatt, Robert Nay, Bradford Cooper, p - Robert Featherstone, Graham White	Wilifried Hartung, Peter Bruch, Udo Poser, Lutz Unger, p - Roger Pyttel	Bruce Robertson, Brian Phillips, Ian MacKenzie, Ralph Hutton, p - Dean Buckboro	Brian Brinkley, John Mills, Michael Bailey, Colin Cunningham
USA-7:35.78w	GER – 7:41.69	SOV – 7:45.76	SWE – 7:47.37	AUS – 7:48.66	GDR – 7:49.11	CAN – 7:53.61	GBR – 7:55.59

Chapter 19

Olympiad XXI - 1976
Montreal, Canada

the Olympic Games returned to North American soil with Montreal, Canada playing host to the twenty-first Olympiad. The Queen of England presided over the Games' Opening Ceremonies.

Attempting to keep the Olympic program more manageable, the IOC eliminated some of the events previously held. Despite this, the Montreal Games featured 198 events, three more than the previous Olympics.

The East German women would emerge as the dominating force in women's swimming. They won 11 of the 13 women's swimming events. The East Germans had never won a swimming gold medal before. Nine of thirteen world records were bettered.

Long before the Games of Montreal, the East Germans had begun studying athletic training, turning it into a true and exact science. Their work would subsequently change the course of training for swimmers worldwide.

Many of these young female swimmers had muscular builds and deep voices. Accusations of steroid use by the East Germans began to surface. Their coaches explained that the swimmers were participants in a rigorous training and weight lifting program.

With the fall of the Berlin Wall in 1990, came new information regarding the steroid controversy. Former East German swim coaches admitted that anabolic steroids were administered to not

SCORE
BOARD

The American Men's Swim Team swept four events: the 200m freestyle, 200m backstroke, 100m and 200m butterfly. In five other events they placed 1-2.

all, but some, of their swimmers. It has since been determined that the East German's athletic program systematically doped their athletes, unbeknownst to many of the athletes themselves.

The 1976 U.S. Men's Swim Team is still considered today the best team ever fielded by the Americans. They seized gold in twelve out of thirteen events. In nine of these events they finished 1-2. They took home 27 out of 35 medals. This prolific medal winning team accounted for over one-third of all gold medals won for the U.S. in Montreal.

Three swimming events were eliminated from the Olympic swimming program in 1976: the men's 400m freestyle relay and both the men and women's 200m individual medley.

SHIRLEY BABASHOFF
UNITED STATES

Shirley Babashoff is one of the United States' most accomplished swimmers. A two-time Olympian, she has two gold and six silver medals to her credit. She was the high point winner at the U.S. Nationals five times and she held eleven world and 39 American records.

In Munich, the fifteen year old Babashoff captured silver in the 100m and 200m freestyle events and a gold medal swimming anchor on the 400m freestyle team.

During the 1976 Montreal Games, Babashoff had three individual second place finishes, which were all bettered by East German swimmers.

The gold medal winning American 4X100m free relay team of K. Peyton, W. Boglioli, J. Sterkel, and S.Babashoff.

One of the most exciting moments at these Games came in the 4X100m freestyle race. Americans Kim Peyton, Wendy Boglioli, Jill Sterkel, and Babashoff seized the moment and touched ahead of the East German women by over one-half second posting a new world record (3:44.82).

L A N E L I N E S

"Back to Back Finishes"

East German backstroke specialist, Ulrike Richter, captured gold in both the 100m and 200m races. Both of these races had the very same outcome: Richter, gold; Birgit Treiber, (GDR) silver; and Canadian Nancy Garapick, bronze.

Richter swam to gold a third time as a member of the 400m medley relay team.

MIKE BRUNER
UNITED STATES

Courtesy of ISHOF

Crowd pleaser Mike Bruner.

In Montreal, American Mike Bruner captured the 200m fly title and collected a second gold medal swimming the first leg of the 800m freestyle relay. World records were set in each of these events.

Bruner was at his peak in 1980 and had been the high point winner at both the indoor and outdoor national meets that year. Swimming for Stanford University he held NCAA titles in both the 200y fly and 1650y freestyle events.

At the 1980 U.S. Olympic Trials this versatile Olympian qualified for three events. Mike Bruner was another American casualty

SCORE
BOARD

The Russian women swept the 200m breaststroke event

Marina Koshevaia, Maryna Yurchenya, and Lyubov Rusanova placed 1-2-3, respectively. Rusanova and Koshevaia placed second and third in the 100m breaststroke final, to East German Hannelore Anke. The Russian women captured five out of the six possible breaststroke medals.

of the Olympic boycott of the Soviet Games and suffered a fate worse than defeat – being denied the opportunity to compete.

KORNELIA ENDER
EAST GERMANY

The brightest star of the East German team was the amazing Kornelia Ender. Ender's Olympic career began with the 1972 Games when she won three silver medals. Four years later she returned to the Games and made Olympic history.

East Germany's Kornelia Ender

Courtesy of ISHOF

In the 100m fly final Ender equaled her own world record. She returned to the pool only twenty-seven minutes later and broke her own world mark in the 200m freestyle final.

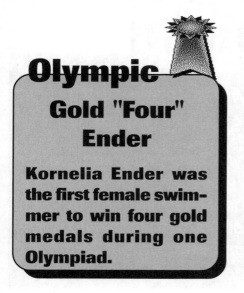

Olympic
Gold "Four"
Ender

Kornelia Ender was the first female swimmer to win four gold medals during one Olympiad.

Ender was named World Swimmer of the Year in 1973, 1975 and 1976. Kornelia married Olympian backstroker Roland Matthes in 1978. Over the span of three Olympiads these two swimming greats won 16 Olympic medals (8-gold, 6-silver & 2-bronze) and set 48 world records.

OFF THE Wall

The After Race

Bruce Furniss shares his most memorable Olympic moment:

"After our 200m freestyle race, John Naber and I were required to "warm down" in preparation for our relay two days later. Our race was the last that evening and we had the press conference, drug control (test), and meetings with family and friends. By the time we arrived at the practice pool, we had the complex to ourselves. We began to warm down very casually, slowly finding our arm strokes and breathing in the same cadence. Eventually our stroke count quickened and we again found ourselves racing. We are still great friends and great competitors to this day. We have always loved our ability to compete against one another regardless of who was watching (or not)."

BRUCE FURNISS
UNITED STATES

Gold medalist Bruce MacFarlane Furniss was nicknamed "The Mongoose," because the mongoose thrives on snakes. Furniss and fellow USC teammate John "The Snake" Naber, had a strong, yet friendly rivalry.

In the 200m freestyle final in Montreal, Naber led the way for the first 190 meters. Furniss made his move, edging out Naber and breaking his own world mark. "Hey, Mongoose, you got the Snake this time," the good natured Naber conceded.

Along with his individual gold, Bruce earned another medal with the 800m freestyle relay team, two incredible accomplishments. It is an incident that took place at the 1980 Olympic Trials however, that Bruce remembers as his proudest:

"My very last individual race of my career was the 200m IM when I failed to touch the wall between back and breaststroke. When the referee, Pat Graham, a man I'd known my entire career, came to inform me of my DQ he asked me whether I touched or not. Every fiber of my being wanted to say, "Yes," but I said, "No," knowing that this moment would be with me for the rest of my life. That

my life. That character confronting moment continues to be the single proudest moment of my career."

Bruce Furniss' older brother Steve, also an Olympian, won a bronze medal in the 200m IM in Munich. It is Steve who Bruce credits as his single greatest mentor, who gave him guidance and encouragement throughout his career.

Courtesy of Bruce Furniss

American Olympian Bruce Furniss

L A N E   L I N E S

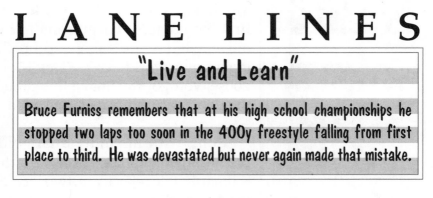

"Live and Learn"

Bruce Furniss remembers that at his high school championships he stopped two laps too soon in the 400y freestyle falling from first place to third. He was devastated but never again made that mistake.

BRIAN GOODELL
UNITED STATES

While still in high school in 1976, seventeen-year-old Brian Goodell captured two individual gold medals. At the Olympic Trials he broke the world marks in the 400m and 1500m freestyle events. He repeated his dual record breaking performances in the finals of the Montreal Olympic Games.

The 1500m freestyle event was an exciting race. American Bobby Hackett lead the event for most of the first 1000 meters. At 1400 meters, Goodell made his move and pulled

Courtesy of Bruce Furniss

Brian Goodell Olympic Champion.

ahead of Hackett and Austraila's Stephen Holland. Goodell held the lead and swam the last 100 meters with a phenomenal time of 57.73.

Brian Goodell, 1977 World Swimmer of the Year, made the 1980 Olympic Team, but due to the American boycott of this Olympiad, was denied the opportunity to compete again in the Games.

L A N E   L I N E S

"Record Breakers"

In the final of the men's 1500m freestyle race all three medalists broke the existing world record of 15:06.66. Brian Goodell (15:02.40) led the pack, followed by American Bobby Hackett (15:03+) and Australian Steve Holland (15:04+).

GARY HALL
UNITED STATES

A three–time Olympian, Gary Hall captured medals in 1968, 1972, and again in 1976. This versatile and seemingly ageless swimmer pursued his medical studies throughout his athletic career requiring him to take "periodic retirements" from swimming.

Hall's Olympic medals were won in three different events. At the 1968 Games, as only a high school student, he took silver in the 400m individual medley. As captain of the 1972 Olympic Team he won another silver in the 200m butterfly and finished his Olympic career in 1976 with a bronze medal in the 100m butterfly. He held ten world and twenty-one national records.

In Montreal, Hall was chosen by the American Olympic Team to carry the flag in the opening ceremony. He was the first swimmer to be given this honor.

Courtesy of ISHOF

"This is an indescribable feeling of honor. I'll be leading the greatest group of athletes in the world, the U.S. Team ... I had goosebumps from my Achilles tendons to my forehead. I was nervous, and when we came out of the tunnel into the light and the crowd began to echo, I started trembling. I hope people didn't notice the flag was shaking." – Gary Hall

Olympian Gary Hall with son, future Olympian, Gary Hall, Jr.

Another Hall made his first Olympic appearance in 1976,

SCORE
BOARD

John Hencken USA

<u>100m Breaststroke</u>
1972 – Bronze – 1:05.61
1976 – Gold – 1:03.11

<u>200m Breaststroke</u>
1972 – Gold – 2:21.55*w*
1976 – Silver – 2:17.26

<u>400m Medley Relay</u>
1972 – swam preliminary heat
1976 – Gold – 3:42.22 *w*

Gary Hall Jr., who was seen riding atop his dad's shoulders. Twenty years later, at the Centennial Games in Atlanta, this Hall too, would be in the Olympic pool etching his name into Olympic history.

JOHN HENCKEN
UNITED STATES

A two-time Olympian, John Hencken broke or equaled his own 100m breaststroke world record three times in Montreal. This Stanford graduate matched his world record in a preliminary round, broke the record in his semi-final round, and both he and second place finisher David Wilkie broke the world mark once again, in the final.

JIM MONTGOMERY
UNITED STATES

Courtesy of ISHOF

Jim Montgomery, a graduate of the University of Indiana, was a major contributor to the American men's "gold rush." The twenty-one year-old Montgomery swam to gold in the 100m freestyle and became the first person to break the 50-second barrier (49.99) in this event. He captured two additional gold medals with the relay teams and a bronze for the 200m freestyle.

JOHN NABER
UNITED STATES

Naber did not start swimming competitively until the age of thirteen. He quickly grew to be 6'6", but was awkward, uncoordinated and somewhat accident prone on dry land. However, John's loose-jointed anatomy and wide feet (11 EEEE) were made for the water. He jokingly referred to them as his "fins."

Eleven weeks before the 1972 Olympics Trials, John Naber cracked his collarbone clowning around on a diving board. He spent eight of those weeks in a shoulder brace and missed making the Olympic Team by a mere 6/10ths of a second.

Courtesy of ISHOF

Five time Olympic medalist John Naber

Nicknamed "The Snake," Naber was the men's swimming star of the Montreal Games. This twenty-year-old backstroke specialist set world records in the finals of both backstroke events. Each of the records survived for seven years. His 200m record made him the first man to break the elusive two-minute barrier.

Naber took home two additional gold medals with each of the relay teams. He also won a silver medal in the 200m freestyle just 55 minutes after winning the 100m backstroke event. Naber considers that 200m free the best race of his career.

> *"My time was better than the previous existing world record, but it was 2/10ths of a second behind Bruce's (Furniss) winning time of 1:50.29. He won the gold, and I got the silver, but I had become the first swimmer to win medals in individual events in one day. I was very proud of that, even though the next day East Germany's Kornelia Ender won the first two of her four gold medals. She out did me, but I was the first."*— *John Naber*

John Naber received the Sullivan Award in 1977 and retired from competitive swimming that year.

LANE LINES

"The Grand Slam"

As coined by John Naber, swimming's "Grand Slam" is a swimmer winning the same event in the same year at the **NCAA** championships, the **AAU** indoor and outdoor championships, the Olympic Trials and the gold ring...the Olympic Games. Naber hit two "Grand Slams" in 1976. He did it in the 100m and the 200m backstroke events.

TIMOTHY SHAW
UNITED STATES

In 1974, Tim Shaw, 17, broke world records in the 200m, 400m and 1500m freestyle events at the AAU national outdoor meet, becoming only the second man in swimming history to hold world records in all three events.

Shaw is one of only a handful of athletes who has won medals in two different Olympic sports. At the 1976 Games, he won a silver medal in swimming for the 400m freestyle event and in 1984 captured a silver medal as a member of the U.S. water polo team. Shaw held 10 world records and was the first swimmer given the F.I.N.A. Prize Eminence. He was also named the 1975 Sullivan Award recipient

PETRA THUMER
EAST GERMANY

Opportunity knocked at the 1976 Games for fifteen-year-old Petra Thumer. Her teammate Barbara Krause, the world record holder in the 400m freestyle, was dropped from the East German team after suffering an angina attack in late June of that year.

Thumer, a relatively unknown swimmer outside of Europe, set records in both the 400m and the 800m freestyle events.

SPLASH BACK
Britain Wins Gold

David Wilkie's 1976 title for the 200m breaststroke was the first win by a British male in 68 years in an Olympic swimming event. "Happy" Henry Taylor won the 400m and the 1500m freestyle in 1908.

DAVID WILKIE
GREAT BRITAIN

David Wilkie's decisive victory in the 200m breaststroke prevented the American Men's Team from a clean sweep of the swimming program in Montreal.

Wilkie graduated from the University of Miami, where he swam for Coach Charlie Hodgson. It is Hodgson that Wilkie credits with being the most instrumental in his success.

A two-time Olympian, Wilkie also collected two silver medals during his swimming career and set three world records (200m IM & 200m breaststroke).

Courtesy of ISHOF

British Olympic Champion David Wilkie

medal count 2

Matt Vogel - USA

100m Butterfly - Gold

400m Medley Relay - Bronze

1976 OLYMPIC SWIMMING FINALS

INDIVIDUAL EVENTS

Gold	Silver	Bronze	Fourth	Fifth	Sixth	Seventh	Eighth
Women 100m Freestyle - World Record (55.73 Kornelia Ender GDR) Olympic Record (58.59 Sandra Neilson USA 1972)							
Kornelia Ender	Petra Priemer	Enith Brigitha	Kim Peyton	Shirley Babashoff	Claudia Hempel	Jill Sterkel	Jutta Weber
GDR – 55.65 w	GDR – 56.49	NED – 56.65	USA – 56.81	USA – 56.95	GDR – 56.99	USA – 57.06	GER – 57.26
Men 100m Freestyle - World Record (50.59 James Montgomery USA) Olympic Record (51.22 Mark Spitz USA 1972)							
James Montgomery	Jack Babashoff	Peter Nocke	Klaus Steinbach	Marcello Guarducci	Joe Bottom	Vladimir Bure	Andrei Krylov
USA– 49.99 w	USA – 50.81	GER – 51.31	GER – 51.68	ITA – 51.70	USA – 52.03	SOV – 52.15	
Women 200m Freestyle - World Record (1:59.78 Kornelia Ender GDR) Olympic Record (2:03.56 Shane Gould AUS 1972)							
Kornelia Ender	Shirley Babashoff	Enith Brigitha	Annelies Maas	Gail Amundrud	Jennifer Hooker	Claudia Hempel	Irina Vlasova
GDR– 1:59.26 w	USA – 2:01.22	NED – 2:01.40	NED – 2:02.56	CAN – 2:03.32	USA – 2:04.20	GDR – 2:04.61	SOV – 2:05.63
Men 200m Freestyle - World Record (1:50.32 Bruce Furniss USA) Olympic Record (1:52.78 Mark Spitz USA 1972)							
Bruce Furniss	John Naber	Jim Montgomery	Andrei Krylov	Klaus Steinbach	Peter Nocke	Gordon Downie	Andrei Bogdanov
USA–1:50.29 w	USA – 1:50.50	USA – 1:50.58	SOV –1:50.73	GER – 1:51.09	GER – 1:51.71	GBR – 1:52.78	SOV –1:53.33

w World Record *o* Olympic Record *p* Preliminary Heat *dq* Disqualified *e* Equal to World Record *eo* Equal to Olympic Record *dns* Did Not Start *dnf* Did Not Finish *ac* Also Competed *r* Relay Lead-off Split *E* Estimated

OLYMPIAD XXI – 1976 – MONTREAL, CANADA

1976 OLYMPIC SWIMMING FINALS

Women 400m Freestyle - World Record (4:11.69 Barbara Krause GDR) Olympic Record (4:00.27 Bradford Cooper AUS 1972)

Men 400m Freestyle - World Record (3:53.08 Brian Goodell USA) Olympic Record (4:00.27 Bradford Cooper AUS 1972)

Women 800m Freestyle - World Record (8:39.63 Shirley Babashoff USA) Olympic Record (8:53.68 K. Rothhammer USA 1972)

Men 1500m Freestyle - World Record (15:06.66 Brian Goodell USA) Olympic Record (15:52.58 Michael Burton USA 1972)

Women 100m Backstroke - World Record (1:01.51 Ulrike Richter GDR) Olympic Record (1:05.78 Melissa Belote USA 1972)

	Gold	Silver	Bronze	Fourth	Fifth	Sixth	Seventh	Eighth
Women 400m Freestyle	Petra Thümer GDR- 4:09.89 w	Shirley Babashoff USA- 4:10.46	Shannon Smith CAN- 4:14.60	Rebecca Perrott NZE- 4:14.76	Kathy Heddy USA- 4:15.50	Brenda Borgh NED- 4:17.43	Annelies Maas NED- 4:17.44	Sabine Kahle GDR- 4:20.42
Men 400m Freestyle	Brian Goodell USA- 3:51.93 w	Tim Shaw USA- 3:52.54	Volodymyr Raskatov SOV- 3:55.76	Djan Madruga Garrido BRA- 3:57.18	Stephen Holland AUS- 3:57.59	Sándor Nagy HUN- 3:57.81	Vladimir Mikheyev SOV- 4:00.79	Stephen Badger CAN- 4:02.83
Women 800m Freestyle	Petra Thümer GDR- 8:37.14 w	Shirley Babashoff USA- 8:37.59	Wendy Weinberg USA- 8:42.60	Rosemary Milgate AUS- 8:47.21	Nicole Kramer USA- 8:47.33	Shannon Smith CAN- 8:48.15	Regina Jäger GDR- 8:50.40	Jennifer Turrall AUS- 8:52.88
Men 1500m Freestyle	Brian Goodell USA- 15:02.40 w	Bobby Hackett USA- 15:03.91	Stephen Holland AUS- 15:04.66	Djan Madruga Garrido BRA- 15:19.84	Vladimir Salnikov SOV- 15:29.45	Max Metzker AUS- 15:31.53	Paul Hartloff USA- 15:32.08	Zoltán Wladár HUN- 15:45.97
Women 100m Backstroke	Ulrike Richter GDR- 1:01.83 o	Birgit Treiber GDR- 1:03.41	Nancy Garapick CAN- 1:03.71	Wendy Hogg-Cook CAN- 1:03.93	Cheryl Gibson CAN- 1:05.16	Nadiya Stavko SOV- 1:05.19	Antje Stille GDR- 1:05.30	Diane Edelijn NED- 1:05.53

1976 OLYMPIC SWIMMING FINALS

	Gold	Silver	Bronze	Fourth	Fifth	Sixth	Seventh	Eighth
Men 100m Backstroke - World Record (56.30 Roland Matthes GDR) Olympic Record (56.58 Roland Matthes GDR 1972)								
	John Naber	Peter Rocca	Roland Matthes	Carlos Berrocal	Lutz Wanja	Bob Jackson	Mark Kerry	Mark Tonelli
	USA – 55.49 w	USA – 56.34	GDR – 57.22	PUR – 57.28	GDR – 57.49	USA – 57.69	AUS – 57.94	AUS – 58.42
Women 200m Backstroke - World Record (2:12.47 Birgit Treiber GDR) Olympic Record (2:19.19 Melissa Belote USA 1972)								
	Ulrike Richter	Birgit Treiber	Nancy Garapick	Nadiya Stavko	Melissa Belote	Antje Stille	Klavdia Studennikova	Wendy Hogg-Cook
	GDR–2:13.43 o	GDR – 2:14.97	CAN – 2:15.60	SOV – 2:16.28	USA – 2:17.27	GDR – 2:17.55	SOV - 2:17.74	CAN – 2:17.95
Men 200m Backstroke - World Record (2:00.64 John Naber USA) Olympic Record (2:02.82 Roland Matthes GDR 1972)								
	John Naber	Peter Rocca	Dan Harrigan	Mark Tonelli	Mark Kerry	Miloslav Rolko	Robert Rudolf	Zoltán Verrasztó
	USA– 1:59.19 w	USA – 2:00.55	USA – 2:01.35	AUS – 2:03.17	AUS – 2:04.07	CZE – 2:05.81	HUN – 2:07.30	HUN – 2:08.23
Women 100m Breaststroke - World Record (1:11.93 Carola Nitschke GDR) Olympic Record (1:13.58 C. Carr USA 1972)								
	Hannelore Anke	Lyubov Rusanova	Marina Koshevaia	Carola Nitschke	Gabriele Askamp	Maryna Yurchenya	Margaret Kelly	Karla Linke
	GDR – 1:11.16	SOV - 1:13.04	SOV - 1:13.30	GDR – 1:13.33	GER – 1:14.15	SOV - 1:14.17	GBR – 1:14.20	GDR – 1:14.21
Men 100m Breaststroke - World Record (1:03.88 John Hencken USA) Olympic Record (1:04.94 Nobutaka Taguchi JPN 1972)								
	John Hencken	David Wilkie	Arvydas Juozaitis	Graham Smith	Giorgio Lalle	Walter Kusch	Duncan Goodhew	Chris Woo
	USA – 1:03.11w	GBR – 1:03.43	SOV - 1:04.23	CAN – 1:04.26	ITA – 1:04.37	GER – 1:04.38	GBR – 1:04.66	USA – 1:05.13

1976 OLYMPIC SWIMMING FINALS

Gold	Silver	Bronze	Fourth	Fifth	Sixth	Seventh	Eighth
Women 200m Breaststroke - World Record (2:34.99 Karla Linke GDR) Olympic Record (2:41.71 B. Whitfield AUS 1972)							
Marina Koshevaia SOV - 2:33.35 w	Maryna Yurchenya SOV - 2:36.08	Lyubov Rusanova SOV - 2:36.22	Hannelore Anke GDR - 2:36.49	Karla Linke GDR - 2:36.97	Carola Nitschke GDR - 2:38.27	Margaret Kelly GBR - 2:38.37	Deborah Rudd GBR - 2:39.01
Men 200m Breaststroke - World Record (2:18.21 John Hencken USA) Olympic Record (2:21.55 John Hencken USA 1972)							
David Wilkie GBR - 2:15.11 w	John Hencken USA - 2:17.26	Richard Colella USA - 2:19.20	Graham Smith CAN - 2:19.42	Charles Keating USA - 2:20.79	Arvydas Juozaitis SOV - 2:21.87	Nikolai Pankin SOV - 2:22.21	Walter Kusch GER - 2:22.36
Women 100m Butterfly - World Record (1:00.13 Kornelia Ender GDR) Olympic Record (1:03.34 Mayumi Aoki JPN 1972)							
Kornelia Ender GDR - 1:00.13 e	Andrea Pollack GDR - 1:00.98	Wendy Boglioli USA - 1:01.17	Camille Wright USA - 1:01.41	Rosemarie Gabriel (Kother) GDR - 1:01.56	Wendy Quirk CAN - 1:01.75	Lelei Fonoimoana USA - 1:01.95	Tamara Shelofastova SOV - 1:02.74
Men 100m Butterfly - World and Olympic Record (54.27 Mark Spitz USA 1972)							
Matt Vogel USA - 54.35	Joe Bottom USA - 54.50	Gary Hall USA - 54.65	Roger Pyttel GDR - 55.09	Roland Matthes GDR - 55.11	Clay Evans CAN - 55.81	Hideaki Hara JPN - 56.34	Neil Rogers AUS - 56.57
Women 200m Butterfly - World Record (2:11.22 R. Gabriel Kother GDR) Olympic Record (2:15.57 Karen Moe USA 1972)							
Andrea Pollack GDR - 2:11.41 o	Ulrike Tauber GDR - 2:12.50	Rosemarie Gabriel Kother GDR - 2:12.86	Karen Moe Thorton USA - 2:12.90	Wendy Quirk CAN - 2:13.68	Cheryl Gibson CAN - 2:13.91	Tamara Shelofastova SOV - 2:14.26	Natalia Popova SOV - 2:14.50

1976 OLYMPIC SWIMMING FINALS

Gold	Silver	Bronze	Fourth	Fifth	Sixth	Seventh	Eighth
Men 200m Butterfly - World Record (1:59.63 Roger Pyttel GDR)						Olympic Record (2:00.70 Mark Spitz USA 1972)	
Mike Bruner	Steven Gregg	Bill Forrester	Roger Pyttel	Michael Kraus	Brian Brinkley	Jorgé Delgado Panchama	Aleksandr Manachinsky
USA– 1:59.23 w	USA – 1:59.54	USA – 1:59.96	GDR – 2:00.02	GER – 2:00.46	GBR – 2:01.49	ECU - 2:01.95	SOV - 2:04.61
Women 400m Individual Medley - World Record (4:48.79 Birgit Treiber GDR)				Olympic Record (5:02.97 G. Neall AUS 1972)			
Ulrike Tauber	Cheryl Gibson	Becky Smith	Birgit Treiber	Sabine Kahle	Donnalee Wennerstrom	Joann Baker	Monique Rodahl
GDR– 4:42.77 w	CAN – 4:48.10	CAN – 4:50.48	GDR – 4:52.40	GDR – 4:53.50	USA – 4:55.34	CAN – 5:00.19	NZE – 5:00.21
Men 400m Individual Medley - World Record (4:26.00 Z.Verrasztó HUN) Olympic Record (4:31.98 G.Larsson /T.McKee 1972)							
Rod Strachan	Tim McKee	Andrei Smirnov	András Hargitay	Graham Smith	Steven Furniss	Andrew Ritchie	Hans-Joachim Geisler
USA– 4:23.68 w	USA – 4:24.62	SOV - 4:26.90	HUN – 4:27.13	CAN – 4:28.64	USA – 4:29.23	CAN – 4:29.87	GER - 4:34.95

1976 OLYMPIC SWIMMING FINALS

RELAY EVENTS

Gold	Silver	Bronze	Fourth	Fifth	Sixth	Seventh	Eighth

Women 400m Medley Relay - World Record (4:13.41 GDR) — Olympic Record (4:20.75 USA 1972)

Gold	Silver	Bronze	Fourth	Fifth	Sixth	Seventh	Eighth
Ulrike Richter, Hannelore Anke, Andrea Pollack, Kornelia Ender *p - Birgit Treiber, Carola Nitschke, Rosemarie Gabriel*	Linda Jezek, Lauri Siering, Camille Wright, Shirley Babashoff *p - Deborah Clarke*	Wendy Hogg, Robin Corsiglia, Susan Sloan, Anne Jardin	Nadiya Stavko, Maryna Yurchenya, Tamara Shelofastova, Larissa Tsareva	Diane Edelijn, Wijda Mazereeuw, Jose Damen, Enith Brigitha *p - Ineke Ran*	Joy Beasley, Margaret Kelly, Susan Jenner, Deborah Hill	Yoshimi Nishigawa, Toshiko Haruoka, Yasue Hatsuda, Sachiko Yamazaki	Michelle Devries, Judith Hudson, Linda Hanel, Jenny Tate
GDR - 4:07.95 w	USA - 4:14.55	CAN - 4:15.22	SOV - 4:16.05	NED - 4:19.03	GBR - 4:23.25	JPN - 4:23.47	AUS - 4:25.91

Men 400m Medley Relay - World and Olympic Records (3:48.16 USA 1972)

Gold	Silver	Bronze	Fourth	Fifth	Sixth	Seventh	Eighth
John Naber, John Hencken, Matt Vogel, Jim Montgomery *p - Peter Rocca, Christopher Woo, Jack Babashoff*	Stephen Pickell, Graham Smith, Clay Evans, Gary MacDonald *p - Bruce Robertson*	Klaus Steinbach, Walter Kusch, Michael Kraus, Peter Nocke *p - Peter Lang, Dirk Braunleder*	James Carter, David Wilkie, John Mills, Brian Brinkley *p - Gary Abraham, Duncan Goodhew, Kevin Burns*	Igor Omelchenko, Arvidas Juozaitis, Yevgeny Seredin, Andrei Krylov *p - Nikolai Pankin, Andrei Bogdanov*	Mark Kerry, Paul Jarvie, Neil Rogers, Peter Coughlan	Enrico Bisso, Giogio Lalle, Paolo Barelli, Marcello Guarducci	Tadashi Honda, Nobutaka Taguchi, Hideaki Hara, Tsuyoshi Yanagidate
USA - 3:42.22 w	CAN - 3:45.94	GER - 3:47.29	GBR - 3:49.56	SOV - 3:49.90	AUS - 3:51.54	ITA - 3:52.92	JPN - 3:54.74

1976 OLYMPIC SWIMMING FINALS

Gold	Silver	Bronze	Fourth	Fifth	Sixth	Seventh	Eighth
Women 400m Freestyle Relay - World Record (3:48.80 GDR)							Olympic Record (3:55.19 USA 1972)
Kim Peyton. Wendy Boglioli. Jill Sterkel. Shirley Babashoff *p* - Jennifer Hooker	Kornelia Ender. Petra Priemer. Andrea Pollack. Claudia Hempel	Gail Amundrud. Barbara Clark. Becky Smith. Anne Jardin *p* - Deborah Clarke	Ineke Ran. Linda Faber. Annelies Maas. Enith Brigitha	Lyubov Kobzova. Irina Vlasova. Marina Kluchnikova. Larissa Tsareva	Guylaine Berger. Sylvie Le Noach. Caroline Carpentier. Chantal Schertz	Pia Martensson. Ylva Persson. Diana Olsson. Ida Hansson *p* - Gunilla Lundberg	Jutta Weber. Marion Platten. Regina Nissen. Beate Jasch *p* - Gudrun Beckmann
USA– 3:44.82 w	GDR – 3:45.50	CAN – 3:48.81	NED – 3:51.67	SOV – 3:52.69	FRA – 3:56.73	SWE – 3:57.25	GER – 3:58.33
Men 800m Freestyle Relay - World Record (7:30.54 USA)							Olympic Record (7:35.78 USA 1972)
Michael Bruner, Bruce Furniss, John Naber, James Montgomery *p* - Douglas Northway, Tim Shaw	Volodymyr Raskatov, Andrei Bogdanov, Sergei Kopliakov, Andrei Krylov *p* - Andrei Smirnov, Vladimir Mikheyev	Alan McClatchey, David Dunne, Gordon Downie, Brian Brinkley	Klaus Steinbach, Peter Nocke, Werner Lampe, Hans-Joachim Geisler *p* - Andreas Schmidt	Roger Pyttel, Wilfried Hartung, Rainer Strohbach, Frank Pfütze	Abdul Ressand, René van der Kuil, André in Het Veld, Henk Elzerman	Pär Arvidsson, Peter Petterson, Anders Bellbring, Bengt Gingsjö	Marcello Guarducci, Roberto Pangaro, Paolo Barelli, Paolo Revelli
USA– 7:23.22 w	SOV – 7:27.97	GBR – 7:32.11	GER - 7:32.27	GDR – 7:38.92	NED – 7:42.56	SWE – 7:42.84	ITA - 7:43.39

Chapter 20

Olympiad XXII - 1980
Moscow, Russia

While Moscow prepared to host the twenty-second Olympiad, troops of the Soviet Union invaded the country of Afghanistan. Politics were thrown into the Olympic arena once again.

World leaders asked the U.S.S.R. to withdraw its troops. They did not, and the result was the boycotting of these Games. In all, 62 nations did not participate, many of them major competitors. It was the smallest number of countries attending in twenty-four years. Among the nations not competing were Canada, Israel, Japan, Kenya, Norway, West Germany and the United States.

Courtesy of ISHOF

Robert Kane, President of the United States Olympic Committee, stated after the U.S.' decision to boycott the Moscow Games, "I am satisfied it was a completely right decision, while feeling desperately sorry for the athletes who have been hurt by it."

The Soviet men dominated the pool, winning seven gold medals. Vladimir Salnikov's lone world record breaking swim was a clear

East German Sweep - Rica Reinisch with teammates Ina Kleber (left) and Petra Riedel (right).

indication that the level of competition for men had been drastically diminished. It was here that the absence of the American swimmers was most apparent.

Olympic 1ST

Aussie Upset

The Australian Men's Swim Team upset the Soviet Union by winning the 400m medley relay, marking the first ever Australian win in this event.

As in Montreal, the East German women continued their swimming domination. They captured nine out of eleven individual titles, finishing 1-2-3 in six finals. The women's events, in contrast to the men's, produced five individual and two relay world records, each set by the East Germans.

While the Moscow Games were well organized, they failed to hold the spirit traditionally associated with the Olympics. The athletes left behind faced the reality of a missed opportunity and the thoughts of what might have been.

INES DIERS
EAST GERMANY

Sixteen-year-old Ines Diers, was the top medal winner of the 1980 Olympic swimming competition, collecting two gold, two silver, and one bronze, for East Germany.

In the 400m freestyle Diers followed teammate Petra Schneider for over 300 meters before pulling ahead to capture her lone individual gold. She added a relay gold to her 1980 collection giving her medals in all five freestyle events.

L A N E   L I N E S

"Back" in the U.S.S.R.

Triple gold medalist Rica Reinisch of East Germany easily won both the 100m and 200m backstroke events, setting new world records in both.

Rica Reinisch broke or equaled the world record in backstroke events four times (three times in the 100m and once in the 200m) during her preliminary, relay, and final swims. She was also a member of the gold medal winning medley relay team.

MICHELLE FORD
AUSTRALIA

At eighteen, Michelle Ford won gold in the 800m freestyle and became one of only two non-East German's to win gold in the women's swimming competition at these Games.

After the 800m freestyle race Ford explained, "My coach said before the race the East Germans had won all those medals and wouldn't it be nice to go out and win one. I thought, yes, it sure would and I did it."

Ford cried tears of joy as she stood on the awards stand, holding

Olympic 1ST

"Russian to be the First"

On the first day of Olympic competition, Sergei Fesenko became the first Russian male ever to win an Olympic swimming event (200m fly). However, the Soviet Men's Team followed suit with six more wins.

her stuffed bear as her country's national anthem played. Michelle would stand on the podium once again, as the bronze medal winner in the 200m butterfly as well.

Duncan Goodhew - Great Britain

100m Breaststroke - Gold

400m Medley Relay - Bronze

As an adolescent, Duncan Goodhew was constantly teased due to an accident that left him bald. He also suffered from the reading disorder dyslexia. He learned to deal with his frustrations and focused on becoming an Olympic swim champion.

L A N E   L I N E S

Fantastic Finishes

World record holder Lina Kaciusýte (SOV) went from last place during the 200m breaststroke at the 50-meter mark to fourth at 100 meters. With 50 meters to go she was still 2-1/2 seconds behind teammate Svetlana Varganova. The seventeen-year-old Kaciusyte, summoned what strength she had left and swam to victory.

Ute Geweniger (GDR), broke her own world record in a preliminary heat of the 100m breaststroke, with a time of 1:10.11. During the final, Geweniger found herself in 5th place at the turn ... and in first at the finish!

BARBARA KRAUSE
EAST GERMANY

Barbara Krause of East Germany began swimming as therapy for orthopedic problems. By 1976 she had become one of East Germany's top swimmers, but was unable to compete at the 1976 Montreal Olympics due to illness. Krause watched from her sick bed as her teammates dominated the women's swim competition. It was a determined Barbara Krause who qualified for the Moscow Olympics.

The 100m freestyle event started with a field of only 30 swimmers. Not since 1932 had this event had so few. Because the field was so small it was decided that the semi-finals would be eliminated. The eight swimmers with the fastest times in the preliminary heats would qualify for the finals, a practice that was adopted and is still used in Olympic competition today.

During her preliminary heat in Moscow, Krause became the first woman to break 55 seconds in the 100m freestyle, breaking her own world record. She again broke her own record with a swim of 54.79 during the final.

Courtesy of ISHOF

Krause acknowledged her teammates Caren Meshuck and Ines Diers, who placed second and third, respectively, in the 100m free. "I

Barbara Krause off the block.

was very pleased to become the first woman under 55 seconds. The new world record was partially due to my team-

Sergei Kopliakov - U.S.S.R.

1976 – Montreal
400m Medley Relay – Silver

1980 – Moscow
200m Freestyle – Gold
800m Freestyle – Gold
400m Medley Relay – Silver

mates who pressed me until the end."

Barbara Krause went on to capture the 200m freestyle title and swim the first leg of the 400m free relay, breaking a world record set by the Americans at the 1978 World Championships.

CAREN METSCHUCK EAST GERMANY

Caren Metschuck captured an individual title in the 100m butterfly in Moscow. It was also the only event in the women's competition in which the Olympic record had not been broken.

Metschuck's silver medal performance in the 100m freestyle event made her the second fastest female swimmer in the world. As the butterfly leg of the 400m medley, and the anchor on the 400m free relay teams, Metschuck swam to two more gold medals. Caren Metschuck won a total of three gold medals and one silver at the 1980 Games.

VLADIMIR SALNIKOV RUSSIA

The 1500m freestyle event was the highlight of the men's swimming com-

OFF THE Wall

Young Guns

At fifteen years and 105 days Rica Reinisch (GDR) was the youngest Olympic Champion of the Moscow Games.

With his win in the 200m backstroke, Sandor Wlador of Hungary, age 17 years and 7 days, was the youngest male champion of these Games.

petition and it was the incredible Vladimir Salnikov who swam to gold. He had three "golden swims" in Moscow, but none compared to the 1500m race.

At the 1400m mark, Salnikov's time was 14:00.22. As his countrymen stood anxiously cheering him on, he swam his final 100 meters in an unbelievable 58.05. Salnikov smashed the existing world record by over four seconds with a final time of 14:58.27.

His achievements were in no way diminished by the boycott. In fact, Vladimir felt that had the American swimmers been present, his times would have been even faster. The silver medalist in the 1500m final, Aleksandr Chaev, was over 16 seconds behind his teammate.

Vladimir Salnikov collected a second individual gold for the 400m freestyle setting a new Olympic mark. Vladimir

OFF THE 𝒲𝒶𝓁𝓁

"Standing O"

After the medal ceremony and media blitz that followed his historic win in Seoul, Salnikov returned to the Olympic Village cafeteria that evening. As he entered the hall, the coaches and athletes of various nations, some **275** of his peers, stopped eating and spontaneously stood to give Vladimir a standing ovation.

L A N E   L I N E S

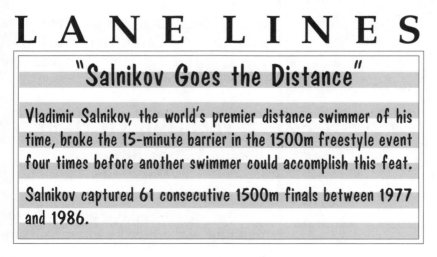

"Salnikov Goes the Distance"

Vladimir Salnikov, the world's premier distance swimmer of his time, broke the 15-minute barrier in the 1500m freestyle event four times before another swimmer could accomplish this feat.

Salnikov captured 61 consecutive 1500m finals between 1977 and 1986.

Vladimir Salnikov one of only three swimmers to win Olympic gold medals eight years apart

cracked the 400m free world record, but not until March of 1992.

Prior to the 1980 Games, a number of Soviet swimmers, including Salnikov, trained in the United States. Sergei Vaitsekhovsky, a Soviet swim coach, graciously acknowledged the American swimmers and coaches for their contribution to the Soviet men's success in the pool.

"The Americans surprised us by not keeping any of their training secrets from us, which means there must still be some decent people left in the world," said Vaitsekhovsky.

As the 1984 Olympics approached, Salnikov held the 400m, 800m and 1500m freestyle world records. Ironically, he would not be able to compete in these Games due to a Soviet boycott. Clearly his absence was felt in the 400m and 1500m races.

Salnikov went on to win 61 consecutive finals in the 1500m freestyle event. His streak came to an end at the 1986 World Championships, when he finished fourth.

By 1987, many thought that Vladimir was ready for retirement, including the Soviet coaches. They had not selected him for the 1988 Olympic Team, no longer viewing him as a medal contender. Salnikov had other ideas. Coached by his wife Marina, he set his sights on Seoul. The Soviet Minister of Sports intervened and Salnikov was placed on the team.

SCORE
BOARD

At the 1980 Olympic Games, the 200m breast-stroke event was swept for the second consecutive Olympiad by the Soviet Women's Team. Lina Kačiušyte, Svetlana Varganova, and Yulia Bogdanova placed 1-2-3 respectively.

At the age of 28, Vladimir Salnikov won the 1500m event and became the oldest Olympic swimming champion since 1932. He joined the ranks of Duke Kahanamoku and Dawn Fraser as the only swimmers to win Olympic gold medals eight years apart.

PETRA SCHNEIDER
EAST GERMANY

Seventeen year-old Petra Schneider's world record setting victory in the 400m individual medley was the most decisive win in the entire women's swimming competition. Schneider touched over ten seconds ahead of second place finisher Sharron Davies of Great Britain.

Petra Schneider missed gold in the 400m freestyle by a mere four tenths of one second, after leading the event for over 300 meters. She was also the holder of the 200m IM world record in 1980, an event that was not on the 1980 Olympic program.

1980 OLYMPIC SWIMMING FINALS

INDIVIDUAL EVENTS

	Gold	Silver	Bronze	Fourth	Fifth	Sixth	Seventh	Eighth
Women 100m Freestyle - World Record (55.41 Barbara Krause GDR)					Olympic Record (55.65 Kornelia Ender GDR 1976)			
	Barbara Krause	Caren Metschuck	Ines Diers	Olga Klevakina	Cornelia van Bentum	Natalya Strunnikova	Guylaine Berger	Agneta Eriksson
	GDR – 54.79 w	GDR – 55.16	GDR – 55.65	SOV – 57.40	NED – 57.63	SOV – 57.83	FRA – 57.88	SWE – 57.90
Men 100m Freestyle - World Record (49.44 Jonty Skinner RSA)					Olympic Record (49.99 James Montgomery USA 1976)			
	Jörg Woithe	Per Holmertz	Per Johansson	Sergei Kopliakov	Raffaele Franceschi	Serhei Krasyuk	René Ecuyer	Graeme Brewer
	GDR – 50.40	SWE – 50.91	SWE – 51.29	SOV – 51.34	ITA – 51.69	SOV – 51.80	FRA – 52.01	AUS – 52.22
Women 200m Freestyle - World Record (1:58.23 C. Woodhead USA)					Olympic Record (1:59.26 Kornelia Ender GDR 1976)			
	Barbara Krause	Ines Diers	Carmela Schmidt	Olga Klevakina	Reggie de Jong	June Croft	Natalya Strunnikova	Irina Aksyonova
	GDR – 1:58.33 o	GDR – 1:59.64	GDR – 2:01.44	SOV – 2:02.29	NED – 2:02.76	GBR – 2:03.15	SOV – 2:03.74	SOV – 2:04.00
Men 200m Freestyle - World Record (1:49.16 Rowdy Gaines USA)					Olympic Record (1:50.29 Bruce Furniss 1976)			
	Sergei Kopliakov	Andrei Krylov	Graeme Brewer	Jörg Woithe	Ron McKeon	Paolo Revelli	Thomas Lejdström	Fabrizio Rampazzo
	SOV – 1:49.81 o	SOV – 1:50.76	AUS – 1:51.60	GDR – 1:51.86	AUS – 1:52.60	ITA – 1:52.76	SWE – 1:52.94	ITA – 1:53.25

w World Record   *o* Olympic Record   *p* Preliminary Heat   *dq* Disqualified   *e* Equal to World Record   *eo* Equal to Olympic Record
dns Did Not Start   *dnf* Did Not Finish   *ac* Also Competed   *r* Relay Lead-off Split   *E* Estimated

OLYMPIAD XXII – 1980 – MOSCOW, U.S.S.R.

1980 OLYMPIC SWIMMING FINALS

	Gold	Silver	Bronze	Fourth	Fifth	Sixth	Seventh	Eighth
Women 400m Freestyle - World Record (4:06.28 Tracey Wickham AUS) Olympic Record (4:09.89 Petra Thümer GDR 1976)								
	Ines Diers GDR– 4:08.76 o	Petra Schneider GDR– 4:09.16	Carmela Schmidt GDR– 4:10.86	Michelle Ford AUS– 4:11.65	Irina Aksyonova SOV– 4:14.40	Annelies Maas NED– 4:15.79	Reggie de Jong NED– 4:15.95	Olga Klevakina SOV– 4:19.18
Men 400m Freestyle - World Record (3:50.49 Peter Szmidt CAN) Olympic Record (3:51.93 Brian Goodell USA 1976)								
	Vladimir Salnikov SOV– 3:51.31 o	Andrei Krylov SOV– 3:53.24	Ivar Stukolkin SOV– 3:53.95	Djan Madruga Garrido BRA– 3:54.15	Daniel Machek CZE– 3:55.66	Sándor Nagy HUN– 3:56.83	Max Metzker AUS– 3:56.87	Ronald McKeon AUS– 3:57.00
Women 800m Freestyle - World Record (8:24.62 Tracey Wickham AUS) Olympic Record (8:37.14 Petra Thümer GDR 1976)								
	Michelle Ford AUS– 8:28.90 o	Ines Diers GDR– 8:32.55	Heike Dähne GDR– 8:33.48	Irina Aksyonova SOV– 8:38.05	Oksana Komissarova SOV– 8:42.04	Pascale Verbauwen BEL– 8:44.84	Ines Geissler GDR– 8:45.28	Yelena Ivanova SOV– 8:46.45
Men 1500m Freestyle - World and Olympic Record (15:02.40 Brian Goodell USA 1976)								
	Vladimir Salnikov SOV– 14:58.27 w	Aleksandr Chayev SOV– 15:14.30	Max Metzker AUS– 15:14.49	Rainer Strohbach GDR– 15:15.29	Borut Petric YUG– 15:21.78	Rafael Escalas ESP– 15:21.88	Zoltán Wladár HUN– 15:26.70	Eduard Petrov SOV– 15:28.24
Women 100m Backstroke - World Record (1:01.51 Ulrike Richter GDR) Olympic Record (1:01.83 Ulrike Richter GDR 1976)								
	Rica Reinisch GDR– 1:00.86 w	Ina Kleber GDR– 1:02.07	Petra Riedel GDR– 1:02.64	Carmen Bunaciu ROM– 1:03.81	Carine Verbauwen BEL– 1:03.82	Larissa Gorchakova SOV– 1:03.87	Monique Bosga NED– 1:04.47	Manuela Carosi ITA– 1:05.10
Men 100m Backstroke - World and Olympic Record (55.49 John Naber USA 1976)								
	Bengt Baron SWE– 56.33	Viktor Kuznetsov SOV– 56.99	Volodymyr Dolhov SOV– 57.63	Miloslav Rolko CZE– 57.74	Sándor Wladár HUN– 57.84	Fred Eefting NED– 57.95	Mark Tonelli AUS– 57.98	Gary Abraham GBR– 58.38

1980 OLYMPIC SWIMMING FINALS

Gold	Silver	Bronze	Fourth	Fifth	Sixth	Seventh	Eighth
Women 200m Backstroke - World Record (2:11.95 Linda Jezek USA)				Olympic Record (2:13.43 Ulrike Richter GDR 1976)			
Rica Reinisch	Cornelia Polit	Birgit Treiber	Carmen Bunaciu	Yolande van der Straeten	Carine Verbauwen	Lisa Forrest	Larissa Gorchakova
GDR – 2:11.77 w	GDR – 2:13.75	GDR – 2:14.14	ROM – 2:15.20	BEL – 2:15.58	BEL – 2:16.66	AUS – 2:16.75	SOV – 2:17.72
Men 200m Backstroke - World and Olympic Record (1:59.19 John Naber USA 1976)							
Sándor Wladár	Zoltán Verrasztó	Mark Kerry	Vladimir Shemetov	Fred Eefting	Michael Söderlund	Douglas Campbell	Paul Moorfoot
HUN – 2:01.93	HUN – 2:02.40	AUS – 2:03.14	SOV – 2:03.48	NED – 2:03.92	SWE – 2:04.10	GBR – 2:04.23	AUS – 2:06.15
Women 100m Breaststroke - World Record (1:10.20 Ute Geweniger GDR)				Olympic Record (1:10.86 H. Anke GDR 1976)			
Ute Geweniger	Elvira Vasilkova	Susanne Nielsson	Margaret Kelly	Eva-Marie Håkansson	Susannah Brownsdon	Lina Kaciušyte	Monica Bonon
GDR – 1:10.22	SOV – 1:10.41	DEN – 1:11.16	GBR – 1:11.48	SWE – 1:11.72	GBR – 1:12.11	SOV – 1:12.21	ITA – 1:12.51
Men 100m Breaststroke - World and Olympic Record (1:02.86 Gerald Mörken)				Olympic Record (1:03.11 John Hencken USA 1976)			
Duncan Goodhew	Arsens Miskarovs	Peter Evans	Aleksandr Fedorovsky	János Dzvonyár	Lindsay Spencer	Pablo Restrepo	Albán Vermes
GBR – 1:03.44	SOV - 1:03.82	AUS – 1:03.96	SOV - 1:04.00	HUN – 1:04.67	AUS – 1:05.04	COL – 1:05.91	HUN – dq
Women 200m Breaststroke - World and Olympic Record (2:28.36 Lina Kaciušyte SOV)				Olympic Record (2:33.35 M. Koshevaia SOV 1976)			
Lina Kaciušyte	Svetlana Varganova	Yulia Bogdanova	Susanne Nielsson	Irena Fleissnerová	Ute Geweniger	Bettina Löbel	Sylvia Rinka
SOV - 2:29.54 o	SOV - 2:29.61	SOV - 2:32.39	DEN – 2:32.75	CZE - 2:33.23	GDR – 2:34.34	GDR – 2:34.51	GDR - 2:35.38
Men 200m Breaststroke - World and Olympic Record (2:15.11 David Wilkie GBR 1976)							
Robertas Šulpa	Albán Vermes	Arsens Miskarovs	Gennady Utenkov	Lindsay Spencer	Duncan Goodhew	Peter Berggren	Jörg Walter
SOV - 2:15.85	HUN – 2:16.93	SOV - 2:17.28	SOV - 2:19.64	AUS – 2:19.68	GBR – 2:20.92	SWE – 2:21.65	GDR - 2:22.39

1980 OLYMPIC SWIMMING FINALS

	Gold	Silver	Bronze	Fourth	Fifth	Sixth	Seventh	Eighth
Women 100m Butterfly - World Record (59.26 Mary T. Meagher USA) Olympic Record (1:00.13 Kornelia Ender GDR 1976)	Caren Metschuck GDR – 1:00.42	Andrea Pollack GDR – 1:00.90	Christiane Knacke GDR – 1:01.44	Ann Osgerby GBR – 1:02.21	Lisa Curry AUS – 1:02.40	Agneta Mårtensson SWE – 1:02.61	Maria del Milagro Paris CRC – 1:02.89	Janet Osgerby GBR – 1:02.90
Men 100m Butterfly - World Record (54.15 Pär Arvidsson SWE)	Pär Arvidsson SWE – 54.92	Roger Pyttel GDR – 54.94	David López-Zubero Purcell ESP – 55.13	Kees Vervoorn NED – 55.25	Yevgeny Seredin SOV – 55.35	Gary Abraham GBR – 55.42	Xavier Savin FRA – 55.66	Aleksei Markovsky SOV – 55.70
Women 200m Butterfly - World Record (2:07.01 Mary T. Meagher USA) Olympic Record (2:11.41 Andrea Pollack GDR 1976)	Ines Geissler GDR – 2:10.44	Sybille Schönrock GDR – 2:10.45	Michelle Ford AUS – 2:11.66	Andrea Pollack GDR – 2:12.13	Dorota Brzozowska POL – 2:14.12	Ann Osgerby GBR – 2:14.83	Agneta Mårtensson SWE – 2:15.22	Alla Grishchenkova SOV – 2:15.70
Men 200m Butterfly - World and Olympic Record (1:59.23 Mike Bruner USA 1976)	Serhei Fesenko SOV – 1:59.76	Philip Hubble GBR – 2:01.20	Roger Pyttel GDR – 2:01.39	Peter Morris GBR – 2:02.27	Mikhail Gorelik SOV – 2:02.44	Kees Vervoorn NED – 2:02.52	Pär Arvidsson SWE – 2:02.61	Stephen Poulter GBR – 2:02.93
Women 400m Individual Medley - World Record (4:38.44 P. Schneider GDR) Olympic Record (4:42.77 U. Tauber GDR 1976)	Petra Schneider GDR – 4:36.29m	Sharron Davies GBR – 4:46.83	Agnieszka Czopek POL – 4:48.17	Grit Släby GDR – 4:48.54	Ulrike Tauber GDR – 4:49.18	Sonya Dangalakova BUL – 4:49.25	Olga Klevakina SOV – 4:50.91	Magdelena Bialas POL – 4:53.30
Men 400m Individual Medley - World Record (4:20.05 Jesse Vassallo USA) Olympic Record (4:23.68 Rod Strachan USA 1976)	Oleksander Sydorenko SOV - 4:22.89	Serhei Fesenko SOV - 4:23.43	Zoltán Verasztó HUN - 4:24.24	András Hargitay HUN - 4:24.48	Djan Madruga Garrido BRA - 4:26.81	Miloslav Rolko CZE - 4:26.99	Leszek Górski POL - 4:28.89	Daniel Machek CZE - 4:29.86

1980 OLYMPIC SWIMMING FINALS

RELAY EVENTS

Women 400m Medley Relay – World and Olympic Record (4:07.95 GDR 1976)

Gold	Silver	Bronze	Fourth	Fifth	Sixth	Seventh	Eighth
Rica Reinisch. Ute Geweniger. Andrea Pollack. Caren Metschuck *p - Sarina* Hulsenbeck	Helen Jameson. Margaret Kelly. Ann Ogerby. June Croft	Yekeba Kruglova. Elvira Vasilkova. Alla Grishchenkova. Natalya Strunnikova *p - Irina* Aksyonova. Olga Klevakina	Annika Uvehall. Eva-Marie Håkansson. Agneta Martensson. Tina Gustafson	Laura Foralosso, Sabrina Seminatore. Cinzia Savi-Scarponi. Monica Vallarin	Lisa Forrest, Lisa Curry. Karen Van De Graaf. Rosemary Brown	Carmen Bunaciu. Brigitte Press. Mariana Parachiv. Irinel Panulescu	Sonya Dangalakova. Tania Bogomilova. Ani Moneva. Dobrinka Mincheva
GDR – 4:06.67w	GBR – 4:12.24	SOV – 4:13.61	SWE – 4:16.91	ITA – 4:19.05	AUS – 4:19.90	ROM – 4:21.27	BUL – 4:22.38

Men 400m Medley Relay - World and Olympic Record (3:42.22 USA 1976)

Gold	Silver	Bronze	Fourth	Fifth	Sixth	Seventh	Eighth
Mark Kerry, Peter Evans, Mark Tonelli, Neil Brooks *p- Glen Patching*	Viktor Kuznetsov, Arsens Miskarovs, Yevgeny Seredin, Sergei Kopliakov, *p-V. Shmetov, A. Fedorovsky, A. Markovsky, Sergei Krasyuk*	Gary Abraham, Duncan Goodhew, David Lowe, T. Martin Smith, *p - Paul Marshall, Mark Taylor*	Dietmar Göhring, Jörg Walter, Roger Pyttel, Jörg Woithe *p- Frank Kühn*	Frédéric Delcourt, Olivier Borios, Xavier Savin, René Ecuyer	Sándor Wladár, Janos Dzvonyar, Zoltán Verrasztó, Gábor Mészáros	Fred Eefting, Albert Boonstra, Kees Vervoorn, Cees Jan Winkel	Romulo Duncan Arantes, Sergio Pinto Ribeiro, Claudo Mamede Kestener, Jorge Luiz Fernandes *p -C iro Marques Delgado*
AUS – 3:45.70	SOV – 3:45.92	GBR – 3:47.71	GDR – 3:48.25	FRA – 3:49.19	HUN – 3:50.29	NED – 3:51.81	BRA – 3:53.23

1980 OLYMPIC SWIMMING FINALS

	Gold	Silver	Bronze	Fourth	Fifth	Sixth	Seventh	Eighth
Women 400m Freestyle Relay - World Record (3:43.43 USA)					Olympic Record (3:44.82 USA 1976)			
	Barbara Krause, Caren Metschuck, Ines Diers, Sarina Hülsenbeck, p- Carmela Schmidt	Carina Ljungdahl, Tina Gustafsson, Agneta Martensson, p- Birgitta Jonsson, Helena Peterson	Cornelia van Bentum, Wilma van Velsen, Reggie de Jong, Annelies Maas	Sharon Davies, Kaye Lovatt, Jacquelina Willmott, June Croft	Lisa Curry, Karen van de Graaf, Rosemary Brown, Michele Pearson	Isabel Reuss, Dagmar Erdman, Teresa Rivera, Helen Plaschinski	Dobrinka Mincheva, Rumiana Nikolova, Ani Kostova, Sonya Dangalakova	Natalia Mas, Margarita Armengol, Laura Flaque, Gloria Casado
	GDR – 3:42.71w	SWE – 3:48.93	NED – 3:49.51	GBR – 3:51.71	AUS – 3:54.16	MEX – 3:55.41	BUL – 3:56.34	ESP – 3:58.73
Men 800m Freestyle Relay - World Record (7:20.82 USA)					Olympic Record (7:23.22 USA 1976)			
	Sergei Kopliakov, Vladimir Salnikov, Ivar Stukolkin, Andrei Krylov, p- Sergei Rusin, Sergei Krasyuk, Yuri Presekin	Frank Pfütze, Jörg Woithe, Detlev Grabs, Rainer Strohbach	Jorge Lutz Fernandes, Marcus Labone Mattioli, Cyro Marques, Djan Madruga Garrido	Michael Söderlund, Pelle Wikström, Per- Alvar Magnusson, Thomas Lejdström, p- Anders Rutkvist, Per- Ola Quist	Paolo Revelli, Raffaele Franceschi, Andrea Ceccarini, Fabrizio Rampazzo, p- Frederic Silvestri	Douglas Campbell, Philip Hubble, T. Martin Smith, Andrew Astbury, p- Mark Taylor, Kevin Lee	Graeme Brewer, Mark Tonelli, Mark Kerry, Ron McKeon, p- Max Metzker	Fabien Noel, Mark Lazzaro, Dominique Petit, Paskal Laget
	SOV – 7:23.50	GDR – 7:28.60	BRA – 7:29.30	SWE – 7:30.10	ITA – 7:30.37	GBR – 7:30.81	AUS – 7:30.82	FRA – 7:36/08

Chapter 21

Olympiad XXIII - 1984
Los Angeles, California, United States

The Eastern Bloc countries, including the Soviet Union and East Germany, did not attend the Los Angeles Games and the level of Olympic competition was affected once again. The greatest loss in the swim arena was felt by the absence of world record holder Vladimir Salnikov.

The 1984 Los Angeles Games were the first to institute private corporation sponsorships. One of the most notable was the "McDonald's Swim Stadium."

At these Games the number of entrants allowed per nation, per event was reduced from three to two. From 1960 to 1980 this ruling changed back and forth, but has remained at two since 1984.

The swimming program saw the return of the 200m individual medley event for both men and women. Also reinstated was the 400m freestyle relay in the men's competition.

The eleven swimming world records set during the 1984 Olympic swimming competition all came from the men's events.

George DiCarlo
U.S.A.

400m Freestyle – Gold
1500m Freestyle – Silver

These were the first Games since 1952 that failed to produce a world mark in the women's swimming competition.

THERESA ANDREWS
UNITED STATES

American Theresa Andrews, 21, was not favored to win gold at the 1984 Games. In fact, she had been a surprise victor at the Olympic Trials. After making the team, Andrews, one of twelve children, committed herself totally to preparing for the Olympics, dropping out of the University of Florida to train full time.

Her race was the 100m backstroke and in the final she was in fourth place at the 50m mark. Andrews pushed past the three swimmers favored in the event to claim victory.

After her Olympic win, Theresa said, "I'm going to give it (gold medal) to Danny. He doesn't know it yet." Theresa's younger brother Danny had been paralyzed the year before when he was struck by a car while riding his bicycle.

Andrews earned yet another gold medal as a member of the U.S. medley relay team.

SPLASH BACK
Streak Snapped

The United States Men's Swim Team failed to medal in the 200m butterfly event. Prior to the 1984 Olympics, the Americans had taken 13 of 18 medals from the 1956 through 1976 Olympic Games in this event.

ALEX BAUMANN
CANADA

To many, Alex Baumann, was the best all around swimmer of his time. In Los Angeles, Baumann gave gold medal performances in both the 400m and 200m individual medley races. In each, he broke his own world record, producing records that would stand for six years.

Courtesy of ISHOF

The victorious Alex Baumann

His win in the 400m individual medley was the first swimming gold medal for Canada in 72 years. The Canadian fans went crazy. A large Canadian flag, held by a group of athletes, could be seen waving on a rooftop at the Olympic Village.

Baumann, who sported a maple leaf tattoo, described his feelings after his historic win, "I was very proud to be a Canadian at that moment. It's been a long grind for me as well as for Canadian swimming and I'm glad we finally hit gold again."

A long grind indeed. Baumann's road to Olympic glory had been a bumpy one. Born in Prague, Czechoslovakia, his family eventually relocated to Sudbury, Ontario, when Alex was a young boy.

Baumann started swimming at the age of nine. He was encouraged by his mother who had been nationally ranked as a breaststroker for Czechoslovakia. He set national 13-14 age group records and in 1981, at the age of sixteen, established his first world record in the 200m IM. At seventeen he already held 38 Canadian records in assorted strokes.

In 1982, Baumann was sidelined with a shoulder injury for several months. Then in 1984, Alex suffered the loss of both his father and his older brother.

Baumann relied heavily on his coach, Jeno Tihanyi, to keep him focused, and on his mother for support. It is her encouragement that Baumann credits for his success. In his career, he set a total of five world records, three for the 200m IM and two in the 400m IM.

RICHARD CAREY
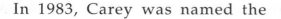
UNITED STATES

At 5' 11", Rick Carey did not fit the prototype of a backstroker, yet his well-developed, muscular arms gave him incredible upper body strength. In 1981, Carey, a high school senior, captured both the 100m and 200m national indoor backstroke titles.

In 1983, Carey was named the

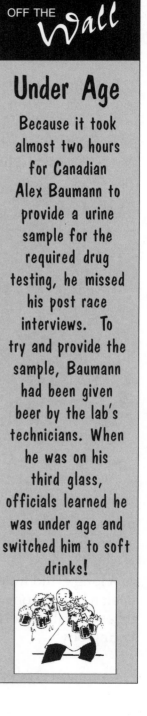

OFF THE **Wall**

Under Age

Because it took almost two hours for Canadian Alex Baumann to provide a urine sample for the required drug testing, he missed his post race interviews. To try and provide the sample, Baumann had been given beer by the lab's technicians. When he was on his third glass, officials learned he was under age and switched him to soft drinks!

Rick Carey's winning form.

Courtesy of ISHOF

"World Swimmer of the Year" by Swimming World magazine. It was the year he broke John Nabers' long standing backstroke world records, set in 1976. Carey arrived in Los Angeles as the current world record holder.

Private by nature, Carey was an intensely competitive perfectionist, demanding more of himself than was expected.

Carey's 200m race at the 1984 Games was a close one. Not until the final lap was he able to pull ahead of the French swimmer, Frederic Delcourt. After the race Carey ignored the roar of the fans and Delcourt, who tried to congratulate him.

At the medal ceremony the other medalists waved and smiled. Carey finally gave a wave after they placed the gold medal around his neck. As they filed out he continued to ignore the crowd, stopping only to kiss his mother.

The media tore Carey apart. Rick explained in a formal apology, "I found it very difficult to smile when my performance didn't live up to my expectations. By not breaking the world record I felt I had not only let myself down but also the crowd...But, please don't get the impression that I didn't appreciate winning. What everyone saw was purely an emotional reaction or over-reaction to Rick Carey's imperfection."

Carey again disappointed himself when he took gold in the

100m backstroke and failed to break his own world record. This time, however, Rick was responsive to the cheering crowd, waving and smiling back.

As the leadoff swimmer in the 400m medley relay, Carey set a new Olympic record for the 100m backstroke. Seeing his time flashed on the board, he thrust his fist in the air. Carey was finally happy. The team went on to set a new world record.

Rick Carey continued to swim after the 1984 Olympic Games taking national indoor and outdoor crowns in 1985 and 1986. He retired from competition in 1986.

L A N E   L I N E S

"Double Dutch"

Petra van Staveren's victory in the 100m breaststroke event was Holland's first swimming gold medal in sixteen years. Petra's teammate Jolanda de Rover's win in the 200m backstroke final, marked the first time the Netherlands had won two swimming titles during one Olympiad. De Rover also captured a bronze medal in the 100m backstroke event.

TRACY CAULKINS
UNITED STATES

Tracy Caulkins of Nashville, Tennessee, was one of the most versatile swimmers in the history of United States swimming. Her accomplishments are almost endless. At various times she was the holder of 48 U.S. national titles (in every stroke), 63 American records, 5 world records, 12 NCAA championships and 3 Olympic gold medals.

It's no wonder that in 1978, at the age of fifteen, Tracy became the youngest person ever to receive the Sullivan Award as the nation's outstanding amateur athlete. That same year she won numerous short and long course titles and three firsts and a second at the World Championships.

Courtesy of ISHOF

The amazing Tracy Caulkins

Favored to win five gold medals, Caulkins was one of the hardest hit by the Moscow boycott. She went on to swim for the University of Florida. In 1982 and 1984, Caulkins won the Honda Broderick Cup, for the United States' outstanding woman college athlete. An excellent student as well, she was named to the 1984 Academic All-American team.

Coming off a lackluster '83 season, Caulkins captured the 200m and 400m IM titles at the United States Swimming International Meet in January of 1984. Having defeated the mighty East German competition, she later stated, "I think a lot of people have counted me out. They better watch out."

Caulkins' first event of the 1984 Olympic Games was the 400m individual medley. The second place finisher, Suzanne Landells of Australia, was some 15 meters behind when Caulkins touched. Tracy had set a new American record and swam a career best for the first time in four years in this event.

"This is one thing I've never had; it's a great way to top off my career. I've dreamt about it so long and here it is," beamed Caulkins. Not known to show her emotions, Tracy talked about the Olympic awards ceremony, "I start getting teary-eyed just talking about it, and I've never felt that way on an awards stand before. It's the experience of a lifetime."

She also acknowledged the absence of East German Kathleen Nord, missing due to the boycott. Caulkins knew that had Nord been there, they would have pushed one another to a faster time.

Caulkins went on to set an Olympic record in the 200m IM, again finishing with her best time in four years. She hadn't lost against an American in this event since 1977 and finished over two seconds ahead of the silver medalist, Nancy Hogshead.

Her peers admire Tracy not only for her accomplishments in the pool, but for the kindness and compassion she demonstrated time and time again for teammates and friends alike. Olympic teammate Rowdy Gaines credited Caulkins with calming him down, at least temporarily, prior to his historic swim in the Olympic 100m freestyle final.

Olympic 1ST

Oh Canada....

Anne Ottenbrite was Canada's first woman swimmer to win an Olympic title. Her victory in the 200m breaststroke came just minutes after teammate Alex Baumann won Canada's first swimming gold in 72 years.

SCORE
BOARD

During the preliminary heat of the 400m freestyle event, West German Thomas Fahrner was trying to swim just fast enough to gain an outside lane in the final. However, he miscalculated and wound up taking ninth and not making the final cut. Swimming in the consolation round just minutes after DiCarlo captured gold and set a new Olympic record, Fahrner beat DiCarlo's winning time. DiCarlo went home with gold and Fahrner the Olympic record, showing the importance of swimming both heats very well.

Nancy Hogshead said of Caulkins, "I can't express to you how much I respect Tracy. She's a nice friend and team leader. She had lunch with Carrie (Steinseifer) because she knew she was nervous. Tracy's like that - kind, behind the scenes."

With a fourth place finish in the 100m breaststroke final, Tracy qualified for a spot on the medley relay team. The team of Theresa Andrews, Mary T. Meagher, Nancy Hogshead, and Caulkins easily won the gold medal.

Just two days after her final swim at the 1984 Olympic Games, Caulkins announced her retirement from competitive swimming. She left behind not only a trophy case full of medals and awards but a legacy of support and kindness that teammates and competitors will always remember.

TIFFANY COHEN
UNITED STATES

Tiffany Cohen was a long distance freestyle specialist. She won her first national title at the age of fifteen and from then on collected one indoor and outdoor title after another.

During the 400m final in Los Angeles, Tiffany, then 18, set an Olympic and American record with the second fastest swim in history. She narrowly missed Australian Tracy Wickham's world record set back in 1978. Cohen had no one pushing her, finishing over three seconds faster than silver medalist Sarah Hardcastle of Great Britain. In the 800m final, Cohen again struck gold and set another Olympic record.

Tiffany Cohen entered the University of Texas that fall, and would continue to swim. Tiffany Cohen retired from swimming in early 1988, passing her distance crown along to American Janet Evans.

VICTOR DAVIS
CANADA

Victor Davis won the 200m breaststroke final by over two seconds against silver medalist Glenn Beringen of Australia. He broke his own world record set less than a month earlier. His new time of 2:13.34, would remain an Olympic record until the 1992 Olympics Games.

The twenty-year-old Canadian's win in the 200m breaststroke was by the largest margin in sixty years for an Olympic final in this event. He went on to capture silver in both the 100m breaststroke event and as a member of the Canadian 400m medley relay team.

Victor Davis returned to the Games in 1988 and placed fourth in the 100m breaststroke and collected his third Olympic silver medal in the 400m medley relay.

Courtesy of ISHOF

Davis readies for the race.

On November 13, 1989, 25 year-old Victor Davis died after being struck by an automobile. A quart of water was taken from lane 5 of the pool where Davis had made Olympic history, to be scattered at sea along with his ashes.

L A N E   L I N E S

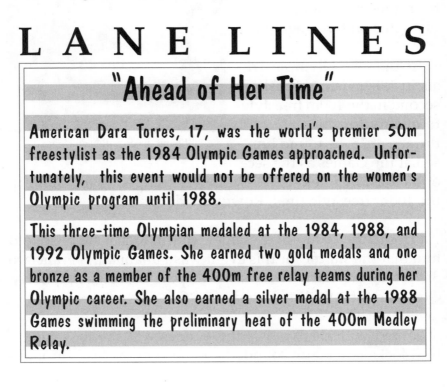

"Ahead of Her Time"

American Dara Torres, 17, was the world's premier 50m freestylist as the 1984 Olympic Games approached. Unfortunately, this event would not be offered on the women's Olympic program until 1988.

This three-time Olympian medaled at the 1984, 1988, and 1992 Olympic Games. She earned two gold medals and one bronze as a member of the 400m free relay teams during her Olympic career. She also earned a silver medal at the 1988 Games swimming the preliminary heat of the 400m Medley Relay.

AMBROSE "ROWDY" GAINES
UNITED STATES

Ambrose "Rowdy" Gaines won his first age group title before his tenth birthday. Gaines, however, gave up swimming competitively in order to play football, baseball, and basketball. He did not return to competitive swimming until his junior year in high school.

Olympic sprinter Rowdy Gaines.

Gaines, a freestyle sprinter, was favored to take three or four gold medals home from the 1980 Moscow Games. The boycott forestalled Gaines' Olympic appearance and he returned to the rigors of training and set his sights on Los Angeles.

At the U.S. Olympic Trials in 1984, Gaines finished second in the 100m freestyle to qualify for the team. At the age of 25, he found himself at the Games as the second oldest in a field of 68 swimmers competing for a lane in the 100m freestyle final. Rowdy made the cut.

Prior to the 100m final, Gaines' coach, Richard Quick, told him that the starter for this event was Panamanian Francisco Silvestri. Silvestri was known to pull the trigger quickly. Quick kept reminding Rowdy to, "Get down."

Armed with this knowledge, Gaines was the first one off the blocks as the gun sounded and he kept the lead throughout the race. Rowdy won his long awaited Olympic gold medal, setting a new Olympic record (49.80).

Gaines went on to anchor both the 400m free and 400m medley relays, garnering two more gold medals, both in world record times.

"I would have said before I came to this meet that the only regret I had in swimming was not going to Moscow. If that's a regret, I can't say that now. Moscow is completely out of my mind now," reflected Gaines. He and teammate Steve Lundquist then joked about being "put out to pasture."

In 1988, Gaines, then 29, just missed qualifying for the Olympic Team and hoped for a comeback in 1992. The summer before those Games, Rowdy was hit with a rare neurological disorder called Guillaine–Barre syndrome. He lay paralyzed in the hospital for two weeks.

SCORE
BOARD

Eighteen year-old American, Mike O'Brien, who swam for the Mission Viejo Club, won the 1500m freestyle title at the Games in Los Angeles. The 1976 Olympic 1500m gold medalist was Brian Goodell, who had also swum for Mission Viejo.

His years of training gave him the strength to fight, and the discipline to endure his long road to rehabilitation. Incredibly, Rowdy went to the 1994 Honolulu Master Championship and set six world records for his age group.

Gaines qualified for the U.S. Olympic Trials in 1996 for both the 50m and 100m freestyle. Instead, he chose to have, "the best seat in the house," as a swim commentator for NBC.

MICHAEL GROSS
WEST GERMANY

A lanky six-foot, seven inches, Michael Gross had arms with a "wing span" of seven feet, four and five-eighths inches. It was his wings that earned him the nickname, "the Albatross."

His win, by two body lengths, in the 200m freestyle, was his country's first swimming gold medal since 1956. Gross won more medals than any other male swimmer in Los Angeles, two gold and two silver.

More than medals, Gross won the hearts and admiration of all whom witnessed his embodiment of the

Courtesy of ISHOF

Michael Gross "The Albatross."

Olympic spirit. After a surprise upset by Australian Jon Sieben, in the 200m butterfly, Gross told the Aussie fans, "To be second in the fastest fly race ever...that's pretty good, I think."

Refusing interviews after his own two gold medal performances, Gross sat next to Sieben, singing the young man's praises to the media. He was more comfortable talking about the accomplishments of others, than of his own.

Prior to the Games in Los Angeles, Gross talked to a journalist from *Sports Illustrated*," "I have nothing to lose in L.A....I have a big chance, really-but only to feel the spirit of the Games, to live with swimmers from other nations in one camp. That is the biggest part of the Games, I think."

At Seoul in 1988, Gross returned and captured the 200m butterfly crown that eluded him in Los Angeles. He also took a bronze, as a member of the 800m freestyle team.

Michael Gross swam for nothing more than fun and self-improvement, and it is this philosophy that earned him a total of six Olympic medals and twelve world records.

NANCY HOGSHEAD
UNITED STATES

Nancy Hogshead has the rare ability to turn tragedy into triumph. After the boycott in 1980, she stayed out of competition for two years. In 1981, as a sophomore at Duke University, the unthinkable happened, the nineteen-year-old was assaulted on campus.

Coached by Mitch Ivey, Hogshead returned to the pool, channeling the intense anger she was feeling into her swimming. A former flyer and IM specialist, Nancy switched her specialty to freestyle. In 1983 she was named the "Comeback Swimmer of the Year."

In Los Angeles, Nancy Hogshead and teammate Carrie Steinseifer finished in a dead heat with a 55.92 in the 100m freestyle final. After a ruling change in 1972, "thousandths of a second" were no longer considered, and so the race stood as a tie.

Hogshead would collect a second gold medal as a member of the 400m freestyle relay. In this event she swam a faster leg than Steinseifer, qualifying her for the anchor spot on the 400m medley relay.

In the 200m individual medley, Nancy finished second for a silver medal, and less than two hours later earned her third gold, swimming anchor on the 400m medley relay team.

In the 200m butterfly race, her fifth and final race of the 1984 Games, Hogshead was struck with a bronchial spasm, yet she managed to place fourth. It was diagnosed later that she suffers from exercise-induced asthma. She would later author <u>Asthma and Exercise</u> and become a spokesperson for the American Lung Association.

Courtesy of ISHOF

Nancy Hogshead, most decorated swimmer of the 1984 Games.

Her advice to today's Olympic hopefuls,

"You'll never be sorry that you went for it 100% — no holds barred – go for it. I had to choose between working to get some work experience on my resume while I was training... or going into debt. I went into debt and made the team versus having something on my resume and no dream fulfilled."

Nancy Hogshead graduated from Georgetown University Law School in 1997.

Olympic 1ST

Swiss Timing

Etienne Dagon won the bronze medal in the 200m breaststroke, Switzerland's first Olympic medal for swimming.

STEVE "LUNK" LUNDQUIST
UNITED STATES

Steve Lundquist was one of a handful of athletes who overcame the disappointment of the 1980 boycott to come back and make the U.S. Team in 1984. Considered one of the premier 100m breaststrokers of the 80's, he lowered the world record in this event five times.

Lundquist captured the gold medal in the first event of the 1984 Olympic Games. The field in the 100m breaststroke event not only included Lundquist's American rival John Moffet, but the 200m breaststroke world record holder, Canadian Victor Davis.

Courtesy of ISHOF

Steve Lundquist's record breaking form.

"Lunk" was the first off the blocks and surfaced two feet ahead of the field, never looking back. He lowered the world record set by Moffet at the U.S. Trials, breaking the 1:02 barrier, and giving America its only individual swimming world record of the Games.

Lundquist and teammate Rowdy Gaines would end their swimming careers in the last event of the 1984 Games. With Rick Carey and Pablo Morales rounding out the 400m medley relay squad, the U.S. handily took gold, blazing to a new world record.

The crowd waved the American flag and chanted "U.S.A.,

U.S.A." for the foursome. Lundquist unrolled a towel that he and his teammates held up for the "home crowd." It read, "America...Thank you for a dream come true."

MARY T. MEAGHER
UNITED STATES

Mary T. Meagher is the greatest women's butterflyer of all time. Remarkably, she still owns the 200m butterfly (2:05.96) long course world record set back in August of 1981. She held the 100m fly record for 18 years until broken in 1999.

Meagher, "Madame Butterfly," swimming to her amazing world record in the 200m butterfly.

Photo by Tim Morse.

Prior to Mary's fifteenth birthday in 1979, she set her first world record in the 200m fly and the following spring did the same in the 100m event.

Meagher qualified for five events, including two relays, on the ill-fated 1980 U.S. Olympic Team. After the boycott, she would continue training in her quest for gold.

As the 1984 Games approached, Mary dropped out of the University of California to train full time with the Mission Viejo Swim Club. The coaches worked on fine tuning her technique and she returned to using a track start off the blocks.

In Los Angeles, Meagher brought her own cheering section, including her parents, one brother, nine sisters, four brother-in-laws, and various friends. They were unmistakable, all sporting their "Mary T" tee shirts.

The 100m fly was Meagher's first event; qualifying first in the final she set a new Olympic record of 59.05. It was the second fastest swim of all time in this event.

During the final, Mary trailed behind teammate Jenna Johnson who had placed first at the U.S. Trials. In the last ten meters Meagher would not be denied, and she surged ahead for the gold.

The medley relay team of Theresa Andrews, Nancy Hogshead, Tracy Caulkins, and Meagher decisively put away the competition. The second place West German team came in three and one–half seconds behind the Americans.

Meagher went on to set a new Olympic record in the 200m butterfly event (2:06.90), a mark that withstood the Centennial Games of 1996. She collected her third gold medal of these Games and she owned the seven fastest times ever recorded in this event. Of her L.A. experience Mary recalls,"

"I guess I'll always envision them as a kind of heaven, sort of a dream world. Only this dream world was real."

Mary T. Meagher returned to the University of California and went on to capture several NCAA titles in the 100y and 200y fly events. In 1987, she was awarded the Honda Broderick Cup, as the country's outstanding female college athlete. Meagher returned to the Olympics in 1988, making her third U.S. Olympic Team and collected a bronze medal for the 200m butterfly event.

Madame Butterfly's legacy and her world records still stand today, untouched by time.

JOHN MOFFET
UNITED STATES

According to his family, John Moffet could swim before he could walk. Moffet beat long time rival Steve Lundquist for the first time ever in the 100m breaststroke event, at the 1984 U.S. Olympic Trials. He did it in style, breaking Lundquist's world record as well.

Then came L.A., where Moffet was the top qualifier in the preliminaries, setting an Olympic record and posting the second fastest swim in this event. Unfortunately, he tore a muscle as he pushed off the wall during his preliminary round and exited the pool limping. By afternoon he could hardly walk.

In spite of the seriousness of his injury, Moffet told ABC-TV, "This is the Olympics, and I'm going to go for it." Steve Lundquist later revealed that Moffet approached him before the final and said, "If something goes haywire with my leg, get the gold for the United States."

John Moffet stood on the block for the Olympic final with his thigh heavily bandaged. Incredibly, he placed fifth. He did not win an Olympic medal, but he won the hearts of all who watched. His quiet, yet heroic performance truly embodied the spirit of the Olympic Games.

JON SIEBEN
AUSTRALIA

At seventeen, Jon Sieben swam to not only the biggest upset of the 1984 Games, but possibly in Olympic history.

OFF THE  *Wall*

"Anne Get Your Crutch"

Infamous for being accident prone, Anne Ottenbrite was unable to swim at the Canadian Olympic Trials due to a dislocation of her kneecap (she was lifting her leg to show off her new shoes and the next thing she knew-no trials). Fortunately, Coach Trevor Tiffany had the foresight to place her on the Olympic team.

Even the Olympic Games did not prevent Anne from getting into some trouble. Ottenbrite was involved in an auto accident and suffered a whiplash injury. Later, while playing a video game, she suffered a minor muscle pull in her thigh. Amazingly, none of these ailments hurt her performance; she left L.A. with three Olympic medals.

His performance in the 200m butterfly was an astounding four seconds faster than his pre-Olympic best.

West German Michael Gross, the world record holder, was considered a "shoe-in." Sieben wasn't believed to be a medal contender. Going into the last lap in fourth place, Sieben saw an opportunity and went for it.

It looked as though Sieben, Gross, Vidal, and Morales had hit the wall simultaneously. The audience and the swimmers looked to the board to see who had won. "I only knew I'd won when I turned around and saw on the board that I'd won," admitted Sieben.

Not only had Sieben beaten "The Albatross," he had broken the world record by one one-hundredth of a second. The crowd gave the young Australian a well-deserved standing ovation. His peers in the water displayed almost as much delight as Sieben himself, after the hard fought race. This was perhaps the greatest gathering of swimmers this event had ever fielded.

CARRIE STEINSEIFER
UNITED STATES

Carrie Steinseifer's dead heat finish with teammate Nancy Hogshead in the 1984 100m freestyle event, gave the United States their first Women's Swimming Championship in an individual event since 1972.

Carrie and Nancy were both awarded gold and Anne-Marie Verstappen received the bronze. No silver medal was awarded.

Olympic 1ST

Seeing Double

Nancy Hogshead and Carrie Steinseifer became the first athletes in Olympic swimming history to each be awarded gold medals in the same event.

The veteran Hogshead and the youngster Steinseifer were roommates during the Olympic Games. Steinseifer, 16, learned that Hogshead started her competitive swim career in 1969 when Carrie was only a year old. Nonetheless, they made a fine team. Carrie took another gold medal with teammates Hogshead, Dara Torres, and Jenna Johnson in the 400m freestyle relay.

CYNTHIA "SIPPY" WOODHEAD
UNITED STATES

In 1976, at the age of twelve, "Sippy" (a name that stuck when her sister could not pronounce Cynthia), entered the first

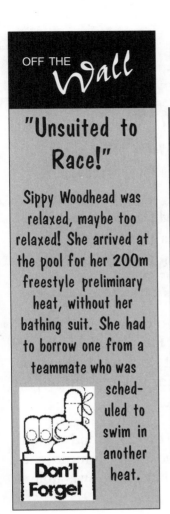

OFF THE *Wall*

"Unsuited to Race!"

Sippy Woodhead was relaxed, maybe too relaxed! She arrived at the pool for her 200m freestyle preliminary heat, without her bathing suit. She had to borrow one from a teammate who was scheduled to swim in another heat.

Don't Forget

of her three Olympic Trials. She placed twenty-fourth in the 200m freestyle.

In 1978 and 1979 Woodhead was the world's best freestyler. Like so many others, her hopes for Olympic glory in 1980 ended with the United States' boycott of the Moscow Games. After struggling through illness, training problems, and injuries, Woodhead, 20, headed for Los Angeles with confidence.

"Sippy" swam to silver in the 200m freestyle, coming in close behind teammate Mary Wayte. A long awaited Olympic medal was finally hers.

MEN'S 800M FREESTYLE RELAY

The men's 800m freestyle relay was considered the most exciting swimming final of these Olympic Games, with the smallest margin of victory ever for this event.

In a preliminary heat the United States "B" relay team of Geoffrey Gaberino, David Larson, Bruce Hayes, and Richard Saeger broke the West Germans' world record, qualifying the United States first with a time of 7:18.87.

U.S. Olympic Coach Don Gambril knew the West Germans would likely put 200m gold medalist Michael Gross in the

LANE LINES

"Worth Her Wayte"

In Los Angeles, nineteen-year-old Mary Wayte pulled ahead in the last 10 meters to touch out teammate Sippy Woodhead for first place in the 200m freestyle.

In 1988, Wayte returned to the Games and placed fourth in the 200m freestyle event, with a faster time than her 1984 winning final. She won a bronze medal at the 1988 Games in the 400m freestyle relay event.

anchor leg of the relay. Hoping to avoid a "touch finish," Gambril changed his team's strategy. He placed his fastest swimmer, 200m freestyle silver medalist Michael Heath, in the lead off spot, hoping to build a lead prior to Gross hitting the water.

Heath did his job, giving David Larson, 25, a body length lead. Larson, who had made the ill fated 1980 Olympic team, swam against West German Dirk Korthals, who was able to cut the American lead to four feet.

Twenty-four year old U.S. Team Captain, Jeff Float, also a member of the 1980 Olympic Team, was next off the blocks. They were up on their feet, cheering him on as he lengthened the American lead to almost three yards. Float touched in at the 600m mark 1.56 seconds ahead of West German Alexander Schwotka.

In spite of a 1.56-second lead, U.S. swimmer Bruce Hayes was up against the fastest 200m freestylist in the world, Michael Gross. As Gross surfaced from his dive he had already cut the lead in half. Hayes, however, had a history of "finishing" in the anchor position.

Gross swam an incredible first 50 meters and by the 100m mark was already even with Hayes. As the American coaches had hoped, Gross didn't swim his race. Normally Gross paced himself over the 200 meters. This time he went out fast, playing catch up with Hayes.

At the final turn, the West German pulled ahead of Hayes by two feet. Undaunted, Hayes pursued Gross, never letting up. The 15,000 spectators were up on their feet, cheering and screaming wildly as Hayes pulled even with Gross, with only 15 meters to go. It appeared that with Gross's long arms, he would have the advantage as the two men battled out the last 10 meters to the finish.

As they both came pounding to the wall, Hayes, with his head down, arms extended underwater, touched the pad. The race was so close the swimmers and spectators alike turned to the scoreboard. The margin of victory was four one–hundreths of a second. The United States had won, setting a new world record of 7:15.69, breaking the record set earlier that day.

In one day the two American free relay teams had shaved five seconds off the previous world record held by the West Germans.

Michael Gross swam an unbelievable split of 1:46.80. It was the fastest split ever recorded. Always the gentleman, Gross had this to say after the race, "I just ran out of gas. That was a really hot race. It was an honorable defeat."

After the foursome received their well-deserved gold medals, Jeff Float, who is hearing impaired, responded to the crowd by signing, "I love you."

1984 OLYMPIC SWIMMING FINALS

INDIVIDUAL EVENTS

	Gold	Silver	Bronze	Fourth	Fifth	Sixth	Seventh	Eighth
Women 100m Freestyle - World and Olympic Record (54.79 Krause GDR 1980)								
	Nancy Hogshead	Carrie Steinseifer	Annemarie Verstappen	Cornelia van Benturn	Michele Pearson	June Croft	Susanne Schuster	Angela Russel
	USA - 55.92	USA - 55.92-Tie	NED - 56.08	NED - 56.43	AUS - 56.83	GBR - 56.90	GER - 57.11	AUS - 58.09
Men 100m Freestyle - World Record (49.36 A. Rowdy Gaines USA) Olympic Record (49.99 James Montgomery USA 1976)								
	Ambrose "Rowdy" Gaines	Mark Stockwell	Per Johansson	Michael Heath	Dano Halsall	Stephan Caron	Dirk Korthals	
	49.80 o	AUS - 50.24	SWE - 50.31	USA - 50.41	SUI - 50.50	FRA - 50.70	GER - 50.93	
Women 200m Freestyle - World Record (1:57.75 Kristin Otto GDR) Olympic Record (1:58.33 Barbara Krause GDR 1980)								
	Mary Wayte	Cynthia Woodhead	Annemarie Verstappen	Michele Pearson	Conelia van Benturn	June Croft	Ina Beyermann	Anna McVann
	USA - 1:59.23	USA - 1:59.50	NED - 1:59.69	AUS - 1:59.79	NED - 2:00.59	GBR - 2:00.64	GER - 2:01.89	AUS - 2:02.87
Men 200m Freestyle - World Record (1:47.55 Michael Gross GER) Olympic Record (1:49.81 Sergei Kopliakov BLR 1980)								
	Michael Gross	Michael Heath	Thomas Fahrner	Jeffrey Float	Alberto Mestre Sosa	Frank Drost	Marco Dell 'Uomo	Peter Dale
	GER - 1:47.44w	USA - 1:49.10	GER - 1:49.69	USA - 1:50.18	VEN - 1:50.23	NED - 1:51.62	ITA - 1:52.20	AUS - 1:53.84

w **World Record**   *o* **Olympic Record**   *p* **Preliminary Heat**   *dq* **Disqualified**   *e* **Equal to World Record**   *eo* **Equal to Olympic Record**
dns **Did Not Start**   *dnf* **Did Not Finish**   *ac* **Also Competed**   *r* **Relay Lead-off Split**   *E* **Estimated**

OLYMPIAD XXIII – 1984 – LOS ANGELES, USA

1984 OLYMPIC SWIMMING FINALS

Gold	Silver	Bronze	Fourth	Fifth	Sixth	Seventh	Eighth
Women 400m Freestyle – World Record (4:06.28 Tracey Wickham AUS)					Olympic Record (4:08.76 Ines Diers GDR 1980)		
Tiffany Cohen	Sarah Hardcastle	June Croft	Kimberly Linehan	Anna McVann	Jolande van der Meer	Birgit Kowalczik	Julie Daigneult
USA – 4:07.10 o	GBR – 4:10.27	GBR – 4:11.49	USA – 4:12.26	AUS – 4:13.95	NED – 4:16.05	GER – 4:16.33	CAN – 4:16.41
Men 400m Freestyle - World Record (3:48.32 Vladimir Salnikov SOV)				Olympic Record (3:51.31 V. Salnikov SOV 1980)			
George DiCarlo	John Mykkanen	Justin Lemberg	Stefan Pfeiffer	Franck Iacono	Darjan Petric	Marco Dell'Uomo	Ronald McKeon
USA – 3:51.23 o	USA – 3:51.49	AUS – 3:51.79	GER – 3:52.91	FRA – 3:54.58	YUG – 3:54.88	ITA – 3:55.44	AUS – 3:55.48
Women 800m Freestyle - World Record (8:24.62 Tracey Wickham AUS)				Olympic Record (8:28.90 Michelle Ford AUS 1980)			
Tiffany Cohen	Michele Richardson	Sarah Hardcastle	Anna McVann	Carla Lasi	Jolande van der Meer	Monica Olmi	Karen Ward
USA – 8:24.95 o	USA – 8:30.73	GBR – 8:32.60	AUS – 8:37.94	ITA – 8:42.45	NED – 8:42.86	ITA – 8:47.32	CAN – 8:48.12
Men 1500m Freestyle - World Record (14:54.76 V. Salnikov SOV)				Olympic Record (14:58.27 V. Salnikov SOV 1980)			
Michael O'Brien	George DiCarlo	Stefan Pfeiffer	Rainer Henkel	Franck Iacono	Stefano Grandi	David Shemilt	Wayne Shillington
USA – 15:05.20	USA – 15:10.59	GER – 15:12.11	GER – 15:20.03	FRA – 15:26.96	ITA – 15:28.58	CAN – 15:31.28	AUS – 15:38.18
Women 100m Backstroke - World and Olympic Record (1:00.86 Rica Reinisch GDR 1980)							
Theresa Andrews	Betsy Mitchell	Jolanda de Rover	Carmen Bunaciu	Aneta Patrascoiu	Svenja Schlicht	Beverley Rose	Carmel Clark
USA – 1:02.55	USA – 1:02.63	NED – 1:02.91	ROM – 1:03.21	ROM – 1:03.29	GER – 1:03.46	GBR – 1:04.16	NZE – 1:04.47
Men 100m Backstroke - World Record (55.19 Richard Carey USA)				Olympic Record (55.49 John Naber USA 1976)			
Richard Carey	David Wilson	Mike West	Gary Hurring	Mark Kerry	Bengt Baron	Donald "Sandy" Goss	Hans Kroes
USA – 55.79	USA – 56.35	CAN – 56.49	NZE – 56.90	AUS – 57.18	SWE – 57.34	CAN – 57.46	NED – 58.07

1984 OLYMPIC SWIMMING FINALS

	Gold	Silver	Bronze	Fourth	Fifth	Sixth	Seventh	Eighth
Women 200m Backstroke - World Record (2:09.91 Cornelia Sirch GDR) Olympic Record (2:11.77 Rica Reinisch GDR 1980)								
	Jolanda de Rover NED - 2:12.38	Amy White USA - 2:13.04	Aneta Patrascoiu ROM - 2:13.29	Georgina Parkes AUS - 2:14.37	Tori Trees USA - 2:15.73	Svenja Schlicht GER - 2:15.93	Carmen Buenaciu ROM - 2:16.15	Carmel Clark NZE - 2:17.89
Men 200m Backstroke - World Record (1:58.86 Richard Carey USA) Olympic Record (1:59.19 John Naber USA 1976)								
	Richard Carey p - 1:58.99 o USA - 2:00.23	Frédéric Delcour FRA - 2:01.75	Cameron Henning CAN - 2:02.37	Ricardo Prado BRA - 2:03.05	Gary Hurring NZE - 2:03.10	Nicolai Klapkarek GER - 2:03.95	Ricardo Aldabe ESP - 2:04.53	David Orbell AUS - 2:04.61
Women 100m Breaststroke - World Record (1:08.51 Ute Geweniger GDR) Olympic Record (1:10.11 U. Geweniger GDR 1980)								
	Petra van Staveren NED - 1:09.88 o	Anne Ottenbrite CAN - 1:10.69	Catherine Poirot FRA - 1:10.70	Tracy Caulkins USA - 1:10.88	Eva-Marie Hakansson SWE - 1:11.14	Hiroko Nagasaki JPN - 1:11.33	Susan Rapp USA - 1:11.45	Jean Hill GBR - 1:11.82
Men 100m Breaststroke - World Record (1:02.13 John Moffet USA) Olympic Record (1:03.11 John Hencken USA 1976)								
	Steve Lundquist USA - 1:01.65 w	Victor Davis CAN - 1:01.99	Peter Evans AUS - 1:02.97	Adrian Moorhouse GBR - 1:03.25	John Moffet USA - 1:03.29	Brett Stocks AUS - 1:03.49	Gerald Mörken GER - 1:03.95	Raffaele Avagnano ITA - 1:04.11
Women 200m Breaststroke - World Record (2:28.36 L. Kaciušyte SOV) Olympic Record (2:29.54 L. Kaciusyte SOV 1980)								
	Anne Ottenbrite CAN - 2:30.38	Susan Rapp USA - 2:31.15	Ingrid Lempereur BEL - 2:31.40	Hiroko Nagasaki JPN - 2:32.93	Sharon Kellett AUS - 2:33.60	Ute Hasse GER - 2:33.82	Susannah Brownsdon GBR - 2:35.07	Kimberly Rhodenbaugh USA - 2:35.51
Men 200m Breaststroke - World Record (2:14.58 Victor Davis CAN) Olympic Record (2:15.11 David Wilkie GBR 1976)								
	Victor Davis CAN - 2:13.34w	Glenn Beringen AUS - 2:15.79	Etienne Dagon SUI - 2:17.41	Richard Schroeder USA - 2:18.03	Ken Fitzpatrick CAN - 2:18.86	Pablo Restrepo COL - 2:18.96	Alexandre Yokochi POR - 2:20.69	Marco Del Prete ITA - dq

1984 OLYMPIC SWIMMING FINALS

Gold	Silver	Bronze	Fourth	Fifth	Sixth	Seventh	Eighth
Women 100m Butterfly - World Record (57.93 Mary T. Meagher USA) Olympic Record (1:00.13 Kornelia Ender GDR 1976)							
Mary Meagher p - 59.05 υ	Jenna Johnson	Karin Seick	Annemarie Verstappen	Michelle MacPherson	Janet Tibbits	Cornelia van Bentum	Ina Beyermann
USA – 59.26	USA – 1:00.19	GER – 1:01.36	NED – 1:01.56	CAN – 1:01.58	AUS – 1:01.78	NED – 1:01.94	GER – 1:02.11
Men 100m Butterfly - World Record (53.38 Pablo Morales USA) Olympic Record (54.27 Mark Spitz USA 1972)							
Michael Gross	Pablo Morales	Glenn Buchanan	Rafael Vidal Castro	Andrew Jameson	Anthony Mosse	Andreas Behrend	Bengt Baron
GER – 53.08 w	USA – 53.23	AUS – 53.85	VEN – 54.27	GBR – 54.28	NZE – 54.93	GER – 54.95	SWE – 55.14
Women 200m Butterfly - World Record (2:05.96 Mary T. Meagher USA) Olympic Record (2:10.44 Ines Geissler GDR 1980)							
Mary T. Meagher	Karen Phillips	Ina Beyermann	Nancy Hogshead	Samantha Purvis	Naoko Kume	Sonja Hausladen	Cornelia van Bentum
USA – 2:06.90υ	AUS – 2:10.56	GER – 2:11.91	USA – 2:11.98	GBR – 2:12.33	JPN – 2:12.57	AUT – 2:15.38	NED – 2:17.39
Men 200m Butterfly - World Record (1:57.05 Michael Gross GER) Olympic Record (1:59.23 Mike Bruner USA 1976)							
Jonathon Sieben	Michael Gross	Rafael Vidal Castro	Pablo Morales	Anthony Mosse	Thomas Ponting	Peter Ward	Patrick Kennedy
AUS – 1:57.04w	GER – 1:57.40	VEN – 1:57.51	USA – 1:57.75	NZE – 1:58.75	CAN – 1:59.37	CAN – 2:00.39	USA – 2:01.03
Women 200m Individual Medley - World Record (2:11.73 U.Geweniger GDR) 1976-1980 - Event Not Held On Olympic Program							
Tracy Caulkins	Nancy Hogshead	Michele Pearson	Lisa Curry	Christiane Pielke	Manuela Dalla Valle	Petra Zindler	Katrine Bomstad
USA – 2:12.64 o	USA – 2:15.17	AUS – 2:15.92	AUS – 2:16.75	GER – 2:17.82	ITA – 2:19.69	GER – 2:19.86	NOR – 2:20.48
Men 200m Individual Medley – World Record (2:02.45 Alex Baumann CAN) Olympic Record (2:07.17 G. Larsson SWE 1972)							
Alex Baumann	Pablo Morales	Neil Cochran	Robin Brew	Steve Lundquist	Andrew Phillips	Nicolai Klapkarek	Ralf Diegel
CAN– 2:01.42 w	USA – 2:03.05	GBR – 2:04.38	GBR – 2:04.52	USA – 2:04.91	JAM – 2:05.60	GER – 2:05.88	GER – 2:06.66

1984 OLYMPIC SWIMMING FINALS

Gold	Silver	Bronze	Fourth	Fifth	Sixth	Seventh	Eighth
Women 400m Individual Medley - World Record (4:36.10 P.Schneider GDR) Olympic Record (4:36.29 Schneider GDR 1980)							
Tracy Caulkins	Suzanne Landells	Petra Zindler	Susan Heon	Nathalie Gingras	Donna McGinnis	Gaynor Stanley	Katrine Bomstad
USA – 4:39.24	AUS – 4:48.30	GER – 4:48.57	USA – 4:49.41	CAN – 4:50.55	CAN – 4:50.65	GBR – 4:52.83	NOR – 4:53.28
Men 400m Individual Medley - World Record (4:17.53 A. Baumann CAN) Olympic Record (4:22.89 O. Sydorenko SOV 1980)							
Alex Baumann	Ricardo Prado	Robert Woodhouse	Jesse Vassallo	Maurizio Divano	Jeffrey Kostoff	Stephen Poulter	Giovanni Franceschi
CAN – 4:17.41w	BRA – 4:18.45	AUS – 4:20.50	USA – 4:21.46	ITA – 4:22.76	USA – 4:23.28	GBR – 4:25.80	ITA – 4:26.05

1984 OLYMPIC SWIMMING FINALS

RELAY EVENTS

Women 400m Medley Relay - World Record (4:05.79 GDR)   Olympic Record (4:06.67 GDR 1980)

Gold	Silver	Bronze	Fourth	Fifth	Sixth	Seventh	Eighth
Theresa Andrews, Tracy Caulkins, Mary T. Meagher, Nancy Hogshead, *p* - Betsy Mitchell, Susan Rapp, Jenna Johnson, Carrie Steinseifer	Svenja Schlicht, Ute Hasse, Ina Beyermann, Karin Seick	Reema Abdo, Anne Ottenbrite, Michelle MacPherson, Pamela Rai	Beverley Rose, Jean Hill, Nicola Fibbens, June Croft	Manuela Carosi, Manuela Dalla Valle, Roberta Lanzarotti, Silvia Persi	Eva Gysling, Patricia Brülhart, Carole Brook, Marie-Thérèse Armentero	Naomi Sekido, Hiroko Nagasaki, Naoko Kume, Kaori Yanase	Anna-Karin Eriksson, Eva-Marie Håkansson, Agneta Eriksson, Maria Kardum
USA – 4:08.34	GER – 4:11.97	CAN – 4:12.98	GBR – 4:14.05	ITA – 4:17.40	SUI – 4:19.02	JPN – *dq*	SWE – *dq*

Men 400m Medley Relay - World Record (3:40.42 USA)   Olympic Record (3:42.22 USA 1976)

Gold	Silver	Bronze	Fourth	Fifth	Sixth	Seventh	Eighth
Richard Carey, Steve Lundquist, Pablo Morales, Rowdy Gaines, *p* - David Wilson, Richard Schroeder, Michael Heath, Thomas Jager	Mike West, Victor Davis, Thomas Ponting, Donald "Sandy" Goss	Mark Kerry, Peter Evans, Glenn Buchanan, Mark Stockwell, *p* - Jonathan Sieben, Neil Brooks	Stefan Peter, Gerald Mörken, Michael Gross, Dirk Korthals, *p* - Andreas Behrend, Alexander Schowtka	Bengt Baron, Peter Berggren, Thomas Lejdström, Per Johansson, *p* - Michael Söderlund	Neil Harper, Adrian Moorhouse, Andrew Jameson, Richard Burrell, *p* - David Lowe	Patrick Ferland, Etienne Dagon, Theophile David, Dano Halsall	Daichi Suzuki, Shigehiro Takashashi, Taihei Saka, Hiroshi Sakamoto
USA – 3:39.30w	CAN – 3:43.23	AUS – 3:43.25	GER – 3:44.26	SWE – 3:47.13	GBR – 3:47.39	SUI – 3:47.93	JPN – *dq*

1984 OLYMPIC SWIMMING FINALS

Women 400m Freestyle Relay – World and Olympic Record (3:42.71 GDR 1980)

	Gold	Silver	Bronze	Fourth	Fifth	Sixth	Seventh	Eighth
Swimmers	Jenna Johnson, Carrie Steinseifer, Dara Torres, Nancy Hogshead, *p* - Jill Sterkel, Mary Wayte	Annemarie Verstappen, Elles Voskes, Desi Reijers, Cornielia van Bentum, *p* - Wilma van Velsen	Iris Zscherpe, Susanne Schuster, Christiane Pielke, Karin Seick	Michele Pearson, Angela Russel, Anna McVann, Lisa Curry, *p* - Janet Tibbits	Pamela Rai, Carol Klimpel, Cheryl McArton, Jane Kerr, *p* - Maureen New	June Croft, Nicola Fibbens, Debra Gore, Annabelle Cripps	Maria Kardum, Agneta Eriksson, Petra Hilder, Karin Furuhed, *p* - Malin Rundgren	Caroline Amoric, Sophie Kamoun, Veronique Jardin, Laurence Bensimon
	USA – 3:43.43	NED – 3:44.40	GER – 3:45.56	AUS – 3:47.79	CAN – 3:49.50	GBR – 3:50.12	SWE – 3:51.24	FRA – 3:52.15

Men 400m Freestyle Relay - World Record (3:19.26 USA)

	Gold	Silver	Bronze	Fourth	Fifth	Sixth	Seventh	Eighth
Swimmers	Christopher Cavanaugh, Michael Heath, Matthew Biondi, Rowdy Gaines, *p* - Thomas Jager, Robin Leamy	Gregory Fasala, Neil Brooks, Michael Delany, Mark Stockwell	Thomas Lejdström, Bengt Baron, Mikael Örn, Per Johansson, *p* - Richard Milton, Michael Söerlund	Dirk Korthals, Andreas Schmidt, Alexander Schowtka, Michael Gross, *p* - Nicolai Klapkarek	David Lowe, Roland Lee, Paul Easter, Richard Burrell	Stephan Caron, Laurent Neuville, Dominique Bataille, Bruno Lesaffre	David Churchill, Blair Hicken, Alex Baumann, Donald "Sandy" Goss, *p* - Levente Mady	Marcello Guarducci, Marco Colombo, Metello Savino, Fabrizio Rampasso, *p* - Raffaele Franceschi
	USA – 3:19.03w	AUS – 3:19.68	SWE – 3:22.69	GER – 3:22.98	GBR – 3:23.61	FRA – 3:24.70	CAN – 3:24.70	ITA – 3:24.97

1976-1980 - Event Not Held On Olympic Program

1984 OLYMPIC SWIMMING FINALS

Gold	Silver	Bronze	Fourth	Fifth	Sixth	Seventh	Eighth
Men 800m Freestyle Relay - World Record (7:20.40 GER)						Olympic Record (7:23.22 USA 1976)	
Michael Heath, David Larson, Jeffrey Float, L. Bruce Hayes *p* - Geoffrey Gamerino, Richard Saeger	Thomas Fahrner, Dirk Korthals, Alexander Schowtka, Michael Gross *p* - Rainer Henkel	Neil Cochran, Paul Easter, Paul Howe, Andrew Astbury	Peter Dale, Justin Lemberg, Ronald McKeon, Graeme Brewer *P* - Thomas Stachewicz	Donald "Sandy" Goss, Wayne Kelly, Peter Szmidt, Alex Baumann *p* - Benoit Clement	Michael Söderlund, Tommy Werner, Anders Holmertz, Thomas Lejdström *p* - Mikael Orn	Hans Kroes, Peter Drost, Edsard Schlingemann, Frank Drost	Stephan Caron, Dominique Bataille, Michel Pou, Pierre Andraca
USA – 7:15.69w	GER – 7:15.73	GBR – 7:24.78	AUS – 7:25.63	CAN – 7:26.51	SWE – 7:26.53	NED – 7:26.72	FRA – 7:30.16

Chapter 22

Olympiad XXIV - 1988
Seoul, Korea

The 1988 Olympic Games were held in Seoul, a city of 10 million people and the capital of South Korea. The government spent 3.1 billion dollars in preparation for these Games. The stadiums, facilities, and equipment were state of the art.

South Korea, which had been devastated by war, had evolved into a modern, industrialized country. Their theme for these Olympic Games was "Harmony and Progress." The Koreans' attention to detail was incredible. Their country was set on "daylight savings time" so that Americans could see their athletes performing in "prime time."

As the Olympic flame was lit during the opening ceremony, five jets flew over the Olympic Stadium, emitting colored

Olympic 1ST Winning Their Firsts

Sixteen-year-old Zhuang Yong of China was a surprise medalist, capturing the silver in the 100m freestyle final. She was the first Chinese swimmer to win an Olympic medal.

Six foot three inch, Silvia Poll, won Costa Rica's first Olympic medal, with her silver medal performance in the 200m freestyle final.

smoke forming the five Olympic rings.

For the first time since Montreal in 1976, the "world" would compete again. "East" and "West" were brought together and there were no boycotts. Almost 10,000 athletes, representing a record breaking 160 countries, came to compete.

The Olympic Swim program expanded, as did many other competitions. The 50m freestyle event was added to both the men and women's docket, making it the largest ever with 31 events (16 men/15 women). The "submarine start" was seen for the first time in Olympic competition, leading to considerable controversy.

The East German women were back to dominate the pool with Kristin Otto winning a record six gold medals. This team would capture ten of the fifteen titles, taking home nearly half of the total medals available on the women's program. As previously mentioned, the East German's accomplishments have been clouded with the admitted steroid use by their country's athletic program. This practice victimized not only the competition, but their own athletes as well.

Only American Janet Evans' three victories prevented a sweep by the Eastern European women. In the men's program, the Americans were able to sweep all three relays. A record number of 21 different countries were awarded medals during the Olympic swimming competition with nine different countries standing on the gold medal platform.

medal count

Chris Jacobs - U.S.A.

400m Free Relay – Gold
400m Medley Relay – Gold
100m Freestyle - Silver

DUNCAN ARMSTRONG
AUSTRALIA

OFF THE Wall

Sneak Preview

Duncan Armstrong entered the Games ranked 46th in the world in the 200m freestyle event. He left with its championship and garnered a silver medal in the 400m freestyle event as well.

The Olympic final in the 200m event in 1988 represented one of the strongest gatherings of competition this event had fielded in some time. It featured 200m freestyle world record holder, Michael Gross of West Germany; the 100m world record holder, American Matt Biondi; and the 400m freestyle world record holder and fastest qualifier, Artur Wojdat of Poland.

During the race, Armstrong found himself in third with 50 meters to go. Coming out of the turn he passed Anders Holmertz of Sweden and, in the final 25 meters, pulled ahead of Biondi for the victory. Coincidentally, both Jon Sieben's and Armstrong's upsets were swum in Australia's "lucky lane six."

Armstrong broke Michael Gross'

The events leading up to the 200m freestyle final are as much a part of the outcome as the race itself. Australia's Duncan Armstrong's coach was Lawrie Laurence.

Prior to the final, Laurence broke into a locked video tape room to replay and study the 200m free preliminary heats. After this "review session," Laurence put together a strategy for Armstrong. He advised Duncan to draft off Biondi, who would undoubtedly take the lead. By doing so, Armstrong would be able to save his energy for the final 50 meters.

Laurence had coached Jon Sieben in 1984, when Sieben defeated Michael Gross in one of the biggest Olympic upsets ever witnessed.

five-year hold on the 200m freestyle world record, with a time of 1:47.25. This also represented Australia's 100th Olympic swimming medal (not counting the obstacle course medal in 1900). After winning, Armstrong proclaimed to his country, "Hello, Australia! We just won the gold and it's a bloody enormous feeling!"

MATT BIONDI
UNITED STATES

Matt Biondi holds the record for winning more Olympic medals than any other American, an honor he shares with swimmer Mark Spitz and shooter Carl Osburn. Competing in three Olympics, he has a total medal count of eleven.

Not a serious swimmer until the age of fifteen, Matt made his first Olympic appearance in Los Angeles. He was relatively unknown, but his anonymity would be short lived. He left L.A. with gold as a member of the 400m freestyle relay team.

Photo by Tim Morse

Holder of eleven Olympic medals, Matt Biondi in victory.

Biondi would represent the University of California at Berkeley in the NCAA's. As the 1988 Olympic Games approached, Matt Biondi was America's brightest hope for Olympic glory.

A private person, Biondi liked the fact that in L.A. he was an unknown and could enjoy the opening ceremonies. Seoul was a different story. He was thrust into the limelight and faced a seven-event schedule. Matt elected not to march in the opening ceremonies.

Matt's first event in Korea was the 200m freestyle. He came in third. Defending himself from a comment made by a television commentator that "Biondi had settled for bronze," he said, "I didn't settle for it, I earned it. I know a lot of people who would love to settle for an Olympic bronze medal."

In the 100m butterfly event, Biondi lead for 99 meters when he misjudged the distance to the wall. Matt elected to glide in kicking instead of taking another stroke, allowing Anthony Nesty of Surinam to slip in and out-touch him for the gold. Matt later reflected, "One hundredth of a second-what if I had grown my fingernails longer?"

It was on to the 100m freestyle. Biondi held the ten fastest times in this event. His time in the final was 48.63, an Olympic record that still stands (1996). His world record time was not beaten until Alexander Popov of Russia did so in 1994.

Biondi's momentum continued. He won the 50m freestyle event, setting a new world record of 22.14. He beat long time rival and friend, American Tom Jager, for the first time in two years in this event. World marks continued to fall, as Biondi went on to set three more with all three relay teams.

When the Olympic Games of Seoul had come to a close, Matt Biondi had seven Olympic medals. He left thinking that his days of Olympic competitive swimming were over and that if he did return, it would be as part of the U.S. Water Polo Team.

Four years later, during the Barcelona Olympics, the world watched Matt Biondi once again mount the starting block. He won a silver medal in the 50m final, and a gold medal for

SCORE

BOARD

The American women have captured gold in the 400m freestyle event at every Olympiad attended with the exception of 1936, 1952 and 1988 where they were the bronze medalists.

swimming the second leg of the 400m freestyle relay. His qualifying swim for the 400m medley relay team earned him yet another gold.

Matt Biondi left Barcelona with three more Olympic medals, earning his place among the world's greatest swimming legends.

TANIA DANGALAKOVA
BULGARIA

Tania Dangalakova, age 23, gave birth to a baby girl in June of 1987 and required surgery in October of that same year. With her husband Jorgi Dangalakova coaching her, she resumed training seriously in January of 1988.

Dangalakova set a new Olympic record at the

First Time for Bulgaria

Tania Dangalakova's win in the 100m breaststroke final represented Bulgaria's first Olympic swimming gold medal ever.

1988 Games, missing the world record in the 100m breaststroke by only four hundredths of a second.

Seventeen-year-old Bulgarian teammmate Antoaneta Frenkova captured the silver medal in the 100m breaststroke. Their 1-2 finish was a first-ever in Olympic history for Bulgaria.

TAMAS DARNYI
HUNGARY

At the age of fifteen, Tamas Darnyi was blinded in one eye during a friendly snowball fight. Several surgeries for the detached retina only restored light sensitivity.

Darnyi came into the Seoul Games as the world record holder in the 200m and the 400m IM. He had not lost a major championship in either of these events in three years.

Tamas Darnyi sweeps I.M. events in back to back Olympics.

Photo by Tim Morse

During the 200m individual medley final, the 21 year-old Darnyi was in third place after 150 meters. As was his style, he powered through the water, clocking a 27.73 in the final freestyle leg to break his own world record. The 400m event was much the same. Darnyi not only captured gold, but set another world mark as well.

As the 1992 Games approached, Darnyi's winning streak was still intact. In Barcelona, he repeated his IM sweep. Tamas Darnyi is the only swimmer to accomplish back to back Olympic championships in both the 200m and 400m individual UWE medley events.

Silke Hörner — Daniela Hunger
German Democratic Republic

Silke Hörner captured the 200m breaststroke title and reclaimed the world record in the process. It was the third time Hörner had broken the record for this event. Hörner captured a bronze medal in the 100m breaststroke and a gold with the medley relay team.

Sixteen-year-old Daniela Hunger of Berlin won two gold medals and one bronze in Seoul. She set a new Olympic record in the 200m IM. Hunger captured a second gold medal as a member of the 400m freestyle relay team and her bronze was won in the 400m individual medley.

UWE DASSLER
GERMAN DEMOCRATIC REPUBLIC

After one of the hardest fought battles in the pool at Seoul, 21 year old Uwe Dassler claimed victory in the 400m freestyle event. All eight competitors had broken Thomas Fahner's 1984 Olympic record just to make the final.

In the final more records would fall. Dassler, followed closely by Duncan Armstrong and Artur Wojdat, broke the world record set by Wojdat earlier that year. Armstrong and Wojdat also eclipsed the old mark.

Dassler left the Games in Seoul with more than a gold, winning a bronze medal for the 1500m free, and a silver with the 800m freestyle relay.

L A N E   L I N E S

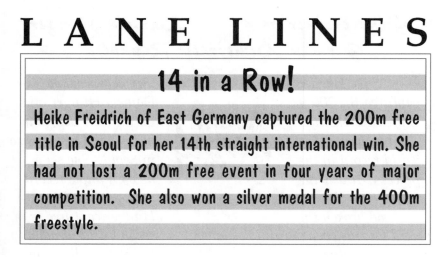

14 in a Row!

Heike Freidrich of East Germany captured the 200m free title in Seoul for her 14th straight international win. She had not lost a 200m free event in four years of major competition. She also won a silver medal for the 400m freestyle.

JANET EVANS
UNITED STATES

Janet Evans was a natural born swimmer who qualified for her first Junior Olympics at the age of eleven. In 1987, at all of 95 pounds and fifteen years of age, Janet set her first world record.

Using what is considered an unorthodox windmill stroke and having to take more strokes overall due to her diminutive size, Evans continued to astound the swimming world.

Evans held the "triple," that is, the 400m, 800m, and 1500m freestyle world records. It had been a decade since that had been accomplished. Evans was the first woman to break the sixteen-minute barrier in the 1500m freestyle, lowering her own world record by over eight seconds to an unbelievable 15.52.10.

In Seoul, it was the seventeen-year-old Evans who would

LANE LINES

Record Breaker[3]

Fifteen-year-old Janet Evans set her first world record in the 800m freestyle, breaking a seven-year-old record. In the 1500m freestyle, she snapped a record that was almost nine years old. Later that year, Evans also captured Tracy Wickham's nine-year-old record in the 400m free event.

win the first gold medal for the United States. She took the 400m individual medley event and collected her second medal in the 400m freestyle, along with a new world record. Her time of 4:03.85 still stands (1996). It was the first time in competition that Evans had actually "negative split" the last 200 meters (2:02.14/2:01.71).

Evans' win in the 800m event gave her three gold medals in Seoul. She out swam East Germany's Astrid Strauss and Australian Julie McDonald, who had placed ahead of Evans a year earlier in this event. Janet Evans was the only American female swimmer to return home from Seoul with gold.

Photo by Tim Morse

The great distance swimmer, Janet Evans, holds more individual Olympic gold medals than any other female U.S. swimmer to date.

In 1992, Evans was once again on the U.S. Olympic Team, qualifying for both the 400m and 800m freestyle events. In Barcelona she became the first person ever to win back to back Olympic gold medals for the 800m event.

In the 400m freestyle race, she captured silver, bringing her six-year winning streak for this event to an end.

For the third time in her incredible career, Janet Evans returned to the Olympic Games in 1996, an amazing feat in itself, but even more so for a distance swimmer. Here she was honored during the Opening Ceremonies with the privilege of carrying the Olympic torch as the last runner, passing it on to former Olympic boxer Muhammad Ali, who lit the Olympic Flame.

Evans placed fifth in the 800m final but missed making the final in the 400m event, with a ninth place finish in the preliminaries. She did not medal in Atlanta, but her world records stood. Janet Evans remains the fastest distance swimmer of all time and her four Olympic individual gold medals are the most won by an American female swimmer to date.

It is hard to believe that a town like Collinsville, Illinois, with no swim club or training pool, could produce an Olympic swimming champion. When

"E-fish-ient Evans"

Prior to the Games in Seoul, Janet Evans was tested for energy efficiency. Dr. John Troup, Director of Sports Medicine and Science for U.S. Swimming said of Janet, "She is the most energy efficient machine in the water today, male or female." He went on to say, "Janet uses less oxygen, or less energy, to swim at a fast pace than anybody I've ever seen. I'll stop short of saying Janet's a fish but physiologically she's very similar."

it comes to Tom Jager, one can quickly become a believer.

Jager ruled the 50m freestyle long before it became an international event at the World Championships in 1986. He won it there and kept on winning it.

Photo by Tim Morse

The infamous Jager Start

"The 50 leaves no room for error. It's an event of nerves, pressure and precision. An extra breath can cost you the race."

Tom Jager

The Games in Seoul would be the first Olympics to see the 50m freestyle on the men's program. Jager, the current world record holder would be there. His biggest rival was fellow American Matt Biondi. The two had previously faced each other 14 times, with Jager winning ten of those races. It had been two years since Biondi had beaten Jager in this event.

The stage was set for a duel in the pool. Jager had another of his phenomenally quick starts, but this time Biondi was able to stay with him and power past Jager to the finish giving America a 1-2 finish.

Jager won two relay gold medals in L.A. for swimming as an alternate in qualifying heats. He captured gold in Seoul with the 400m free relay team, swimming the second fastest leg and helping the team set a world record. A second gold was his at these same Games, with the medley relay team. Jager swam in the preliminary heat that qualified the U.S. Team.

In 1992, Tom Jager qualified for his third consecutive Olympiad. He captured gold as a member of the 400m freestyle relay team and once again stood on the blocks in the 50m final with the best in the world. He earned a bronze behind Russian Alexander Popov and longtime rival Matt Biondi.

Jager's world record time of 21.81 seconds for the 50m freestyle, set in March of 1990, still stands today, making Tom Jager the fastest swimmer of all time.

Tom Jager's and Matt Biondi's contributions to the sport of swimming go far beyond the pool. Each was a force behind the movement to allow swimmers to reap financial rewards for their athletic success. F.I.N.A. now allows athletes to accept endorsement money and limited assistance from their national federations. This ruling enables swimmers to extend their swimming careers.

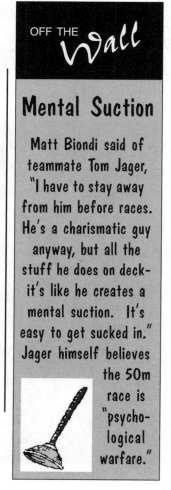

OFF THE *Wall*

Mental Suction

Matt Biondi said of teammate Tom Jager, "I have to stay away from him before races. He's a charismatic guy anyway, but all the stuff he does on deck—it's like he creates a mental suction. It's easy to get sucked in." Jager himself believes the 50m race is "psychological warfare."

ADRIAN MOORHOUSE
GREAT BRITAIN

In 1976, Great Britain's David Wilkie swam to gold in the 200m breaststroke in the Montreal Games. Back in England, a

SCORE
BOARD

"New Wave Breaststrokers"

Both Hungarian József Szabó and American Mike Barrowman, competed in the 200m breaststroke final in Seoul, using the new "wave-action" technique.

Gold	József Szabó	HUN	2:13.52
Silver	Nicholas Gillingham	GBR	2:14.12
Bronze	Sergio Lopez	SPA	2:15.21
4th Place	Michael Barrowman	USA	2:15.45

twelve-year-old named Adrian Moorhouse anxiously watched on television and thought, "I want one of those."

Eight years later, Moorhouse was in Los Angeles trying to do just that. He finished fourth in the 100m breaststroke final and out of medal contention. Before returning home, Moorhouse's former Sunday school teacher sent him a telegram reading, "Very bad luck, all proud of you. There will be a next time."

As the Seoul Games approached Moorhouse was the undisputed favorite. During 1986, 1987, and 1988, he had put out the fastest times in the world and qualified first in the preliminaries in Seoul. He was just one race away.

It didn't come easy. At the 50m mark Adrian was in sixth

place. He reached down inside and gave it all he had. At the finish he looked up, uncertain, only to find that he had edged out Hungarian Károly Güttler by just one hundredth of a second.

It took twelve years but Adrian Moorhouse had his gold. In the box that holds his Olympic medal, he placed that insightful telegram from 1984, "There will be a next time."

ANTHONY NESTY
SURINAM

Olympic 1ST
First Time for Surinam

Surinam's first Olympic medal came with Anthony Nesty's 100m butterfly win. This victory marked the first Olympic gold medal by a black swimmer.

The small country of Surinam, whose entire population numbers 380,000, has only one Olympic-size swimming pool. As the Seoul Games approached, Surinam had yet to win its first Olympic medal in any sport. Anthony Nesty changed all that with his win in the 100m butterfly, upsetting Matt Biondi by one inch!

Returning home, Nesty was given a hero's welcome. He returned to the Games in 1992 and won a bronze medal in the same event.

KRISTIN OTTO
GERMAN DEMOCRATIC REPUBLIC

After the disappointment of East Germany's boycott of the L.A. Games, Kristin Otto suffered a cracked vertebra in her neck. Recovering in 1985, she returned to the rigors of train-

Courtesy of ISHOF

Kristin Otto, winner of six gold medals.

ing, ignoring warnings from her doctors.

At the World Championships in 1986, she proved she was back. She won four gold and two silver medals. In two of those races, Otto swam in events she had never before swum in international competition.

When the Games in Seoul arrived, they marked the end of an eleven-year journey for Otto, a journey that began with her being appointed to a state run sports school in East Germany at the age of eleven.

Otto's individual event victories showed her amazing versatility. She won gold medals in the 100m freestyle, 100m backstroke and 100m butterfly. In its first Olympic appearance, the 50m freestyle also saw Otto emerge as something of a surprise victor.

Otto and teammates set Olympic records in both **Olympic 1ST**

Golden Olympian

In Seoul, 22-year old Kristin Otto made a place for herself in Olympic history. She accomplished what no other female athlete had, winning six Olympic gold medals in one Olympiad. This amazing feat remains untied and unbroken to this day.

the 400m free and 400m medley relays, easily out-swimming the competition. Surprisingly, no world records were set in either of the relays or in any of Otto's individual victories. Kristin Otto was voted the "Outstanding Competitor" of the 1988 Olympic Games.

SPLASH BACK

A Twelve Year Medal Reunion

Jill Sterkel won her first medal at the 1976 Games. With her bronze medal performance in 1988 she became the first female swimmer ever to win Olympic medals twelve years apart.

JILL STERKEL
UNITED STATES

At the age of 27, Jill Sterkel was the co-captain and, oldest member of the U.S. swimming squad going to Seoul. Just making the team gave her a spot in Olympic swimming history. Never before had a swimmer qualified for four consecutive Olympiads.

In 1976, as a member of the 400m freestyle relay team, Jill captured her first gold medal. That victory represented a hard fought battle and was the only gold won by the American's Women's Swim Team that year. Then, as a member of the U.S. 1980 Olympic Team, Sterkel faced the disappointment of the boycott.

At the Games of Los Angeles, Jill earned gold as an alternate with the 400m free relay squad. That foursome's qualifying race in the preliminaries came in over three seconds faster than the second place team. Sterkel's split of 55.42 during the qualifying heat was the fastest running split swum, including the finals.

Jill Sterkel, first swimmer from the U.S. to qualify for four consecutive Olympic Games.

Photo by Tim Morse

Four years later Sterkel once again represented her country at the Olympic Games. Jill qualified for the 50m freestyle and tied for third, with fifteen-year-old Katrin Meissner, of East Germany. Both were awarded a bronze medal, clocking in at 25.71 seconds. Jill Sterkel earned another bronze in Seoul as an alternate on the 400m freestyle relay team.

LANE LINES

A Close Second

In the 50m freestyle final, American Leigh Ann Fetter, finished just behind bronze medalist Jill Sterkel, who was an assistant swim coach at Texas where Fetter swam.

DAVID WHARTON
UNITED STATES

David Wharton was America's hope for a medal in the 400m individual medley. He held the world record briefly in August of 1987, only to have it broken five days later by Tamas Darnyi. It was Darnyi who would again deny him. Wharton earned silver in Seoul.

On one occasion Wharton swam a 16,000m IM at practice, taking him almost four hours to complete the nine-mile swim. At another practice session, Wharton swam for a total of 65,000 yards. He swam two hours on and one hour off over a 24-hour period!

Wharton, who is hearing impaired, returned to the Games in 1992 and once again swam in the 400m final. He just missed adding a bronze medal to the silver he had captured in Seoul, finishing just two one hundredths of a second short of third.

THE 100M BACKSTROKE FINAL

The Olympic 100m backstroke final produced more than medals. The top three contenders used the controversial submarine start, where a swimmer pushes off and stays submerged for an extended period of time.

On March 15, 1988, Igor Poliansky of the Soviet Union broke Rick Carey's 100m backstroke world record. The following night, Poliansky repeated the feat, and four months later brought the time down to 55 seconds flat.

Along came American David Berkoff, who broke the world record twice in August at the U.S. Olympic Trials. During the 1988 Olympic preliminary heat Berkoff again set a new world record for the 100m back event. In addition to the submarine start he used a dolphin kick, kicking 32 times while still underwater.

A third factor was Daichi Suzuki of Japan. Suzuki had been training using the submarine start for seven years. The players were there and the race was on in Seoul.

Poliansky, Berkoff, and Suzuki were still submerged at the

30-meter mark. At 35 meters, Berkoff was the last to surface and was in first place. He had had a slow start and was not as far ahead of the field as he had anticipated.

Suzuki closed in on Berkoff's lead and began to pass the American with only 10 meters to go. The gold was Suzuki's, the silver Berkoff's, while Poliansky earned the bronze. Berkoff's world record remained unbroken.

Poliansky collected a gold medal for the 200m backstroke event. Berkoff would return to the Games in 1992 and collect a bronze medal in the 100m event.

After the 1988 Olympic Games, F.I.N.A. changed the back-stroke start rules, stating that a swimmer would be disqualified should he or she stay submerged beyond the 10-meter mark. That rule was later amended to 15 meters.

SPLASH BACK
The Gold Returns to Japan

At the 1984 Olympic Games, Daichi Suzuki of Japan placed eleventh in the 100m backstroke. Suzuki returned in 1988 to win Japan's first swimming Olympic gold medal since Nobutaka Taguchi's win in the 100m breaststroke event at the 1972 Games.

1988 OLYMPIC SWIMMING FINALS

Gold	Silver	Bronze	Fourth	Fifth	Sixth	Seventh	Eighth

INDIVIDUAL EVENTS

Women 50m Freestyle - World Record (24.98 Yang Wenyi CHN) — 1896-1984 - Event Not Held On Olympic Program

Gold	Silver	Bronze	Fourth	Fifth	Sixth	Seventh	Eighth
Kristin Otto	Yang Wenyi	Katrin Meissner	Jill Sterkel	Leigh Ann Fetter	Tamara Costache	Catherine Plewinski	Karen Van Wirdum
GDR - 25.49 o	CHN - 25.64	GDR - 25.71	USA - 25.71	USA - 25.78	ROM - 25.80	FRA - 25.90	AUS - 26.01

Men 50m Freestyle - World Record (22.23 Tom Jager USA) — 1906-1984 - Event Not Held On Olympic Program

Gold	Silver	Bronze	Fourth	Fifth	Sixth	Seventh	Eighth
Matthew Biondi	Thomas Jager	Gennady Prigoda	Dano Halsall	Stefan Volery	Vladimir Tkashenko	Frank Henter	Andrew Baildon
USA - 22.14 w	USA - 22.36	SOV - 22.71	SUI - 22.83	SUI - 22.84	SOV - 22.88	GER - 23.03	AUS - 23.15

Women 100m Freestyle - World Record (54.73 Kristin Otto GDR) — Olympic Record (54.79 B. Krause GDR 1980)

Gold	Silver	Bronze	Fourth	Fifth	Sixth	Seventh	Eighth
Kristin Otto	Zhuang Yong	Catherine Plewinski	Manuela Stellmach	Silvia Poll	Karin Brienesse	Dara Torres	Cornelia van Bentum
GDR - 54.93	CHN - 55.47	FRA - 55.49	GDR - 55.52	CRC - 55.90	NED - 56.15	USA - 56.25	NED - 56.54

Men 100m Freestyle - World Record (48.42 Matt Biondi USA) — Olympic Record (49.80 Rowdy Gaines USA 1984)

Gold	Silver	Bronze	Fourth	Fifth	Sixth	Seventh	Eighth
Matt Biondi	Christopher Jacobs	Stephan Caron	Gennady Prigoda	Yuri Bashkatov	Andrew Baildon	Per Johansson	Tommy Werner
USA - 48.63 o	USA - 49.08	FRA - 49.62	SOV - 49.75	SOV - 50.08	AUS - 50.23	SWE - 50.35	SWE - 50.54

Women 200m Freestyle - World Record (1:57.55 H. Friedrich GDR) — Olympic Record (1:58.33 B. Krause GDR 1980)

Gold	Silver	Bronze	Fourth	Fifth	Sixth	Seventh	Eighth
Heike Friedrich	Silvia Poll	Manuela Stellmach	Mary Wayte	Natalya Trefilova	Mitzi Kremer	Stephanie Ortwig	Cecile Prunier
GDR - 1:57.65 o	CRC - 1:58.67	GDR - 1:59.01	USA - 1:59.04	SOV - 1:59.24	AUS - 2:00.23	GER - 2:00.73	FRA - 2:02.88

w World Record   o Olympic Record   p Preliminary Heat   dq Disqualified   e Equal to World Record   eo Equal to Olympic Record
dns Did Not Start   dnf Did Not Finish   ac Also Competed   r Relay Lead-off Split   E Estimated

OLYMPIAD XXIV – 1988 – SEOUL, SOUTH KOREA

1988 OLYMPIC SWIMMING FINALS

Gold	Silver	Bronze	Fourth	Fifth	Sixth	Seventh	Eighth

Men 200m Freestyle - World and Olympic Record (1:47.44 Michael Gross GER 1984)

Gold	Silver	Bronze	Fourth	Fifth	Sixth	Seventh	Eighth
Duncan Armstrong	Anders Holmertz	Matt Biondi	Artur Wojdat	Michael Gross	Steffen Zesner	Troy Dalbey	Thomas Fahrner
AUS - 1:47.25 w	SWE - 1:47.89	USA - 1:47.99	POL - 1:48.40	GER - 1:48.59	GDR - 1:48.77	USA - 1:48.86	GER - 1:49.19

Women 400m Freestyle - World Record (4:05.45 Janet Evans USA) Olympic Record (4:07.10 Tiffany Cohen USA 1984)

Gold	Silver	Bronze	Fourth	Fifth	Sixth	Seventh	Eighth
Janet Evans	Heike Friedrich	Anke Möhring	Tami Bruce	Janelle Elford	Isabelle Arnould	Stephanie Ortwig	Natalya Trefilova
USA - 4:03.85 w	GDR - 4:05.94	GDR - 4:06.62	USA - 4:08.16	AUS - 4:10.64	BEL - 4:11.73	GER - 4:13.05	SOV - 4:13.92

Men 400m Freestyle - World Record (3:47.38 Artur Wojdat POL) Olympic Record (3:51.23 George DiCarlo USA 1984)

Gold	Silver	Bronze	Fourth	Fifth	Sixth	Seventh	Eighth
Uwe Dassler	Duncan Armstrong	Artur Wojdat	Matthew Cetlinski	Mariusz Podkoscielny	Stefan Pfeiffer	Kevin Boyd	Anders Holmertz
GDR - 3:46.95w	AUS - 3:47.15	POL - 3:47.34	USA - 3:48.09	POL - 3:48.59	GER - 3:49.96	GBR - 3:50.16	SWE - 3:51.04

Women 800m Freestyle - World Record (8:17.12 Janet Evans USA) Olympic Record (8:24.95 Tiffany Cohen USA 1984)

Gold	Silver	Bronze	Fourth	Fifth	Sixth	Seventh	Eighth
Janet Evans	Astrid Strauss	Julie McDonald	Anke Möhring	Tami Bruce	Janelle Elford	Isabelle Arnould	Antoaneta Strumenlieva
USA - 8:20.20 o	GDR - 8:22.09	AUS - 8:22.93	GDR - 8:23.09	USA - 8:30.86	AUS - 8:30.94	BEL - 8:37.47	BUL - 8:41.05

Men 1500m Freestyle - World Record (14:54.76 V.Salnikov SOV) Olympic Record (14:58.27 Salnikov SOV 1980)

Gold	Silver	Bronze	Fourth	Fifth	Sixth	Seventh	Eighth
Vladimir Salnikov	Stefan Pfeiffer	Uwe Dassler	Matthew Cetlinski	Mariusz Podkoscielny	Rainer Henkel	Kevin Boyd	Darjan Petric
SOV - 15:00.40	GER - 15:02.69	GDR - 15:06.15	USA - 15:14.76	POL - 15:14.76	GER - 15:18.19	GBR - 15:21.16	YUG - 15:37.12

Women 100m Backstroke - World Record (1:00.59 Ina Kleber GDR) Olympic Record (1:00.86 R. Reinisch GDR 1980)

Gold	Silver	Bronze	Fourth	Fifth	Sixth	Seventh	Eighth
Kristin Otto	Krisztina Egerszegi	Cornelia Sirch	Betsy Mitchell	Beth Barr	Silvia Poll Ahrens	Nicole Livingstone	Marion Aizpors
GDR - 1:00.89	HUN - 1:01.56	GDR - 1:01.57	USA - 1:02.71	USA - 1:02.78	CRC - 1:03.34	AUS - 1:04.15	GER - 1:04.19

1988 OLYMPIC SWIMMING FINALS

Men 100m Backstroke - World Record (54.91 David Berkoff USA) Olympic Record (55.49 John Naber USA 1976)

	Gold	Silver	Bronze	Fourth	Fifth	Sixth	Seventh	Eighth
Name	Daichi Suzuki	David Berkoff p - 54.51 w	Igor Polyansky	Sergei Zabolotnov	Mark Tewksbury	Frank Baltrusch	Frank Hoffmeister	Sean Murphy
Time	JPN - 55:05	USA - 55.18	SOV - 55.20	SOV - 55.37	CAN - 56.09	GDR - 56.10	GER - 56.19	CAN - 56.32

Women 200m Backstroke - World Record (2:08.60 Betsy Mitchell USA) Olympic Record (2:11.77 R. Reinisch GDR 1980)

	Gold	Silver	Bronze	Fourth	Fifth	Sixth	Seventh	Eighth
Name	Krisztina Egerszegi	Kathrin Zimmerman	Cornelia Sirch	Cynthia "Beth" Barr	Nicole Livingstone	Andrea Hayes	Jolanda de Rover	Svenja Schlicht
Time	HUN - 2:09.29 o	GDR - 2:10.61	GDR - 2:11.45	USA - 2:12.39	AUS - 2:13.43	USA - 2:15.02	NED - 2:15.17	GER - 2:15.94

Men 200m Backstroke - World Record (1:58.14 Igor Polyansky SOV) Olympic Record (1:58.99 R. Carey USA 1984)

	Gold	Silver	Bronze	Fourth	Fifth	Sixth	Seventh	Eighth
Name	Igor Polyansky	Frank Baltrusch	Paul Kingsman	Sergei Zabolotnov	Dirk Richter	Jens-Peter Berndt	Daniel Veatch	Rogerio Romero
Time	SOV - 1:59.37	GDR - 1:59.60	NZE - 2:00.48	SOV - 2:00.52	GDR - 2:01.67	GER - 2:01.84	USA - 2:02.26	BRA - 2:02.28

Women 100m Breaststroke - World Record (1:07.91 S. Hörner GDR) Olympic Record (1:09.88 P. van Staveren NED 1984)

	Gold	Silver	Bronze	Fourth	Fifth	Sixth	Seventh	Eighth
Name	T. Dangalakova Bogomilova	Antoaneta Frenkeva	Silke Hörner	Allison Higson	Yelena Volkova	Tracey McFarlane	Huang Xiaomin	Annett Rex
Time	BUL - 1:07.95 o	BUL - 1:08.74	GDR - 1:08.83	CAN - 1:08.86	SOV - 1:09.24	USA - 1:09.60	CHN - 1:10.53	GDR - 1:10.67

Men 100m Breaststroke - World and Olympic Record (1:01.65 Lundquist USA 1984)

	Gold	Silver	Bronze	Fourth	Fifth	Sixth	Seventh	Eighth
Name	Adrian Moorhouse	Károly Güttler	Dmitri Volkov	Victor Davis	Tamás Debnár	Richard Schroeder	Gianni Minervini	Christian Poswiat
Time	GBR - 1:02.04	HUN - 1:02.05	SOV - 1:02.20	CAN - 1:02.38	HUN - 1:02.50	USA - 1:02.55	ITA - 1:02.93	GDR - 1:03.43

Women 200m Breaststroke - World Record (2:27.27 Allison Higson CAN) Olympic Record (2:29.54 L. Kaciušyte SOV 1980)

	Gold	Silver	Bronze	Fourth	Fifth	Sixth	Seventh	Eighth
Name	Silke Hörner	Huang Xiaomin	Antoaneta Frenkeva	T. Dangalakova Bogomilova	Yulia Bocharova	Ingrid Lempereur	Allison Higson	Manuela Dalla Valle
Time	GDR - 2:26.71w	CHN - 2:27.49	BUL - 2:28.34	BUL - 2:28.43	SOV - 2:28.54	BEL - 2:29.42	CAN - 2:29.60	ITA - 2:29.86

1988 OLYMPIC SWIMMING FINALS

Men 200m Breaststroke - World and Olympic Record (2:13.34 Victor Davis CAN 1984)

Gold	Silver	Bronze	Fourth	Fifth	Sixth	Seventh	Eighth
József Szabó	Nicholas Gillingham	Sergio Lopez	Michael Barrowman	Valery Lozyk	Vadim Alekseyev	Jonathan Cleveland	Péter Szabó
HUN - 2:13.52	GBR - 2:14.12	ESP - 2:15.21	USA - 2:15.45	SOV - 2:16.16	SOV - 2:16.70	CAN - 2:17.10	HUN - 2:17.12

Women 100m Butterfly - World Record (57.93 Mary T. Meagher USA) Olympic Record (59.05 Mary T. Meagher USA 1984)

Gold	Silver	Bronze	Fourth	Fifth	Sixth	Seventh	Eighth
Kristin Otto	Birte Weigang	Qian Hong	Catherine Plewinski	Janel Jorgensen	Cornelia van Bentum	Mary T. Meagher	Wang Xiaohong
GDR - 59.00 o	GDR - 59.45	CHN - 59.52	FRA - 59.58	USA - 1:00.48	NED - 1:00.62	USA - 1:00.97	CHN - 1:01.15

Men 100m Butterfly - World Record (52.84 Pablo Morales USA) Olympic Record (53.08 Michael Gross GER 1984)

Gold	Silver	Bronze	Fourth	Fifth	Sixth	Seventh	Eighth
Anthony Nesty	Matthew Biondi	Andrew Jameson	Jonathan Sieben	Michael Gross	Jay Mortenson	Thomas Ponting	Vadym Yaroshchuk
SUR - 53.00 o	USA - 53.01	GBR - 53.30	AUS - 53.33	GER - 53.44	USA - 54.07	CAN - 54.09	SOV - 54.60

Women 200m Butterfly - World Record (2:05.96 Mary T. Meagher USA) Olympic Record (2:06.90 Meagher USA 1984)

Gold	Silver	Bronze	Fourth	Fifth	Sixth	Seventh	Eighth
Kathleen Nord	Birte Weigang	Mary T. Meagher	Stela Pura	Trina Radke	Kiyomi Takahashi	Wang Xiaohong	Cornelia van Bentum
GDR - 2:09.51	GDR - 2:09.91	USA - 2:10.80	ROM - 2:11.28	USA - 2:11.55	JPN - 2:11.62	CHN - 2:12.34	NED - 2:13.17

Men 200m Butterfly - World Record (1:56.24 Michael Gross GER) Olympic Record (1:57.04 Jonathon Sieben AUS 1984)

Gold	Silver	Bronze	Fourth	Fifth	Sixth	Seventh	Eighth
Michael Gross	Benny Nielsen	Anthony Mosse	Thomas Ponting	Melvin Stewart	David Wilson	Jon Kelly	Anthony Nesty
GER - 1:56.94 o	DEN - 1:58.24	NZE - 1:58.28	CAN - 1:58.91	USA - 1:59.19	AUS - 1:59.20	CAN - 1:59.48	SUR - 2:00.80

Women 200m Individual Medley - World Record (2:11.73 U.Geweniger GDR) Olympic Record (2:12.64 T.Caulkins USA 1984)

Gold	Silver	Bronze	Fourth	Fifth	Sixth	Seventh	Eighth
Daniela Hunger	Yelena Dendberova	Noemi Lung	Jodie Clatworthy	Marianne Muis	Aneta Patrascoiu	Lin Li	Whitney Hedgepeth
GDR - 2:12.59 o	SOV - 2:13.31	ROM - 2:14.85	AUS - 2:16.31	NED - 2:16.40	ROM - 2:16.70	CHN - 2:17.42	USA - 2:17.99

1988 OLYMPIC SWIMMING FINALS

	Gold	Silver	Bronze	Fourth	Fifth	Sixth	Seventh	Eighth

Men 200m Individual Medley - World Record (2:00.56 Tamás Darnyi HUN) Olympic Record (2:01.42 A.Baumann CAN 1984)

Gold	Silver	Bronze	Fourth	Fifth	Sixth	Seventh	Eighth
Tamás Darnyi	Patrick Kühl	Vadym Yaroshchuk	Mikhail Zubkov	Peter Bermel	Robert Bruce	Raik Hannemann	Gary Anderson
HUN - 2:00.17w	GDR - 2:01.61	SOV - 2:02.40	SOV - 2:02.92	GER - 2:03.81	AUS - 2:04.34	GDR - 2:04.82	CAN - 2:06.35

Women 400m Individual Medley - World Record (4:36.10 P.Schneider GDR)Olympic Record (4:36.29 P. Schneider GDR 1980)

Gold	Silver	Bronze	Fourth	Fifth	Sixth	Seventh	Eighth
Janet Evans	Noemi Lung	Daniela Hunger	Yelena Dendeberova	Kathleen Nord	Jodie Clatworthy	Lin Li	Donna Procter
USA - 4:37.76	ROM - 4:39.46	GDR - 4:39.76	SOV - 4:40.44	GDR - 4:41.64	AUS - 4:45.86	CHN - 4:47.05	AUS - 4:47.51

Men 400m Individual Medley - World Record (4:15.42 T. Darnyi HUN)   Olympic Record (4:17.41 Alex Baumann CAN 1984)

Gold	Silver	Bronze	Fourth	Fifth	Sixth	Seventh	Eighth
Tamás Darnyi	David Wharton	Stefano Battistelli	József Szabó	Patrick Kühl	Jens-Peter Berndt	Luca Sacchi	Peter Bermel
HUN - 4:14.75w	USA - 4:17.36	ITA - 4:18.01	HUN - 4:18.15	GDR - 4:18.44	GER - 4:21.71	ITA - 4:23.23	GER - 4:24.02

RELAY EVENTS

Women 400m Medley Relay - World Record (4:03.69 GDR)   Olympic Record (4:06.67 GDR 1980)

Gold	Silver	Bronze	Fourth	Fifth	Sixth	Seventh	Eighth
Kristin Otto. Silke Hörner. Birte Weigang. Katrin Meissner. p - Cornelia Sirch. Manuela Stellmach	Beth Barr. Tracey McFarlane. Janel Jorgensen. Mary Wayte. p - Betsy Mitchell. Mary Meagher. Dara Torres	Lori Melien. Allison Higson. Jane Kerr. Andrea Nugent. p - Keltie Duggan. Patricia Noall	Nicole Livingstone. Lara Hooiveld. Fiona Alessandri. Karin Van Wirdum	Jolanda de Rover. Linda Moes. Cornelia van Bentum. Karin Brienesse	Bistra Gospodinova. Tania Dangalakova. Bogomilova. Neviana Miteva. Natasha Hristova	Svenja Schlicht. Britta Dahm. Gabi Rehaa. Marion Aizpors	Lorenza Vigarani. Manuela Dalla Valle. Ilaria Tocchini. Silvia Persi
GDR - 4:03.74 e	USA 0 4:07.90	CAN - 4:10.49	AUS - 4:11.57	NED - 4:12.19	BUL - 4:12.36	GER - 4:12.89	ITA - 4:13.85

1988 OLYMPIC SWIMMING FINALS

Gold	Silver	Bronze	Fourth	Fifth	Sixth	Seventh	Eighth
Men 400m Medley Relay - World Record (3:38.28 USA)						Olympic Record (3:39.30 USA 1984)	
David Berkoff, Richard Schroeder, Matthew Biondi, Christopher Jacobs *p* - Jay Mortenson, Thomas Jager	Mark Tewksbury, Victor Davis, Thomas Ponting, Donald "Sandy" Goss	Igor Polyansky, Dmitri Volkov, Vadym Yaroshchuk, Gennady Prigoda *p* - Sergei Zabolotnov, Valery Lozik, Konstantin Peltrov, Nikolai Yevseyev	Frank Hoffmeister, Alexander Mayer, Michael Gross, Björn Zikarsky *p* - Mark Warnecke	Daichi Suzuki, Hironobu Nagahata, Hiroshi Miura, Shigeo Ogata	Carl Wilson, Ian Mcadam, Jonathon Sieben, Andrew Baildon	Hans Kroes, Ronald Dekker, Frank Drost, Patrick Dybiona	Neil Harper, Adrian Moorhouse, Andrew Jameson, Mark Foster *p* - Gary Binfield, Roland Lee
USA - 3:36.93w	CAN - 3:39.28	SOV - 3:39.96	GER - 3:42.98	JPN - 3:44.36	AUS - 3:45.85	NED - 3:46.85	GBR - *dq*
Women 400m Freestyle Relay - World Record (3:40.57 GDR)						Olympic Record (3:42.71 GDR 1980)	
Kristin Otto, Katrin Meissner, Daniela Hunger, Manuela Stellmach *p* - Sabina Schulze, Heike Friedrich	Marianne Muis, Mildred Muis, Cornelia van Bentum, Karin Brienesse *p* - Diana van der Plaats	Mary Wayte, Mitzi Kremer, Laura Walker, Dara Torres *p* - Paige Zemina, Jill Sterkel	Xia Fujie, Yang Wenyi, Lou Yaping, Zhuang Yong	Yelena Dendeberova, Svetlana Issakova, Natalya Trefilova, Svitlana Kopchykova *p* - Inna Abramova	Kathy Bald, Patricia Noall, Andrea Nugent, Jane Kerr *p* - Kristen Topham, Allison Higson	Stephanie Ortwig, Marion Aizpors, Christiane Pielke, Karin Seick *p* - Katja Ziliox	Gitta Jensen, Pia Sorensen, Mette Jacobsen, Annette Moldrup Jorgensen
GDR - 3:40.63 *o*	NED - 3:43.39	USA - 3:44.25	CHN - 3:44.69	SOV - 3:44.99	CAN - 3:46.75	GER - 3:46.90	DEN - 3:49.25

1988 OLYMPIC SWIMMING FINALS

Men 400m Freestyle Relay - World Record (3:17.08 USA)   Olympic Record (3:19.03 USA 1984)

Gold	Silver	Bronze	Fourth	Fifth	Sixth	Seventh	Eighth
Christopher Jacobs, Troy Dalbey, Thomas Jager, Matthew Biondi, p - Brent Lang, Douglas Gjertsen, Shaun Jordan	Gennady Prigoda, Yuri Bashkatov, Nikolai Yevseyev, Vladimir Tkachenko, p - Raimundas Ma·uolis, Aleksei Borislavsky	Dirk Richter, Thomas Flemming, Lars Hinneburg, Steffen Zesner	Stephan Caron, Christophe Kalfayan, Laurent Neuville, Bruno Gutzeit	Per Johansson, Tommy Werner, Joakim Holmquist, Göran Titus, p - Richard Milton	Michael Gross, Thomas Fahrner, Björn Zikarsky, Peter Sitt	Michael Fibbens, Mark Foster, Roland Lee, Andrew Jameson, p - Torsten Wiegel	Roberto Gleria, Giorgio Lamberti, Fabrizio Rampazzo, Andrea Ceccarini
USA - 3:16.53w	SOV - 3:18.33	GDR - 3:19.82	FRA - 3:20.02	SWE - 3:21.07	GER - 3:21.65	GBR - 3:21.71	ITA - 3:22.93

Men 800m Freestyle Relay - World Record (7:13.10 GER)   Olympic Record (7:15.69 USA 1984)

Gold	Silver	Bronze	Fourth	Fifth	Sixth	Seventh	Eighth
Troy Dalbey, Matthew Cetlinski, Douglas Gjertsen, Matthew Biondi, p - Craig Oppel, Daniel Jorgensen	Uwe Dassler, Sven Lodziewski, Thomas Flemming, Steffen Zesner, p - Lars Hinneburg	Erik Hochstein, Thomas Fahrner, Rainer Henkel, Michael Gross, p - Peter Sitt, Stefan Pfeiffer	Thomas Stachewicz, Ian Brown, Jason Plummer, Duncan Armstrong, p - Martin Roberts	Roberto Gleria, Giorgio Lamberti, Massimo Trevisan, Valerio Giambalvo, p - Fabrizio Rampazzo	Anders Holmertz, Tommy Werner, Michael Söderlund, Christer Wallin, p - Henrik Jangvall	Michel Pou, Franck Iacono, Olivier Fougeroud, Ludovic Depickere, p - Stephan Caron, Laurent Neuville	Turlough O'Hare, Donald "Sandy" Goss, Donald Haddow, Gary Vandermeulen, p - Darren Ward
USA - 7:12.51	GDR - 7:13.68	GER - 7:14.35	AUS - 7:15.23	ITA - 7:16.00	SWE - 7:19.10	FRA - 7:24.69	CAN - 7:24.91

Chapter 23

Olympiad XXV - 1992
Barcelona, Spain

the 1992 Summer Olympic Games were held in Barcelona, Spain. These Games represented a truly global gathering of the world's best athletes, with a record 172 nations participating.

There were no boycotts to diminish the spirit or level of competition. South African athletes came to the Olympic Games for the first time since 1960. A total of 10,563 athletes participated in the 257 events offered.

L A N E   L I N E S

Rewriting the Record Books

Ten World records and 21 Olympic records were set during the swimming competition in Barcelona. In eight of these swim finals, the world record holders were out touched at the finish.

Nine different countries would be represented on the gold medal podium for men and women combined. Nineteen countries would bring home Olympic swimming medals.

SPLASH BACK
Hungary Devours Gold

1952 Gold Medalists	*1992 Gold Medalists*
100m Freestyle - Katalin Szöke	*100m Backstroke - Krisztina Egerszegi*
400m Freestyle - Valéria Gyenge	*200m Backstroke - Krisztina Egerszegi*
200m Breaststroke - Éva Székely	*400m IM - Krisztina Egerszegi*
400m Freestyle Relay - Women's Team	*200m & 400 IM - Tamas Darnyi*

MIKE BARROWMAN
UNITED STATES

In 1988 at the Seoul Olympics, Mike Barrowman took the top qualifying spot in the 200m breaststroke, but finished fourth in the final. That disappointment fueled his fire for the next four years.

Photo by Tim Morse

> *"Since then, everyday, all I've thought about was the Olympic Games. The only plans I've had were for July 29th, 1992."*
> —*Mike Barrowman*

Entering the U.S. Olympic Trials in 1992, Barrowman had not been

In 1992 Mike Barrowman's name followed the seven fastest times in the 200m breaststroke event.

OFF THE $\mathcal{Wall}$

Goldie Lawn

Mike Barrowman returned to his home in Potomac, Maryland, to find that his neighbors had celebrated his Olympic success by painting his entire front lawn gold.

defeated in his specialty, the 200m breaststroke, since Seoul. Roque Santos touched him out, but the second spot gave him his place on the U.S. Olympic squad.

In Barcelona, Barrowman was unstoppable. He led the race from start to finish, breaking his own record. This race marked the sixth time he had lowered the world record. Barrowman's name followed the seven fastest times ever recorded for this event.

"I've done everything I wanted to in the 200m breaststroke," stated Barrowman, "I've accomplished the Triple Crown—I have a world record, a world championship and an Olympic Championship."

NELSON DIEBEL
UNITED STATES

Swimmer Nelson Diebel described himself during his early years, as "a rebel without a clue." Expelled from various schools for delinquent behavior, Diebel landed at Peddie, a private high school in New Jersey. There, under Coach Chris Martin, Diebel grew into a world class swimmer.

At the Trials in 1992, Diebel was not only the surprise winner of the 100m breaststroke, but set a new American record as well. He broke Steve Lundquist's 7 ½-year-old record, but was not favored to medal at the Games.

Diebel's victory in the 100m breaststroke was the first gold medal of these Games for the United States. As a member of the medley relay team he would clinch a second gold, as the squad matched the world record set by the United States at the 1988 Games.

Over his six-year swimming career, Diebel had more than the occasional "disagreement" with his coaches. After his Olympic win, Coach Martin was asked if he knew

Nelson Diebel 100m breaststroke champion.

Photo by Tim Morse

what it takes to be an Olympic Champion. Martin responded, "I thought I did, until Nelson won."

OFF THE *Wall*

"Crash Landing"

In 1988 Nelson Diebel broke both his wrists while attempting to dive into the school pool from the spectator section. He lost his

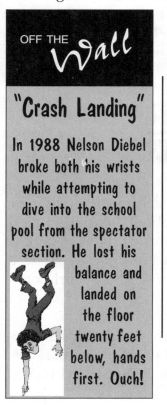

balance and landed on the floor twenty feet below, hands first. Ouch!

NICOLE HAISLETT
UNITED STATES

Nicole Haislett, a University of Florida standout, qualified for both the 100 and 200 meter free events in Barcelona. Haislett was the favorite to win the 200m event, until the fourteen-year-old German, Franziska van Almsick, stunned the crowd, qualifying first.

The German teenager went out even faster in the final, swimming close to the lane line between lanes four and five, just as she had done in her preliminary swim. In lane five, the veteran Haislett proceeded to hug the shared lane line and stayed at van Almsick's shoulder, drafting off of her.

This strategic error likely cost van Almsick the gold medal. Haislett expended less energy as she continued drafting off van Almsick during most of the race. Haislett made her move in the final 15 meters, pulling even with van Almsick 10 meters from the wall. At 5 meters, Nicole pulled slightly ahead to capture the gold medal.

Haislett's winning time of 1:57.90 in the 200m freestyle broke the oldest standing American record, set back in 1979 by Olympian "Sippy" Woodhead (1:58.23). Nicole collected two additional gold medals as a member of the 400m freestyle relay, and the qualifying 400m medley relay team.

L A N E   L I N E S

First Time for Everything

Prior to the Games in Barcelona, Dagmar Hase was known as a backstroke specialist. However, her upset victory in the 400m freestyle final over American record holder Janet Evans earned her far more fame. This was the first time Hase had swum the 400m freestyle event at a major meet. Hase collected two additional silver medals swimming the backstroke.

KYOKO IWASAKI
JAPAN

Kyoko Iwasaki of Japan entered Barcelona ranked 12th in the world for the 200m breaststroke. The petite teenager, just shy of 100 pounds, was matched up against world record holder Anita Nall.

These breaststrokers shared the same birthday, Kyoko turned 14 and Anita 16 only six days before their Olympic final. Nall lead until the final meters of the race when Iwasaki, using her strong kick, came from behind to capture gold. With this win, Kyoko became the youngest swimming champion in Olympic history.

Qian Hong - China

Qian Hong of China medaled in both her 1988 and 1992 Olympic performances. At Seoul, the 100m fly title eluded her and she placed third. Hong was determined to strike gold in Barcelona. Qian overtook American Crissy Ahmann-Leighton in the final few meters to win gold and set a new Olympic record.

RONALD KARNAUGH
UNITED STATES

U.S. Olympian Ronald Karnaugh wasn't scheduled to swim until the last day of the swimming competition. This allowed him the opportunity to participate in the opening ceremonies in Barcelona. Due to the good people of Maplewood, New Jersey, who raised money for the trip, the Karnaugh family was there to watch Ron march.

Karnaugh's proud father Peter, a retired truck driver, was at the railing taking photographs as Ron marched by with the American delegation. Shortly afterward, the elder Karnaugh returned to the bleachers where he suffered a fatal heart attack.

Five days later, the courageous Karnaugh pulled himself together to qualify in the 200m IM. He entered this event with the second fastest recorded time of 1992. Karnaugh was in medal contention until the final 50 meters of his race, but finished in sixth place.

Ron Karnaugh's story is not about medals. It is a story of inner strength that best exemplifies the spirit of the Olympic Games.

China's National Swimming Team recruited Lin Li when she was only twelve years old. She went on to become a three-time Olympian, making her first appearance in Seoul at eighteen. Though she did not medal, she set a national record for

SCORE
B O A R D

U.S. Relay Streak Ends

The United States Men's Swimming Team had won the 800m freestyle relay final at every Olympic Game since 1960 (with the exception of the 1980 boycott). Their winning streak of seven Olympic titles came to an end in Barcelona, when the Russian Team of Dimitri Lepikov, Vladimir Pyshnenko, Veniamin Tayanovich and Yevgeny Sadovyi broke the world record set by the Americans in Seoul.

China in the 400m individual medley.

In Barcelona, Lin held off Summer Sanders in the final meters of the 200m individual medley to win the gold. Lin's time of 2:11.65 broke the longest standing world record (11 years) on the books. This versatile swimmer also took silver in both the 200m breaststroke and the 400m IM.

At the Olympic Games in Atlanta, Lin, now 25, returned to defend her Olympic crown in the 200m IM. She finished with bronze, but her world record, set in Barcelona, withstood the Olympic competition.

PABLO MORALES
UNITED STATES

In 1984, Pablo Morales was called "swimming's rising superstar." In Los Angeles the 19 year-old Morales was overpowered by West Germany's Michael Gross in the 100m fly. Both Morales and Gross broke the world record. Morales went home with another silver in the 200m IM, and gold as a member of the medley relay team.

Photo by Tim Morse

A pensive Pablo Morales.

Morales retired from swimming in 1988 after narrowly missing a place on the U.S. Olympic Team. He remained the world record holder in the 100m butterfly. Three years later, Pablo resumed the rigors of training. He took leave from Cornell Law School, giving himself seven months to prepare for the 1992 U.S. Trials.

Morales returned to train with his former Stanford coach, Skip

Kenney, who would be instrumental in his comeback. During this time Pablo suffered the loss of this mother, Bianca, who had been waging a courageous fight against cancer. Having almost drowned as a child, it was Bianca who insisted her children learn to swim.

At the 1992 Olympic Trials Morales would not be denied. He took the top qualifying seed in the 100m fly and was voted captain of the 1992 U.S. Olympic Team. As he entered these, his second Games, his 1986 100m fly world record still stood.

Eight years after Los Angeles, at the age of 27, Pablo Morales captured his long-awaited gold. He later shared, "When I was up on the victory stand, I was thinking that my mother would want to be here to experience this, and I know that she was with me in spirit. This was my time at last."

During his Olympic career Pablo Morales collected three gold and two silver medals. He returned to Cornell Law School and received his law degree. However, his contributions to swimming continue. Never far from the pool, Pablo is now coaching at San José State University in California.

ANITA NALL
UNITED STATES

On March 4, 1992, at the U.S. Olympic Trials, 15-year-old Anita Nall set a new world record in the 200m breaststroke...twice! Nall became the youngest swimmer to set a world record since Mary T. Meagher, nearly

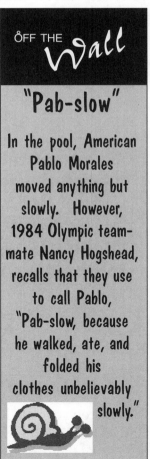

ÖFF THE *Wall*

"Pab-slow"

In the pool, American Pablo Morales moved anything but slowly. However, 1984 Olympic teammate Nancy Hogshead, recalls that they use to call Pablo, "Pab-slow, because he walked, ate, and folded his clothes unbelievably slowly."

thirteen years earlier.

In Barcelona, Nall swam to bronze in her specialty, the 200m breaststroke. Two days later, the young Olympian swam to silver in the 100m breaststroke, setting a new American record in the process. As a member of the medley relay team she shared gold and a new world record.

Anita Nall returned home from the Olympic Games with three Olympic medals, ready to start her junior year at Towson Catholic High School.

Photo by Tim Morse

Anita Nall, youngest swimmer to set a world record since Mary T. Meagher, nearly 13 years earlier.

L A N E   L I N E S

Frequent Flyer

Crissy Ahmann-Leighton, who garnered a silver medal in the 100m butterfly, swam the second fastest fly relay leg ever as a member of the U.S. medley team in Barcelona. She put away the competition and the team went on to a set a world record. Her sizzling split of 58.58 seconds was second only to the greatest "flyer" ever, Mary T. Meagher.

KIEREN PERKINS
AUSTRALIA

Eighteen year-old Kieren Perkins of Australia entered the 1992 Games holding the world record in the 400m, the 800m (not on the men's Olympic program), and the 1500m freestyle events.

Photo by Tim Morse

Kieren Perkins is — first to the wall!

Nine years earlier Kieren suffered a gash on the calf of his left leg that required 86 stitches. His doctor felt swimming would aid the healing process of the injured muscle. So began his swimming career. At sixteen he became only the third person ever to break the 15-minute barrier in the 1500m event.

In Barcelona, Yevgeny Sadovyi touched out the young Australian in the 400m free final. Both swimmers had broken the world record.

Returning to the pool for the 1500m final, Perkins blew his competition out of the water, finishing 11.81 seconds ahead of teammate Glen Houseman. Perkins shattered his own world record by almost five seconds.

Perkins returned to Olympic competition in 1996, still in possession of the world record for the 1500m freestyle. He narrowly qualified, but in the final, Perkins took the lead in lane eight and never looked back. He clinched gold for his second consecutive Olympic victory in this event.

YELENA RUDKOVSKAYA
RUSSIA

Yelena Rudkovskaya, of Belarus, a tenacious breaststroker, continued with her swimming career despite the declining economic conditions in her country. Hard times directly affected most athletic programs.

Her parents would often go to the training camp to supplement the horrendous food given the athletes. Then, a year before the Games, her coach relocated to Israel. Despite this adversity, Yelena never lost sight of her Olympic dream...to win a medal.

Rudkovskaya won gold in the 100m breaststroke, placed fourth in the 200m breaststroke and collected a bronze with her teammates in the medley relay. Yelena Rudkovskaya had been rewarded and her dreams fulfilled.

Anders Holmertz - Sweden

Anders Holmertz of Sweden swam in three Olympiads. A mid-distance freestyle specialist, he qualified for a total of eleven Olympic swimming finals, including five relay teams. He collected one bronze and four silver medals in his career.

YEVGENY SADOVYI
RUSSIA

Yevgeny Sadovyi entered the Olympic Games with a ranking of 12th in the 400m freestyle and 5th in the 200m free. He felt his best chance for gold was in the 400m, even though he would be facing the world record holder from Australia, Kieren Perkins.

In the 200m free final, nineteen-year-old Sadovyi, took the lead in the last several meters of the race. He missed the world record by one hundredth of a second, but clinched an Olympic record and a gold medal.

The 400m freestyle final came down to a dual between Perkins and Sadovyi, who battled it out stroke by stroke as they sprinted to the finish. Sadovyi touched the wall first. Both swimmers had broken the existing world record.

Sadovyi, who had been promised a house by a private sponsor should he win gold, knew he would see wealth. His gold in the 400m and with the 800m freestyle relay team brought Sadovyi's medal total to three and he became the most decorated male swimmer of the 1992 Games.

SUMMER SANDERS
UNITED STATES

Photo by Tim Morse

Summer Sanders in training.

Bob Sanders boasts that his daughter Summer could swim a 25-yard lap at the age of three. At four she was competing for California's Roseville Sugar Bears.

Sanders missed qualifying for the 1988 Olympic Team by twenty-seven hundredths of a second. Prior to the trials she had never qualified for a final at a national meet. Summer returned home from the trials more determined than ever.

As a freshman at Stanford University she was fortunate enough to be coached by Richard Quick. At the Olympic Trials in 1992, Summer qualified for four individual events.

In Barcelona, Sanders was the most decorated female swimmer of the Games. She captured a silver medal in the 200m IM, and a bronze in the 400m IM. Sanders, the reigning 200m butterfly world champion, won her individual Olympic gold in a fiercely fought final, pulling ahead in the last few meters.

Having swum the qualifying round of the 400m medley race, Sanders earned yet another gold as part of this team. After completing her grueling Olympic schedule, she was asked, "What are you going to do now?" "I just want to sit down and relax," Sanders responded, "I want to enjoy the feeling that nobody expects me to do any thing great tomorrow."

In Atlanta, Summer Sanders was a swimming commentator for NBC. She went on to become the host of "Figure it Out," a game show on the popular kid's network, Nickelodeon.

OFF THE $\mathcal{wall}$

"Double Take"

As the swimmers touched the pads, at the finish of the 100m freestyle final in Barcelona, they turned to the scoreboard. Aleksandr Popov (49.02) had placed first, France's Stephan Caron (49.50) second, and Jon Olsen (USA) third (49.51). The timing device in Gustavo Borges' (BRA) lane malfunctioned. They reviewed the videotapes of the race and determined Borges had placed fourth.

Incredibly, prior to the 100m free ceremony the film was reviewed yet again. Officials determined that they had mistakenly watched Biondi's fourth place finish, not Borges'! Borges was subsequently awarded the silver medal, with Caron beating Olsen out by one hundredth of a second for the bronze medal.

MELVIN STEWART
UNITED STATES

Photo by Tim Morse

Melvin Stewart's flying style.

As a young age-group swimmer in South Carolina, Melvin Stewart was taught to breathe to the side when swimming the butterfly. It was a technique that he used throughout his career and is the factor to which he attributes his success.

In his junior year of high school Stewart had the opportunity to attend Mercersburg Academy, a school that had fifteen Olympic swimmers on its alumni list. Tuition was $14,000 a year, a cost too steep for the Stewart family. A generous former alumnus, George Baxter, stepped in and paid Stewart's way. A bond was formed with the Baxters, who took Melvin in as one of their own.

Stewart was a member of the 1988 and 1992 U.S. Olympic teams. He entered the Barcelona Games as the world record holder in the 200m fly. He had not lost this event in a major competition since his fifth place finish in Seoul.

He easily captured the gold and set a new Olympic record in the 200m butterfly, finishing one and one half second ahead of Danyon Loader of New Zealand. Stewart had a fifth place finish in the 100m fly and a bronze medal as a member of the 800m freestyle relay team.

After his win, Stewart pledged his gold medal to the 76-year-old "Mr. B.," his mentor. Derek Kennedy, Stewart's friend and former roommate, perhaps said it best of Melvin Stewart; "Swimming for him really is self-expression. Melvin feels joy when he swims."

MARK TEWKSBURY
CANADA

Two-time Olympian Mark Tewksbury knew that American world record holder Jeff Rouse was the man to beat in Barcelona, having lost to Rouse at the World Championships.

Tewksbury's training was grueling. His coach, Derek Snelly, focused on Mark's underwater technique and had him swimming in temperatures similar to Barcelona's heat. Coach Snelly also increased Mark's yardage up to 20 kilometers a day.

The long days of training were rewarded. When all was said and done, Tewksbury out-touched Rouse for the Olympic title in the 100m backstroke event. Entering the Games with a personal best of 55.19, Tewksbury left with a new Olympic record of 53.98.

Mark Tewksbury won Canada's only individual medal in Barcelona. As the leadoff swimmer for Canada's medley relay team, he collected a bronze, as well. With his 1988 silver Olympic medal waiting at home, Tewksbury added the gold and bronze that completed his set.

Olympic 1ST

First Time for Finland

Antti Kasvio won Finland's first Olympic swimming medal, with his third place "finnish" in the 200m freestyle.

JENNY THOMPSON
UNITED STATES

Jenny Thompson is one of the greatest relay anchors in Olympic history. A two-time Olympian, she anchored four American teams to gold. In 1992, the 400m free and 400m medley relay teams had two world records to go with their wins.

In March of 1992, Thompson became the first American female swimmer in 59 years to hold a world record in the 100m freestyle event (during the two decades prior, the East Germans had dominated this event). In Barcelona that year, she swam to silver in the 100m free.

One of the most memorable moments of the 1992 Games was watching Thompson and teammates Nicole Haislett, Dara Torres and Angel Martino, swim a blazing 3:39.46 in the 400m freestyle relay final. Thompson came from behind swimming the final leg in 54.01, the fastest relay leg in women's swimming history to that date.

Jenny Thompson is congratulated by 1996 teammates Trina Jackson, Cristina Teusher, and Sheila Taormina as they become the first Olympic Champions in the 4X200m free relay.

The team annihilated the six-year-old record by over a second. Not since 1976 had an American Women's Team brought home a world mark in this event.

In the 400m medley relay, the squad of Lea Loveless, Anita

Nall, Crissy Ahmann-Leighton and Thompson took the lead immediately and never looked back. They smashed the eight-year-old world record by 1.15 seconds, giving this event back to the Americans.

In Atlanta four years later, the American women were not favored to capture any of the three relay championship titles. Nevertheless, they won all three and Jenny Thompson collected gold for her contribution in each, setting new Olympic records with both the 400m and 800m free squads.

Prior to their 400m freestyle relay win, Thompson and teammates watched Americans Botsford and Hedgepeth receive their medals for the 100m backstroke event. "We were watching in the waiting room as they played the National Anthem, and that really pumped us up for the race," Thompson said, "Nothing can compare to the crowd out there and the noise. All the flags waving around ... it is great inspiration!"

Thompson also made history with the team of Trina Jackson, Cristina Teuscher and Sheila Taormina, as the first Olympic Champions in the 4X200m women's freestyle relay.

Jenny's five Olympic gold medals are the most won by an American female swimmer. On August 23, 1999, Jenny Thompson broke Mary T. Meagher's 18 year-old world mark of 57.93 for the 100m butterfly long course. She swam an incredible 57.88 and now looks to bring this speed to Sydney.

YANG WENYI
CHINA

At the April 1988 Asian Games, Yang Wenyi cracked the 25-second barrier in the women's 50m freestyle, with a time of 24.98.

Olympic 1ST

China's First Gold Medal

Zhuang Yong came in second behind Kristin Otto during the 100m freestyle final in 1988. In Barcelona she led the 100m freestyle from start to finish, set a new Olympic record, and became China's first Olympic swimming gold medalist. Yong also won two silver medals in Barcelona.

The pressure mounted on the 16-year-old Wenyi as she entered the Seoul Games as the world record holder. In the 50m final, the unstoppable Kristin Otto charged ahead, with Yang holding on for a second place finish.

Yang was not considered a serious contender for gold in Barcelona. In the years following Seoul she had continued to compete, but hadn't threatened the 25-second barrier again. She qualified sixth for the final with a time of 25.84.

The pistol sounded and Yang Wenyi blasted off the blocks, putting her in front of the other swimmers. Never letting up, she won by a meter, breaking her own world record, a record that would withstand the rigors of Atlanta.

MARTIN ZUBERO
SPAIN

Martin Zubero was born and raised in Jacksonville, Florida. His father was a citizen of Spain, giving Zubero dual citizenship. He chose to swim for Spain, as did his brother, David, who in 1980 became Spain's first Olympic swimming medalist.

Martin Zubero first represented Spain at the Seoul Games, but did not medal. Then came Barcelona, the perfect setting for Zubero's Olympic triumph. Before a sellout crowd, he set a new Olympic record in the 200m backstroke. This Zubero brother now had the honor of being Spain's first Olympic swimming champion!

In 1996 Martin Zubero made his third consecutive appearance at the Olympic Games. Qualifying for both the 100m and the 200m backstroke finals, he finished fourth and sixth, respectively. The 200m backstoke world record Zubero set back in 1991 remained intact.

L A N E   L I N E S

Biondi and Jager Together Again... and Again

With the American team's 400m free relay win in Barcelona, Jager and Biondi became the first U.S. swimmers ever to win the same Olympic event three times. Jager and Biondi became the first male Olympic swimmers to win gold medals in three Olympiads.

1992 OLYMPIC SWIMMING FINALS

INDIVIDUAL EVENTS

Gold	Silver	Bronze	Fourth	Fifth	Sixth	Seventh	Eighth

Women 50m Freestyle - World Record (24.98 Yang Wenyi CHN) — Olympic Record (25.49 Kristin Otto GDR 1988)

Gold	Silver	Bronze	Fourth	Fifth	Sixth	Seventh	Eighth
Yang Wenyi	Zhuang Yong	Angel Martino	Catherine Plewinski	Jenny Thompson	Natalya Meshcheryakova	Simone Osygus	Inge de Bruijn
CHN – 24.79n	CHN – 25.08	USA – 25.23	FRA – 25.36	USA – 25.37	MDA – 25.47	GER – 25.74	NED – 25.84

Men 50m Freestyle - World Record (21.81 Tom Jager USA) — Olympic Record (22.14 Matt Biondi USA 1988)

Gold	Silver	Bronze	Fourth	Fifth	Sixth	Seventh	Eighth
Aleksandr Popov	Matt Biondi	Tom Jager	Christopher Kalfayan	Peter Williams — Tie - 4th place	Mark Foster	Gennady Prigoda	Nils Rudolph
RUS – 21.91o	USA – 22.09	USA – 22.30	FRA – 22.50	RSA – 22.50	GBR – 22.52	RUS – 22.54	GER – 22.73

Women 100m Freestyle - World Record (54.48 Jenny Thompson USA) — Olympic Record (54.79 B. Krause GDR 1980)

Gold	Silver	Bronze	Fourth	Fifth	Sixth	Seventh	Eighth
Zhuang Young	Jenny Thompson	Franziska van Almsick	Nicole Haislett	Catherine Plewinski	Le Jingyi	Simone Osygus	Karin Brienesse
CHN – 54.64o	USA – 54.84	GER – 54.94	USA – 55.19	FRA – 55.72	CHN – 55.89	GER – 55.93	NED – 56.59

Men 100m Freestyle - World Record (48.42 Matt Biondi USA) — Olympic Record (48.63 Matt Biondi USA 1988)

Gold	Silver	Bronze	Fourth	Fifth	Sixth	Seventh	Eighth
Aleksandr Popov	Gustavo Borges	Stephan Caron	Jon Olsen	Matt Biondi	Tommy Werner	Christian-Alex. Tröger	Gennady Prigoda
RUS – 49.02	BRA – 49.43	FRA – 49.50	USA – 49.51	USA – 49.53	SWE – 49.63	GER – 49.84	RUS – 50.25

Women 200m Freestyle - World Record (1:57.55 H. Friedrich GDR) — Olympic Record (1:57.65 Friedrich GDR 1988)

Gold	Silver	Bronze	Fourth	Fifth	Sixth	Seventh	Eighth
Nicole Haislett	Franziska van Almsick	Kerstin Kielgass	Catherine Plewinski	L. Liliana Dobrescu	Suzu Chiba	Olha Kirichenko	Lu Bin
USA – 1:57.90	GER – 1:58.00	GER – 1:59.67	FRA – 1:59.88	ROM – 2:00.48	JPN – 2:00.64	UKR – 2:00.90	CHN – 2:02.10

w World Record **o** Olympic Record **p** Preliminary Heat **dq** Disqualified **e** Equal to World Record **eo** Equal to Olympic Record **dns** Did Not Start **dnf** Did Not Finish **ac** Also Competed **r** Relay Lead-off Split **E** Estimated

OLYMPIAD XXV – 1992 – BARCELONA, SPAIN

1992 OLYMPIC SWIMMING FINALS

	Gold	Silver	Bronze	Fourth	Fifth	Sixth	Seventh	Eighth
Men 200m Freestyle - World Record (1:46.69 Giorgio Lamberti ITA) Olympic Record (1:47.25 D.Armstrong AUS 1988)	Yevgeny Sadovyi RUS - 1:46.70 *o*	Anders Holmertz SWE - 1:46.86	Antti Kasvio FIN - 1:47.63	Artur Wojdat POL - 1:48.24	Vladimir Pyshnenko RUS - 1:48.32	Joe Hudepohl USA - 1:48.36	Steffen Zesner GER - 1:48.84	Doug Gjertsen USA - 1:50.57
Women 400m Freestyle - World and Olympic Record (4:03.85 Janet Evans USA)	Dagmar Hase GER - 4:07.18	Janet Evans USA - 4:07.37	Hayley Lewis AUS - 4:11.22	Erika Hansen USA - 4:11.50	Kerstin Kielgass GER - 4:11.52	Isabelle Arnould BEL - 4:13.75	Malin Nilsson SWE - 4:14.10	Suzu Chiba JPN - 4:15.71
Men 400m Freestyle - World Record (3:46.47 Kieren Perkins AUS) Olympic Record (3:46.95 Uwe Dassler GDR 1988)	Yevgeny Sadovyi RUS - 3:45.00 *w*	Kieren Perkins AUS - 3:45.16	Anders Holmertz SWE - 3:46.77	Artur Wojdat POL - 3:48.10	Ian Brown AUS - 3:48.79	Sebastian Wiese GER - 3:49.06	Stefan Pfeiffer GER - 3:49.75	Danyon Loader NZL - 3:49.97
Women 800m Freestyle - World Record (8:16.22 Janet Evans USA) Olympic Record (8:20.20 Janet Evans USA 1988)	Janet Evans USA - 8:25.52	Hayley Lewis AUS - 8:30.34	Jana Henke GER - 8:30.99	Philippa Langrell NZL - 8:35.57 *o*	Irene Dalby NOR - 8:37.12	Olga Splichalová CZE - 8:37.66	Erika Hansen USA - 8:39.25	Isabelle Arnould BEL - 8:41.86
Men 1500m Freestyle - World Record (14:48.40 Kieren Perkins AUS) Olympic Record (14:58.27 Salnikov RUS 1980)	Kieren Perkins AUS - 14:43.48w	Glen Housman AUS - 14:55.29	Jörg Hoffmann GER - 15:02.29	Stefan Pfeiffer GER - 15:04.28	Ian Wilson GBR - 15:13.35	Igor Majcen SLO - 15:19.12	Lawrence Frostad USA - 15:19.41	Viktor Andreyev RUS - 15:33.94
Women 100m Backstroke - World Record (1:00.31 K. Egerszegi HUN) Olympic Record (1:00.86 R. Reinisch GDR 1980)	Krisztina Egerszegi HUN– 1:00.68 *o*	Tünde Szabó HUN - 1:01.14	Lea Loveless USA - 1:01.43	Nicole Livingstone Stevenson AUS - 1:01.78	Elizabeth "Janie" Wagstaff USA - 1:01.81	Joanne Meehan AUS - 1:02.07	Nina Zhivanevskaya RUS - 1:02.36	Yoko Koikawa JPN - 1:03.23

1992 OLYMPIC SWIMMING FINALS

Men 100m Backstroke - World Record (53.93) Jeff Rouse USA)
Olympic Record (54.51 David Berkoff USA 1988)

Gold	Silver	Bronze	Fourth	Fifth	Sixth	Seventh	Eighth
Mark Tewksbury	Jeff Rouse	David Berkoff	Martin López-Zubero	Vladimir Selkov	Franck Schott	Rodolfo Falcón Cabrera	Dirk Richter
CAN – 53.98o	USA – 54.04	USA – 54.78	ESP – 54.96	RUS – 55.49	FRA – 55.72	CUB – 55.76	GER – 56.26

Women 200m Backstroke - World Record (2:06.62 K. Egerszegi HUN)
Olympic Record (2:09.29 K. Egerszegi HUN 1988)

Gold	Silver	Bronze	Fourth	Fifth	Sixth	Seventh	Eighth
Krisztina Egerszegi	Dagmar Hase	Nicole Livingstone Stevenson	Lea Loveless	Anna Simcic	Tünde Szabó	Sylvia Poll Ahrens	Leigh Habler
HUN – 2:07.06o	GER – 2:09.46	AUS – 2:10.20	USA – 2:11.54	NZL – 2:11.99	HUN – 2:12.94	CRC – 2:12.97	AUS – 2:13.68

Men 200m Backstroke - World Record (1:56.57 Martin L. Zubero ESP)
Olympic Record (1:58.99 R. Carey USA 1984)

Gold	Silver	Bronze	Fourth	Fifth	Sixth	Seventh	Eighth
Martin López-Zubero	Vladimir Selkov	Stefano Battistelli	Hajime Itoi	William "Tripp" Schwenk	Tino Weber	Tamás Deutsch	Stefaan Maene
ESP – 1:58.47o	RUS – 1:58.87	ITA – 1:59.40	JPN – 1:59.52	USA – 1:59.73	GER – 1:59.78	HUN – 2:00.06	BEL – 2:00.91

Women 100m Breaststroke - World Record (1:07.91 S. Hörner GDR)
Olympic Record (1:07.95 T. Dangalakova BUL 1988)

Gold	Silver	Bronze	Fourth	Fifth	Sixth	Seventh	Eighth
Yelena Rudkovskaya	Anita Nall	Samantha Riley	Guylaine Cloutier	Jana Dörries	Gabriella Csépe	Manuela Dalla Valle	Daniela Brendel
BLR – 1:08.00	USA – 1:08.17	AUS – 1:09.25	CAN – 1:09.71	GER – 1:09.77	HUN – 1:10.19	ITA – 1:10.39	GER – 1:11.05

Men 100m Breaststroke - World Record (1:01.29 Norbert Rózsa HUN)
Olympic Record (1:01.65 Lundquist USA 1984)

Gold	Silver	Bronze	Fourth	Fifth	Sixth	Seventh	Eighth
Nelson Diebel	Norbert Rózsa	Philip Rogers	Akira Hayashi	Vassily Ivanov	Dmitri Volkov	Nicholas Gillingham	Adrian Moorhouse
USA – 1:01.50o	HUN – 1:01.68	AUS – 1:01.76	JPN – 1:01.86	RUS – 1:01.87	RUS – 1:02.07	GBR – 1:02.32	GBR – 1:02.33

Women 200m Breaststroke - World Record (2:25.35 Anita Nall USA)
Olympic Record (2:26.71 Silke Horner GDR 1988)

Gold	Silver	Bronze	Fourth	Fifth	Sixth	Seventh	Eighth
Kyoko Iwasaki	Lin Li	Anita Nall	Yelena Rudkovskaya	Guylaine Cloutier	Nathalie Giguere	Manuela Dalla Valle	Alicja Peczak
JPN – 2:26.65o	CHN – 2:26.85	USA – 2:26.88	BLR – 2:28.47	CAN – 2:29.88	CAN – 2:30.11	ITA – 2:31.21	POL – 2:31.76

1992 OLYMPIC SWIMMING FINALS

	Gold	Silver	Bronze	Fourth	Fifth	Sixth	Seventh	Eighth

Men 200m Breaststroke - World Record (2:10.60 Mike Barrowman USA)

Gold	Silver	Bronze	Fourth	Fifth	Sixth	Seventh	Eighth
Mike Barrowman	Norbert Rózsa	Nicholas Gillingham	Sergio López Miró	Károly Güttler	Philip Rogers	Kenji Watanabe	Akira Hayashi
USA – 2:10.16 w	HUN – 2:11.23	GBR – 2:11.29	ESP – 2:13.29	HUN – 2:13.32	AUS – 2:13.59	JPN – 2:14.70	JPN – 2:15.11

Olympic Record (2:13.34 V. Davis CAN 1984)

Women 100m Butterfly - World Record (57.93 Mary T. Meagher USA)

Gold	Silver	Bronze	Fourth	Fifth	Sixth	Seventh	Eighth
Qian Hong	C. Ahmann-Leighton	Catherine Plewinski	Wang Xiaohong	Susan O'Neill	Summer Sanders	Franziska van Almsick	Rie Shito
CHN – 58.62 o	USA – 58.74	FRA – 59.01	CHN – 59.10	AUS – 59.69	USA – 59.82	GER – 1:00.70	JPN – 1:01.16

Olympic Record (59.00 Kristin Otto GDR 1988)

Men 100m Butterfly - World Record (52.84 Pablo Morales USA)

Gold	Silver	Bronze	Fourth	Fifth	Sixth	Seventh	Eighth
Pablo Morales	Rafal Szukala	Anthony Nesty	Pavel Khnykin	Melvin Stewart	Marcel Gery	Martin López-Zubero	Vladislav Kulikov
USA – 53.32	POL – 53.35	SUR – 53.41	UKR – 53.81	USA – 54.04	CAN – 54.18	ESP – 54.19	RUS – 54.26

Olympic Record (53.00 Anthony Nesty SUR 1988)

Women 200m Butterfly - World Record (2:05.96 Mary T. Meagher USA)

Gold	Silver	Bronze	Fourth	Fifth	Sixth	Seventh	Eighth
Summer Sanders	Wang Xiaohong	Susan O'Neill	Mika Haruna	Ric Shito	Ina "Angie" Wester-Krieg	Mette Jacobsen	Ilaria Tocchini
USA – 2:08.67	CHN – 2:09.01	AUS – 2:09.03	JPN – 2:09.88	JPN – 2:10.24	USA – 2:11.46	DEN – 2:11.87	ITA – 2:13.78

Olympic Record (2:06.90 Meagher USA 1984)

Men 200m Butterfly - World Record (1:55.69 Melvin Stewart USA)

Gold	Silver	Bronze	Fourth	Fifth	Sixth	Seventh	Eighth
Melvin Stewart	Danyon Loader	Franck Esposito	Rafal Szukala	Keiichi Kawanaka	Denis Pankratov	Robert Pinter	Martin Roberts
USA – 1:56.26 o	NZL – 1:57.93	FRA – 1:58.51	POL – 1:58.89	JPN – 1:58.97	RUS – 1:58.98	ROM – 1:59.34	AUS – 1:59.64

Olympic Record (1:56.94 M. Gross GDR 1988)

Women 200m Individual Medley - World Record (2:11.73 U. Geweniger GDR)

Gold	Silver	Bronze	Fourth	Fifth	Sixth	Seventh	Eighth
Lin Li	Summer Sanders	Daniela Hunger	Yelena Dendeberova	Elli Overton	Marianne Limpert	Nancy Sweetman	Ewa Synowska
CHN – 2:11.65 w	USA – 2:11.91	GER – 2:13.92	RUS – 2:15.47	AUS – 2:15.76	CAN – 2:17.09	CAN – 2:17.13	POL – 2:18.85

Olympic Record (2:12.59 D. Hunger GDR 1988)

1992 OLYMPIC SWIMMING FINALS

	Gold	Silver	Bronze	Fourth	Fifth	Sixth	Seventh	Eighth
Men 200m Individual Medley - World Record (1:59.36 Tamás Darnyi HUN)					Olympic Record (2:00.17 T. Darnyi HUN 1988)			
	Tamás Darnyi	Gregory Burgess	Attila Czene	Jani Sievinen	Christian Gessner	Ronald Karnaugh	Matthew Dunn	Gary Anderson
	HUN - 2:00.76	USA - 2:00.97	HUN - 2:01.00	FIN - 2:01.28	GER - 2:01.97	USA - 2:02.18	AUS - 2:02.79	CAN - 2:04.30
Women 400m Individual Medley - World Record (4:36.10 P. Schneider GDR)					Olympic Record (4:36.29 P. Schneider 1980)			
	Krisztina Egerszegi	Lin Li	Summer Sanders	Hayley Lewis	Hideko Hiranaka	Daniela Hunger	Eri Kimura	Ewa Synowska
	HUN - 4:36.54	CHN - 4:36.73	USA - 4:37.58	AUS - 4:43.75	JPN - 4:46.24	GER - 4:47.57	JPN - 4:47.78	POL - 4:53.32
Men 400m Individual Medley - World Record (4:12.36 T. Darnyi HUN)					Olympic Record (4:14.75 T. Darnyi HUN 1988)			
	Tamás Darnyi	Eric Namesnik	Luca Sacchi	David Wharton	Christian Gessner	Patrick Kühl	Sergei Marinyuk	Takahiro Fujimoto
	HUN - 4:14.23 o	USA - 4:15.57	ITA - 4:16.34	USA - 4:17.26	GER - 4:17.88	GER - 4:19.66	MDA - 4:22.93	JPN - 4:23.86

RELAY EVENTS

	Gold	Silver	Bronze	Fourth	Fifth	Sixth	Seventh	Eighth
Women 400m Medley Relay - World Record (4:03.69 GDR)						Olympic Record (4:03.74 GDR 1988)		
	Lea Loveless, Anita Nall, Christine Ahmann-Leighton, Jenny Thompson p - E. Wagstaff, M. Kleine, S. Sanders, N. Haislett	Dagmar Hase, Jana Dörries, Franziska van Almsick, Daniela Hunger p - Daniela Brendel, Bettina Ustrowski, Simone Osygus	Nina Zhivanevskaya, Yelena Rudkovskaya, Olga Kirichenko, Natalya Meshcheryakova p - Y. Shubina	Lin Li, Lou Xia, Qian Hong, Le Jingyi p - He Cihong	Nicole Livingstone, Samantha Riley, Susan O'Neill, Lisa Curry-Kenny p - Joanne Meehan	Nicole Dryden, Guylaine Cloutier, Kristin Topham, Andrea Nugent	Yoko Koikawa, Kyoko Iwasaki, Yoko Kando, Suzu Chiba	Ellen Elzerman, Kira Bulten, Inge de Bruijn, Marianne Muis
	USA - 4:02.54 w	GER - 4:05.19	SOV - 4:06.44	CHN - 4:06.78	AUS - 4:07.01	CAN - 4:09.26	JPN - 4:09.92	NED - 4:10.87

1992 OLYMPIC SWIMMING FINALS

	Gold	Silver	Bronze	Fourth	Fifth	Sixth	Seventh	Eighth
Men 400m Medley Relay - World and Olympic Records (3:36.93 USA 1988)								
	USA-3:36.93ew	SOV – 3:38.56	CAN – 3:39.66	GER – 3:40.19	FRA – 3:40.51	HUN – 3:42.03	AUS – 3:42.65	JPN - 3:43.25
	Jeff Rouse, Nelson Diebel, Pablo Morales, Jon Olsen, *p* - David Berkoff, Hans Dersch, Melvin Stewart, Matt Biondi	Vladimir Selkov, Vasily Ivanov, Pavel Khnykin, Aleksandr Popov, *p* - Vladislav Kulikov, Dmitri Volkov, Vladimir Pyshnenko	Mark Tewksbury, Jonathan Cleveland, Marcel Gery, Stephen Clarke, *p* - Thomas Ponting	Tino Weber, Mark Warnecke, Christian Keller, *p* - Bengt Zikarsky	Franck Schott, Stephane Vossart, Bruno Gutzeit, Stephan Caron, *p* - Franck Esposito, Christophe Kalfayan	Tamás Deutsch, Norbert Rózsa, Péter Horváth, Béla Szabados	Thomas Stachewicz, Philip Rogers, Jonathon Sieben, Christopher Fydler	Hajime Itoi, Akira Hayashi, Keiichi Kawanaka, Tsutomu Nakano
Women 400m Freestyle Relay - World Record (3:40.57 GDR)						Olympic Record (3:40.63 GDR 1988)		
	USA– 3:39.46 w	CHN - 3:40.12	GER - 3:41.60	SOV – 3:43.68	NED – 3:43.74	DEN - 3:47.81	SWE - 3:48.47	CAN - 3:49.37
	Nicole Haislett, Dara Torres, Angel Martino, Jenny Thompson, *p* - Ashley Tappin, Christine Ahmann-Leighton	Zhuang Yong, Lu Bin, Yang Wenyi, Le Jingyi, *p* - Zhao Kun	Franziska van Almsick, Simone Osygus, Daniela Hunger, Manuela Stellmach, *p* - Kerstin Kielgass, Annette Hadding	Natalya Meshcheryakova, Svetlana Leshukova, Yelena Dendeberova, Yelena Shubina, *p* - Yevgenya Yermakova	Diana van de Plaats, Mildred Muis, Marianne Muis, Karin Brienesse, *p* - Inga de Bruijn	Gitta Jensen, Mette Jacobsen, Berit Puggaard, Mette Nielsen, *p* - Annette Poulsen	Eva Nyberg, Louise Karlsson, Ellenor Svensson, Malin Nilsson, *p* - Linda Olofsson	Marianne Limpert, Nicole Dryden, Andrea Nugent, Allison Higson

1992 OLYMPIC SWIMMING FINALS

Men 400m Freestyle Relay - World and Olympic Record (3:16.53 USA 1988)

Gold	Silver	Bronze	Fourth	Fifth	Sixth	Seventh	Eighth
Joe Hudepohl, Matt Biondi, Tom Jager, Jon Olsen *p* - Shaun Jordon, Joel Thomas	Pavel Khnykin, Gennady Prigoda, Yuri Bashkatov, Aleksandr Popov *p* - Vladimir Pyshnenko, Veniamin Tayanovich	Christian-Alexander Tröger, Dirk Richter, Steffen Zesner, Mark Pinger *p* - Andreas Szigat, Bengt Zikarsky	Christophe Kalfayan, Franck Schott, Frederic Lefevre, Stephan Caron *p* - Ludovic Depickere, Bruno Gutzeit	Tommy Werner, Håkan Karlsson, Fredrik Letzler, Anders Holmertz *p* - Göran Titus	José Souza-Junior, Gustavo Borges, Emmanuel Fortes Nascimento, Cristiano Michelena	Roland Lee, Mark Foster, Michael Fibbens, Paul Howe	Christopher Fydler, Andrew Baildon, Thomas Stachewicz, Darren Lange
USA – 3:16.74	SOV – 3:17.56	GER – 3:17.90	FRA – 3:19.16	SWE – 3:20.10	BRA – 3:20.99	GBR – 3:21.75	AUS – 3:22.04

Men 800m Freestyle Relay - World and Olympic Record (7:12.51 USA 1988)

Gold	Silver	Bronze	Fourth	Fifth	Sixth	Seventh	Eighth
Dmitri Lepikov, Vladimir Pyshnenko, Veniamin Tayanovich, Yevgeny Sadovyi *p* - Aleksei Kudryavtsev, Yuri Mukhin	Christer Wallin, Anders Holmertz, Tommy Werner, Lars Frölander	Joe Hudepohl, Melvin Stewart, Jon Olsen, Douglas Gjertsen *p* - Scott Jaffe, Daniel Jorgenson	Peter Sitt, Steffen Zesner, Andreas Szigat, Stefan Pfeiffer *p* - Christian Tröger	Roberto Gleria, Giorgio Lamberti, Massimo Trevisan, Stefano Battistelli *p* - Emanuele Idini, Piermaria Siciliano	Paul Palmer, Steven Mellor, Stephen Akers, Paul Howe	Gustavo Borges, Emmanuel Fortes Nascimento, Teofilo Laborne Ferreira, Cristiano Michelena	Ian Brown, Deane Pieters, Kieren Perkins, Duncan Armstrong *p* - Martin Roberts
SOV – 7:11.95 *w*	SWE – 7:15.51	USA – 7:16.23	GER – 7:16.58	ITA – 7:18.10	GBR – 7:22.57	BRA – 7:24.03	AUS – *dq*

Chapter 24

Olympiad XXVI - 1996
Atlanta, Georgia, United States

for the second time in twelve years the Summer Olympic Games were held in the United States. Atlanta, Georgia was a surprising choice for the Centennial Games. Greece, the birthplace of both the ancient and modern Olympic Games, was the sentimental favorite. The I.O.C., however, opted for the "City of Hospitality."

An estimated 1.7 billion dollars were spent to stage the Atlanta Games, which would be viewed globally by close to 3.5 billion people. An unprecedented number of athletes, more than 11,000, represented 197 nations.

Both the men and women's swimming programs held 13 individual and 3 relay events. Olympic medals were won by swimmers from 19 different countries, an Olympic record in itself. Ten of these nations took home gold. In all, four world records were shattered during the seven days of swimming competition.

Olympic 1ST
Medal Madness

Ireland's Michelle Smith won her country's first swimming medal. Costa Rica's Claudia Poll, Danyon Loader of New Zealand, and Fred de Burghgraeve of Belgium also won their country's first Olympic swimming gold medals.

The United States Team entered these Games as underdogs. Not one American record had been broken at the U.S. Trials. The men were favored only in the 100m back, 400m IM, and 400m freestyle relay events. The American women were not expected to strike gold in Atlanta.

This U.S. Swim Team was nothing short of spectacular, garnering 13 gold medals, seven by the women, six by the men. In all, the United States won 26 Olympic swimming medals, due in large part to the 15,000 partisan fans who packed the swim venue on a nightly basis.

L A N E   L I N E S

MVP Award

Head swim coach, Skip Kenney, said, "In basketball, they give out a sixth man award... and if there were a sixth man here, it would have to be the crowd."

On July 27, 1996, these Games were marred by the explosion of a pipe bomb, set-off in Centennial Olympic Park a popular downtown gathering spot. The explosion was responsible for the deaths of two people and the injury of 113 others.

With flags at half mast, the Olympic Games continued. Centennial Park was reopened three days later. Over 30,000 people were present at the morning ceremony, and by day's end almost 350,000 people had passed through the park.

The tradition of the Olympic Games continued despite this tragedy, as it had done in Munich in 1972. Spectators and athletes alike were not to be denied their Olympic moment.

AMANDA BEARD
UNITED STATES

Fourteen-year-old Amanda Beard was a bright new star on the American team in Atlanta. As a mere high school sophomore, she won individual silvers in both the 100m and 200m breaststroke events, setting a new American record in the 100m final (1:08.09).

Photo by Tim Morse

Fourteen-year-old Amanda Beard set a new American record in the 100m final.

Beard also took home gold as a member of the championship medley relay team. "Home" for Amanda includes her family, four birds, two cats, two rabbits and one dog! As dedicated to animals as she is to her swimming, Amanda donates part of her allowance to a local animal shelter.

BROOKE BENNETT
UNITED STATES

When she was just six years old, Brooke Bennett and her father Keith used to watch the movie Top Gun before her races. Brooke explained this pre-race ritual, "Turn and burn. Turn and burn, just like the fighter pilots," they'd say. Her dad would then ask her, "Who's gonna win?" Her reply, "Me!"

After capturing the 400m, 800m and 1500m freestyle titles

at the U.S. Nationals in August 1995, Brooke Bennett was disappointed when she missed qualifying in the 400m event at the U.S. Olympic Trials. The teenager bounced back, qualifying first in the 800m free event, sending her to Atlanta.

As a determined 16-year-old, Brooke entered Atlanta with only one goal in mind: to win gold. Mission accomplished! Bennett easily out swam her competition, finishing over two seconds ahead of second place finisher Dagmar Hase of Germany.

On the podium, Brooke's thoughts turned to her late grandfather, James Lane, who had taught her to swim. "He was very proud to say he started my swimming career. I know he's jumping up and down as he watches over me," remarked Bennett.

Jon Olsen - United States

Veteran Olympian, Jon Olsen, 26, was elected co-captain of the 1996 U.S. Men's Olympic Swim Team. A freestyle specialist, Jon Olsen earned one Olympic bronze medal and four gold medals over two Olympiads.

In Barcelona he won gold medals anchoring both the 400m medley and free relay teams, and a bronze with the 800m free relay squad. In 1996, as the lead-off swimmer in the 400m free relay, and as a qualifier for the 800m free relay team, Olsen added two more gold medals before closing his Olympic career.

BETH BOTSFORD
UNITED STATES

On day three of the competition Beth Botsford became the first woman from the U.S. to win a gold medal in Atlanta. Beth's win in the 100m backstroke guaranteed her a berth on the 400m

Botsford, 15, credited coach Murray Stevens with keeping her "all together" during the competition. Botsford returned home to North Baltimore with her two gold medals and resumed her high school studies at Garrison Forrest School.

Photo by Tim Morse

Silver and Gold for Hedgepeth and Botsford.

BRAD BRIDGEWATER
UNITED STATES

Late in 1994, backstroker Brad Bridgewater was unhappy with both his academic and swimming performances while at the University of Texas. He made a decision that would ultimately change the course of both. Brad transferred to the University of Southern California (USC) in the spring of 1995.

The move to USC revitalized Bridgewater. With the guidance of USC coach Mark Schubert, Brad prepared for the U.S. Olympic Trials. There he qualifed first in his event, the 200m backstroke.

The 200m backstroke field featured no clear-cut favorites as race day approached. Bridgewater qualified first in the morning preliminary heats.

In the final, the twenty-three-year-old Bridgewater took the lead by the 100m mark. Brad touched first, followed closely by teammate Tripp Schwenk and Italy's Emanuele Merisi.

SCORE
BOARD
Shattered

During the 1996 Centennial Games, three national records were set during the 100m breaststroke final. Jeremy Linn (silver medalist) set an American record (1:00.77), Mark Warnecke (bronze medalist) set a German record, and Zeng Qilian (seventh place finisher) set a new Chinese record (1:02.01).

ATTILA CZENE
HUNGARY

At the Games of Barcelona, Attila Czene of Hungary was not considered a serious medal contender. Czene hoped only to qualify for the 200m IM final. It was his teammate and world record holder, Tamas Darnyi, who "owned" this event.

The tenacious eighteen-year-old, Czene, held his own in the final, remaining in contention until the last 50 meters of the race. His time was a quarter of a second off gold. The young man from Hungary, who merely wanted to qualify, went home with an Olympic bronze medal.

Czene returned to the Olympic Games in Atlanta to compete once more in his specialty, the 200m IM. Again, he was not a favorite.

Attila's preliminary swim did not go well, and, as a result, he was positioned in an outside lane that evening for the final. After the backstroke leg of this event, Czene began to forge ahead in what was described as "outside smoke." Jan Sievinen of Finland, the current world record holder, challenged the Hungarian, but it was Czene who touched the pad first, setting a new Olympic record in the process.

As he was coming down the home stretch during his race, Czene recalled the advice that his coach, Tamas Szechy, had given him, "Don't think, just swim!" That's just what he did.

JOSH DAVIS
UNITED STATES

Texan Josh Davis, 23, won more gold medals than any other American male Olympian at the Games in Atlanta. This freestyle specialist swam in both the 800m and 400m freestyle relay finals, and the 400m medley relay morning prelim to earn his three gold medals.

Photo by Tim Morse

400m freestyle relay gold medalists: G. Hall, B.Schumacher, J. Davis and J. Olsen.

Silver medalist Eric Namesnik congratulates teammate Tom Dolan.

THOMAS DOLAN
UNITED STATES

Tom Dolan's quest to etch his name into the Olympic record books didn't come easy. The versatile swimmer from Arlington, Virginia has suffered since childhood from exercise-induced asthma and reflux. He has a very narrow trachea that, combined with the asthma, greatly limits his oxygen intake. There have been times that

L A N E   L I N E S

Belgian Doesn't Waffle

Fred de Burghgraeve made his first Olympic appearance in Barcelona at the age of nineteen, placing 34th in the 100m breaststroke preliminary round. Four years later, the swimmer from Belgium was the man to beat, as he blazed to a new world record (1:00.60) in the morning qualifying heat in Atlanta. De Burghgraeve won Belgium's first swimming gold medal in a race that boasted the fastest breaststroke field ever assembled in Olympic history.

Dolan has tried swimming through an attack and subsequently passed out. Despite his affliction, Dolan persevered. In 1994 he broke Tamas Darnyi's 400m IM world record at the World Championships in Rome.

His marathon practice sessions (85,000 - 105,000m a week) led to rumors that he was suffering from chronic fatigue syndrome just prior to the 1996 Olympic Trials. At the Trials, Dolan finished atop the qualifiers in the 200m IM, 400m IM and the 400m freestyle events.

At the age of 20, Dolan captured the first gold medal for the U.S. in Atlanta with his win in the 400m IM. The race was a duel between Dolan and Michigan teammate, Eric Namesnik. At the 200-meter mark, both swimmers were even. By 300 meters, Namesnik had almost a half-second lead over the six foot, six inch Dolan.

In the final 50 meters Namesnik was still in the lead, but Dolan had narrowed the gap. They charged to the wall and it was Dolan out touching his longtime nemesis, Namesnik.

"Keep striving, keep praying, keep smiling," was advice Dolan's dad had given him. Tom Dolan added, "That's what I do in swimming and in life."

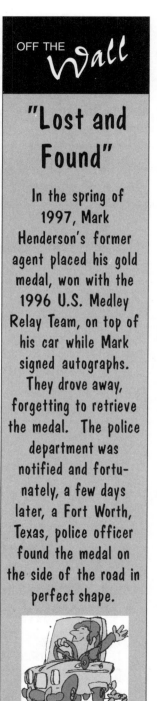

OFF THE $\mathcal{wall}$

"Lost and Found"

In the spring of 1997, Mark Henderson's former agent placed his gold medal, won with the 1996 U.S. Medley Relay Team, on top of his car while Mark signed autographs. They drove away, forgetting to retrieve the medal. The police department was notified and fortunately, a few days later, a Fort Worth, Texas, police officer found the medal on the side of the road in perfect shape.

SPLASH BACK
Dejavu

The Australian great, Dawn Fraser, is the only other swimmer ever to have accomplished what Krisztina Egerszegi did in Atlanta: winning an individual gold medal, in the same event, in three consecutive Olympiads.

KRISZTINA EGERSZEGI
HUNGARY

Krisztina Egerszegi is a member of the elite group of athletes whose careers spanned three Olympiads. Her nickname is Mouse, a translation of "eger" in Hungarian that befits her shy personality.

In 1988, Egerszegi, at 99 pounds (42 pounds lighter than the nearest competitor), blew past the field in the Olympic 200m backstroke final. It had been 36 years since a female Hungarian had won a gold medal.

With this victory, Egerszegi, at the age of fourteen, became the youngest swimmer in Olympic his-

Photo by Tim Morse

Three-time Olympic Backstroke Champion Krisztina Egerszegi.

tory to win an individual swimming gold medal. This "mighty mouse" collected a silver medal in the 100m backstroke at these games, as well.

In 1992, Krisztina, now the seasoned veteran, returned to the Olympic stage. As the current world record holder of both the 100m and 200m backstroke events, Egerszegi, as expected, handily won both finals.

The eighteen-year-old Hungarian collected her third gold medal in Barcelona when she pushed ahead in the final 50 meters of the 400m IM to upset Lin Li of China.

Krisztina still held the world record in the 200m back as she entered the Centennial Olympic Games. She swam into the record books with her third historic win in this event. She also won bronze in the 400m IM final.

Krisztina Egerszegi has won more individual gold medals than any other female Olympian (5). On August 16, 1996, Egerszegi's 22nd birthday, she announced her intention to retire from major competition.

LANE LINES

To Compete or Not to Compete

Despite being ranked number one in the 100m back at the 1996 Games, Egerszegi surprisingly opted not to compete in this event. She did, however, go on to win a bronze medal in the 400m IM final. It was noted that her lead-off time for the backstroke leg of the 400m IM, was 1:01.05; faster than the gold medal performance of American Beth Botsford in the 100m backstroke final (1:01.19).

GARY HALL, JR.
UNITED STATES

Gary Hall, Jr., carries on not only his father's name, but also a tradition of Olympic swimming. The elder Hall represented the United States in 1968, 1972 and 1976. "Junior's" introduction to the Olympic Games came as a two-year-old. The toddler rode atop his father's shoulders, poolside at the 1976 Montreal Games twenty years earlier.

Leading up to the Olympic Trials, the younger Hall was not known for a strong training ethic. However, at the U.S. Trials, the talented sprinter qualified first in the 50m and second in the 100m freestyle events, respectively.

Photo by Tim Morse

The 400m relay team of Jeremy Linn, Gary Hall Jr., Jeff Rouse and Mark Henderson.

Hall was a major player in two of the most anxiously awaited races of the swimming competition in Atlanta. He was up against the outspoken world record holder and defending Olympic champion, Aleksandr Popov of Russia.

The 100m freestyle final ignited the 15,000 spectators, as Hall and Popov blazed down their respective lanes. Hall, as is his custom, was first off the blocks and hit the 50m wall first. Popov came out of his turn ahead of the American. Fifteen meters from the finish Hall caught the Russian superstar, only to be touched out by seven hundredths of a second.

The 50m free final was no less exciting. In this race, it was

Popov who got the jump off the blocks. Hall caught him midway, but was unable to stay with him in the last 10 meters, taking his second silver medal of the 1996 Atlanta Games.

Hall's relay events were a different story. It was here with his relay splits that he finally defeated Popov. As Hall's proud parents cheered him on, Gary anchored the 400m medley and the 400m free relay to gold. Hall's 47.45 split in the 400m free relay was the fastest swim ever for that distance (relay legs cannot be sanctioned as records unless it is the lead-off swimmer).

L A N E L I N E S

Like Father, Like Son

Gary Hall, Jr. anchored the U.S. Men's 400m Freestyle Relay Team to a new world record in August, 1995, at the Pan Pacific meet. With the setting of this record, Hall and his father became the only father and son to hold world records in swimming.

WHITNEY HEDGEPETH
UNITED STATES

Backstroke specialist Whitney Hedgepeth, as a 1988 Olympian, finished 8th in the 200 IM. At the 1992 U.S. Trials only the first and second place finishers made the Olympic Team. Hedgepeth missed qualifying with a third place finish in both the 200m freestyle and 200m backstroke events

Hedgepeth retired from competition soon after those Trials and went on to become a sixth grade teacher in Austin, Texas. In 1994, Whitney came out of retirement and resumed training, in hopes of making the 1996 Team.

Her Trials were outstanding, with a first place finish in the 100m and a second in the 200m backstroke. At each race she was flanked by high schooler Beth Botsford.

In Atlanta, Whitney Hedgepeth, age 25, won silver medals in both backstroke finals. She also collected a gold medal for swimming the morning qualifying round for the victorious U.S. 400m medley relay team. Ever the teacher, Whitney taught the world to be patient with one's dreams.

PENELOPE HEYNS
SOUTH AFRICA

Photo by Tim Morse

Penelope Heyns of South Africa, the only woman to set a new world mark in the swimming competiton in Atlanta.

Penelope Heyns, 21, of Amanzimototi, South Africa, struck gold twice in the Games of Atlanta. She entered as the current world record holder in the 100m breaststroke, having broken Australian Samantha Riley's world record earlier in the year.

Four years earlier in Barcelona, Heyns had finished 33rd and 34th in the breaststroke events. Heyns came to the United States in 1993, as a student at the University of Nebraska. She continues to train in the U.S.

With her win in the 100m breaststroke on day two of the swimming competition, Penelope became the first swimmer in forty-four years to win a gold medal for South Africa. Not only did Heyns capture gold, she shattered her own world record during the 100m breaststroke prelim, with a 1:07.02.

Heyns returned to the pool two days later to win the 200m breaststroke title and set a new Olympic record. Her lead in that race was so great that even though American Amanda Beard swam the final 50 meters almost two seconds faster, she still failed to catch Heyns.

Penny Heyns was the only woman during the seven days of Olympic swimming competition in Atlanta to set a new world record.

Daniel Kowalski - Australia

Daniel Kowalski, 21, was Australia's most decorated male swimmer of the 1996 Olympic Games. Known as a middle to long distance swimmer, he collected bronze medals in both the 200m and 400m freestyle events. On the final day of competition he captured a silver medal in the 1500m free, finishing behind fellow countryman Kieren Perkins

LE JINGYI
CHINA

Le Jingyi of China is a two-time Olympian. In her Olympic debut in Barcelona, she finished sixth in the 100m freestyle. At 21, she entered the Atlanta Games as the current world record holder in both the 50m and 100m freestyle events. Le had her sites set on gold.

The first event of the Atlanta Games was the women's 100m freestyle event. Jingyi captured the title and set a new Olympic record (54.50).

The American 400m free relay team considered Jingyi their biggest obstacle to gold. Surprisingly, she was chosen to swim the first leg of the final. She put her team out front, but her teammates were unable to hold off the strong American squad and finished with the silver.

The very last day of the swimming competition brought the 50m freestyle final. Le led throughout, but was touched out at the wall by American Amy Van Dyken. Le Jingyi returned to China as her country's most decorated Olympian of the 1996 Olympic Games.

DANYON LOADER
NEW ZEALAND

Photo by Tim Morse

Danyon Loader shows off New Zealand's first Olympic Swimming gold medal.

Danyon Loader represented New Zealand in both the 1992 and 1996 Olympic Games. At seventeen he made his first notch in Olympic history. Loader swam like never before, crushing his pre-Olympic time by 3.6 seconds, winning silver in the 200m butterfly event.

After Barcelona, Loader switched his focus from butterfly to freestyle. Danyon, attended the University of Southern California, and came to Atlanta as a serious contender in both the 200m and 400m freestyle, events where there were no clear favorites.

On the first day of swimming competition the ponytailed

Loader captured gold in the 200m free final by a decisive margin, claiming New Zealand's very first Olympic swimming gold medal.

Loader returned to the pool on the fourth day of the Games. By the last lap of the 400m freestyle final, Danyon was simply out of reach. Finishing ahead of Paul Palmer (GBR) by over a full second, Loader clinched a second gold.

Danyon Loader left Atlanta with two new national records and two gold medals to add to his Olympic accomplishments.

L A N E   L I N E S

Sister Act

Claudia Poll won Costa Rica's first Olympic gold medal with her victory over world record holder Franziska van Almsick (GER), in the 200m freestyle final in Atlanta. Claudia Poll returned home to a hero's welcome. Close to 1.5 million of her countrymen celebrated with an eight-hour parade in her honor.

At the 1988 Olympic Games, Claudia's older sister, Silvia Poll Ahrens, won the silver medal in the same event, earning Costa Rica's first Olympic medal.

Claudia Poll celebrates Costa Rica's first gold medal.

Photo by Tim Morse

ANGEL MARTINO
UNITED STATES

At the U.S. Olympic Trials in 1988, Angel (Meyers) Martino, became the center of controversy. Qualifying for three events, she was subsequently disqualified for testing positive for steroids. Denying the allegations, Angel believed the positive test resulted from prescribed medication.

Photo by Tim Morse

A. Martino, B. Botsford and A. Beard congratulate A. Van Dyken in their 400m medley relay team victory.

Martino persevered and qualified for the 1992 U.S. Olympic Team. In Barcelona, she captured a bronze medal in the 50m freestyle event, swimming her fastest time ever. She won gold as a member of the 400m free relay squad, swimming the second fastest leg on the team.

This seasoned veteran qualified for three individual events at the 1996 Olympic Trials. In Atlanta, Martino won individual bronze medals in both the 100m freestyle and 100m butterfly events. She was just touched out for a third bronze in the 50m freestyle final. Angel also captured gold with the 400m freestyle and medley relay teams.

Angel honored Trish Henry, a volunteer at the Games who had undergone radiation treatments for cancer only two days earlier. "You are my hero, and my thoughts are with you," said Martino, as she gave Henry her newly acquired bronze medal.

LANE LINES

"No Teen Angel"

With her victories as a member of the 400m freestyle and 400m medley relay teams, Angel Martino, 29, became the oldest American swimmer to win an Olympic gold medal.

ERIC NAMESNIK
UNITED STATES

Eric Namesnik, of Butler, Pennsylvania, is one of America's premier individual medley swimmers. Placing sixth at the U.S. Trials in 1988, he had to wait until 1992 to make his first Olympic appearance. As theAmerican record holder, Namesnik won a silver medal in the 400m IM in Barcelona.

A graduate of the University of Michigan, Namesnik continued to train with Club Wolverine and Coach Jon Urbanchek. As the Atlanta Games approached, Eric's strongest competition came from Wolverine teammate, Tom Dolan.

Namesnik and Dolan each respected the fact that they had

Curtis Myden - Canada

Curtis Myden of Canada won bronze medals in both the 200m and 400m IM's. His 400m IM swim set a new Canadian record and earned Canada's only swimming medals of the Atlanta Games.

pushed one another to become the fastest 400m IM swimmers in the world. Dolan and Namesnik finished 1-2 respectively, in Atlanta.

SUSAN O'NEILL
AUSTRALIA

Australian Susan O'Neill began her Olympic career at the 1992 Games in Barcelona, where she captured her first Olympic medal, taking bronze in the 200m butterfly.

O'Neill, 23, entered the 1996 Olympic Games and won silver and bronze medals, as a member of Australia's 400m medley relay and 800m free relay squads. She also placed fifth in both the 200m free and 100m butterfly finals.

Having dominated the 200m butterfly event for the last three years, O'Neill had one thing on her mind, and it had to wait until day seven. She disappointed no one, finishing over two seconds ahead of silver medalist and teammate, Petra Thomas, to capture the Olympic title. Her victory represented Australia's first swimming gold medal of the 1996 Olympic Games.

On February 17th, 1999, Susan O'Neill broke the 18 year–old women's short course 200m butterfly mark held by Mary T. Meagher. O'Neill now has her sights set on Meagher's long-course record.

SPLASH BACK

In 1968 Lynette McClements became Australia's first female swimmer to capture an Olympic gold medal in a butterfly event. This was an unmatched feat until Susan O'Neill's victory in the 200m butterfly in Atlanta.

DENIS PANKRATOV
RUSSIA

Denis Pankratov is a butterfly specialist from Volgograd, Russia, who competed at both the 1992 and 1996 Games.

Growing up in the city of Stalingrad (now Volgograd), Pankratov started competitive swimming at the age of

Denis Pankratov flys from the blocks to a new world record.

Photo by Tim Morse

seven. The conditions he trained in were less than ideal. He had no access to indoor training facilities and at times trained in near arctic conditions.

> *"The pool water flowed from the dressing room, under a wall and outside. Everyday we would jump into that water and swim outside into the cold air. On some days we could not see the coach because so much steam would be rising from the water. On clearer days we would see our coach on deck wearing a hat, scarf, heavy coat, gloves and boots, giving us directions while holding a snowball. Those were tough, yet memorable times."*
>
> —Denis Pankratov

In his first Olympic appearance in Barcelona, the young Pankratov placed sixth in the 200m fly final. In August of 1995, he broke the 100m fly world record, held by Pablo Morales. Earlier that year he set the world record in the 200m fly, as well.

Then came Atlanta. His fourth place swim in the qualifying round for the 200m butterfly caused concern, but by evening's end Pankratov was golden. On day five of the Olympic swimming competition, Pankratov not only won the 100m butterfly final, but broke his own world record with a time of 52.27. He was one of only two men to set individual world records in Atlanta, and he left no doubt who ruled the fly.

As a member of Russia's 400m medley relay team, Pankratov added a silver medal to his collection. Looking ahead, we are likely to see Denis Pankratov on the starting blocks at the Games of 2000 in Sydney, Australia, set to defend both his Olympic titles.

SPLASH BACK
Back to Back

With Aleksandr Popov's back to back Olympic 100m freestyle wins, he joined the ranks of swimming greats Johnny Weissmuller (1924 & 1928) and Duke Kahanamoku (1912 & 1920).

ALEKSANDR POPOV
RUSSIA

Photo by Tim Morse

The "Russian Rocket" sighs relief after his hard fought 100m free victory.

He is nicknamed the "Russian Rocket" and he is the only swimmer to win both the 50m and 100m freestyle events in two consecutive Olympiads. Aleksandr Popov is the greatest freestyle sprinter in Olympic history to date.

In Popov's first event of the Barcelona Games, the 20 year-old Russian faced the American powerhouse, Matt Biondi. Biondi had not lost a major 100m freestyle final in eight years.

Popov, however, was the top qualifier, setting the stage for an exciting final. At the 50m mark Popov was in sixth place and Biondi was leading the pack. In the final 50 meters Popov turned it on, swimming 24.99 (the first-ever, sub-25 in the last 50 meters) for a decisive win.

The 50m free final was expected to be a duel between American Biondi and Tom Jager. Popov upset both great sprinters, setting a new Olympic record of 21.91. He added two silver medals to his accomplishments with the Russian 400m free, and medley relay teams.

Popov arrived in Atlanta as the undisputed favorite in the 100m event, but had only the third fastest swim of the year over the 50m distance. He ranked behind Americans Gary Hall, Jr. and David Fox.

Both the 100m and 50m races proved to be a battle between Popov and Hall. In both, Popov lunged to the wall to out touch the American. As he had done in Barcelona, Popov earned two more silver medals with his teammates in the 400m free and medley relay races.

OFF THE *Wall*

"Turn-over"

Aleksandr Popov began competitive swimming as a backstroker, at the age of eight. Years later, Soviet coach Gennadi Touretski, observing the teenager backstroking in the pool, declared, "Turn him over and he'll be a big star...the man to beat Biondi." Popov "turned over" and what a star he has become.

Not long after the Atlanta Games, a Moscow watermelon vendor stabbed Popov. He underwent surgery for the wound, recovered, and by December of 1996 had resumed training.

In a career now spanning two Olympiads, Aleksandr Popov has collected eight Olympic medals. Popov now resides in Australia where he continues to train. "The Iceman," as he is known in some circles (a tribute to his calmness before his races), hopes to be back on the starting blocks at the Sydney Games.

JEFF ROUSE
UNITED STATES

Photo by Tim Morse

Jeff Rouse strokes to gold in the 100m backstroke event.

Jeff Rouse, a native of Fredericksburg, Virginia, rose from the ranks of age-group swimming to become the most dominant 100m backstroker of the 90's. As of 1996, Rouse had been ranked number one in the world for the 100m backstroke event for eight consecutive years. He also collected (6) NCAA Titles during his collegiate career.

A Stanford graduate, Rouse arrived in Barcelona as the world record holder in the 100m backstroke (53.93), and the only man to ever swim this event in less than 54 seconds.

During the final of this event, Rouse held first place, just ahead of Canada's Mark Tewksbury for most of the race.

In the final meters, the two were side by side, but it was Tewksbury who wound up the victor. Barcelona was full of such upsets. Rouse was one of eight world record holders who fell short of gold in their specialty event.

Undaunted, Rouse came back and sparked the 400m medley relay team to gold. He broke his own world record, swimming a blazing 53.86 seconds in that final.

As the 1996 Games approached, Rouse was still ranked number one in his specialty. At the U.S. Olympic Trials the twenty-six year old Rouse was beaten, but his second place finish insured his spot on the Olympic Team. He was elected co-captain of the men's team, along with Jon Olsen.

With the home crowd behind him in Atlanta, Rouse was destined for gold. He led the 100m backstroke final from start to finish, staying well ahead of his closest competitor.

SCORE
BOARD

9 Years - 9 Records

On the last day of the swimming competition the U.S. 400m medley relay team was, for the first time, considered "underdogs". The team of Jeff Rouse, Jeremy Linn, Mark Henderson and Gary Hall, Jr., set a world record in this event. This was the ninth consecutive Olympiad in which the United States Men's medley relay team set or equaled a world record (note: the United States did not attend the 1980 Games).

After the medal ceremony, an exuberant Rouse hurdled the fence in front of the spectator section to celebrate with his parents and sister, Renee.

Rouse was instrumental in the 400m medley relay final. His sub-54 second opening leg gave the U.S. team more than a one and one half second lead. A world record was theirs (4:02.88).

Jeff Rouse has collected a total of three Olympic gold and one silver medal. He led the American medley relay team to two world records and also set a world record in the 100m backstroke event during his Olympic career.

NORBERT ROZSA
HUNGARY

In the morning qualifying round of the 100m breaststroke event during the 1992 Games, world record holder Norbert Rozsa placed eighth. In the final that evening, Rozsa was beaten by American Nelson Diebel, but hung on for the silver medal. Rosza captured a second silver in Barcelona, in the 200m breaststroke.

A seasoned veteran, Rozsa arrived in Atlanta poised for gold. On the first day of the Olympic swim competition, Rosza unexpectedly failed to make the 100m breaststroke final. Disappointed, he spent the next four days with his coach Tamas Szechy, preparing mentally and physically for the 200m event.

Rozsa's victory in the 200 was decisive, finishing over one half second faster than silver medalist and teammate, Karoly Guttler. Norbert Rozsa had his gold and Hungary's first gold medal of these Games.

WILLIAM "TRIPP" SCHWENK
UNITED STATES

Tripp Schwenk, whose nickname comes from being the third William Schwenk, is another American athlete who competed in both Barcelona and Atlanta. A backstroker, Schwenk took silver in the 200m event, and placed fifth in the 100m distance in Atlanta.

After the 200m backstroke ceremony, Schwenk realized he had been awarded the women's 50m freestyle medal. He quipped, "I'd better give it back before Le Jingyi finds out and kicks my butt."

As members of the 400m "B" medley relay team, Schwenk, Kurt Grote, John Hargis, and Josh Davis, qualified the U.S. for the final. The "A" team went on to win, giving Schwenk a gold medal to add to his Olympic silver.

MICHELLE SMITH
IRELAND

Michelle Smith represented Ireland at the 1988, 1992 and 1996 Olympic Games. Smith, who failed to qualify for the finals in 1988 and 1992, swam away with three gold medals and one bronze in Atlanta.

Smith's best finish in 1988 was 17th in the backstroke. In Barcelona, her top performance was in the 400m IM, where she finished 26th. All things considered, Smith was not expected to medal in Atlanta.

On the first day of swimming competition, Smith became the

first Irish woman ever to win an Olympic medal. She won the gold decisively in the 400m IM, and, with it, began a swirl of controversy that surrounds her to this day.

Smith continued in Atlanta with another surprising gold medal performance in the 400m freestyle final. On the fifth day of competition, swimming in lane 8, Smith came from behind in the last leg of the 200m IM to touch out her competitors for her third gold medal. She added a bronze medal to her collection for the 200m fly.

To the Irish media she became known as "the greatest sports story in Irish history." In the swimming community, suspicion surrounding her recent, dramatic reductions in times continues. Prior to 1996, Smith had never swum the 400m freestyle event under 4:26, yet she clocked in at 4:07.25 during the Olympic final, representing a 19-second drop in a year's time.

Smith was coached by Eric de Bruin a Dutch discus thrower, who had been banned from competition for four years, after testing positive for steroid use. De Bruin, now Smith's husband, had never before coached a swimmer.

Smith's post race substance tests were negative and she adamantly denied taking performance-enhancing drugs. In 1998 Michelle Smith was suspended by F.I.N.A from competing in any national or international competition for the next four years. Smith was cited for manipulating urine samples used in doping control.

FRANZISKA VAN ALMSICK
GERMANY

Born and raised in Berlin, Germany, Franziska van Almsick started swimming at the tender age of five. She was selected to attend an East German school for gifted athletes, where academics came second to training.

With the fall of the Berlin Wall in 1989 came the unification of Germany. Van Almsick's training program was subsequently modified as East and West united and school became the main focus. At 13, she was awarded a scholarship as Germany's most promising young athlete.

At 14, van Almsick easily qualified for the 1992 Games, where she collected two silver and two bronze medals. Van Almsick returned to Germany and continued her rise in the swimming world. In 1993, at the European Championships, van Almsick collected seven medals, six of them gold, the most ever won by an individual at that meet.

Arriving in Atlanta as the world record holder, van Almsick was favored to capture the 200m freestyle. She had been the premier swimmer in this event for close to four years. In the final Costa Rica's Claudia Poll beat Van Almsick, but Van Almsick's world record stood.

After her second place finish, the eighteen-year-old van Almsick was philosophical about the pressures of being favored, "It's much harder to defend than it is to chase," she said.

As a part of Germany's 400m and 800m free relay squads, van Almsick added a bronze and silver, respectively, to her Atlanta medal count.

L A N E L I N E S

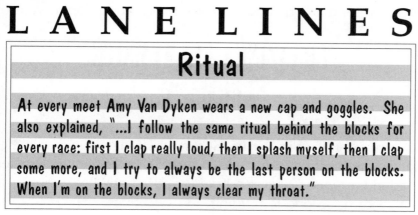

Ritual

At every meet Amy Van Dyken wears a new cap and goggles. She also explained, "...I follow the same ritual behind the blocks for every race: first I clap really loud, then I splash myself, then I clap some more, and I try to always be the last person on the blocks. When I'm on the blocks, I always clear my throat."

AMY VAN DYKEN
UNITED STATES

Amy Van Dyken was diagnosed with asthma at only 18 months of age. As with Tom Dolan, Amy's story is one of inspiration. At the recommendation of her doctor, she was encouraged to swim to build up her lungs.

Amy was twelve years old before she could complete a full lap of 25 yards without stopping. Her asthma was (and still is) so bad that this accomplishment was the fulfillment of one of Amy's young goals. By 14, Amy was swimming competitively, despite taunts from her teammates.

On her first day of competition in Atlanta, Amy swam to a personal best in the 100m freestyle final (55.11), finishing fourth. She later provided one of the most exciting races of these Games. The six-foot Van Dyken touched out

Photo by Tim Morse

Amy Van Dyken, most decorated female Olympian at the 1996 Centennial Games, celebrates her victory in the 50m free event.

China's Liu Limin for the 100m butterfly title. The margin of victory was a mere one hundredth of a second and with teammate Angel Martino capturing the bronze, the results were sweet for the U.S.

After a second gold medal performance in the 50m freestyle, Van Dyken declared, "This is for all the nerds out there," alluding to some of the difficulties she had endured while growing up. "For all the kids out there struggling, if they can keep plugging away at it, something good will always come out of it," was her advice.

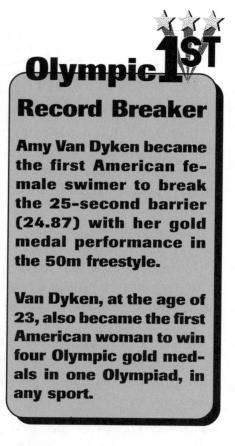

Olympic 1ST
Record Breaker

Amy Van Dyken became the first American female swimer to break the 25-second barrier (24.87) with her gold medal performance in the 50m freestyle.

Van Dyken, at the age of 23, also became the first American woman to win four Olympic gold medals in one Olympiad, in any sport.

Don Van Dyken, Amy's dad, shared; "Today Amy spends much of her free time speaking to young asthmatics, telling them not to give up, but to try to accomplish their goals, living normal lives, doing things normal people do. She tells them to take control of their asthma, not to let it control them."

"... be a humble winner. Whenever you win, you have to beat someone else. Never gloat. Think of each race as a chance to learn about your sport and yourself."

-Amy Van Dyken

Golden relay team of Angel Martino, Catherine Fox, Amy Van Dyken and Jenny Thompson.

OFF TO THE RACES
400M WOMEN'S FREESTYLE FINAL

The United States Women's 400m freestyle relay team of Angel Martino, Amy Van Dyken, Catherine Fox and Jenny Thompson were up against a very powerful Chinese team in Atlanta.

It was the team of Le Jingyi, Chao Na, Nian Yun and Shan Ying that was favored. Le and Shan were members of the Chinese foursome that held the world record (3:37.91), set back in September of 1994.

In a surprise move, the 100m gold medalist Jingyi was the lead-off swimmer for the Chinese Team. She swam against Angel Martino, who kept the American Team within striking distance.

Van Dyken went on to swim the fastest split of these Games

(the second fastest relay split of all time in this event), putting her team ahead by over 3/4 of a second. Fox, who had only qualified for the team that same morning, was able to stave off Yun in the third leg to keep the Americans in the lead.

In the final leg it was Jenny Thompson, swimming the second fastest split of the final, who was first to the wall, the team setting a new Olympic record (3:29.29). After the race Thompson said, "I felt really confident when I knew we had the lead. No one was going to pass me, no matter what."

400M MEN'S FREESTYLE FINAL

The pressure was on in Atlanta for the U.S. Men's relay team. The United States men had won every final since the event's inception in 1964 (with the exception of 1980 boycotted Games).

The race proved nothing short of sensational. The U.S. team of Jon Olsen, Josh Davis, Brad Schumacher and Gary Hall, Jr., was in third place after 300 meters. The crowd of 15,000 sat at the edge of their seats as Gary Hall, Jr., left the blocks for the final 100m leg.

The thirty-two year winning streak now rested on Hall's shoulders. Swimming the fastest 100m free split of all time (47.45), Hall hit the wall first. The Americans set a new Olympic record (3:15.41), with Russia in second and Germany taking the bronze.

1996 OLYMPIC SWIMMING FINALS

INDIVIDUAL EVENTS

Gold	Silver	Bronze	Fourth	Fifth	Sixth	Seventh	Eighth
Women 50m Freestyle - World Record (24.51 Le Jingyi CHN)					Olympic Record (24.79 Yang Wenyi CHN 1992)		
Amy Van Dyken	Le Jingyi	Sandra Volker	Angel Martino	Leah Martindale	Linda Olofsson	Shan Ying	Natalya Meshcheryakova
USA – 24.87	CHN – 24.90	GER – 25.14	USA – 25.31	BAR – 25.49	SWE – 25.63	CHN – 25.70	RUS – 25.88
Men 50m Freestyle - World Record (21.81 Tom Jager USA)					Olympic Record (21.91 Aleksandr Popov RUS 1992)		
Aleksandr Popov	Gary Hall, Jr.	Fernando Scherer	Jiang Chengji	Brendon Dedekind	David Fox	Francisco Sanchez	Ricardo Busquets
RUS – 22.13	USA – 22.26	BRA – 22.29	CHN – 22.33	RSA – 22.59	USA – 22.68	VEN – 22.72	PUR – 22.73
Women 100m Freestyle - World Record (54.01 Le Jingyi CHN)					Olympic Record (54.51 Zhuang Yong CHN 1992)		
Le Jingyi	Sandra Volker	Angel Martino	Amy Van Dyken	Franziska van Almsick	Sarah Ryan	Mette Jacobsen	Karin Brienesse
CHN – 54.50 o	GER – 54.88	USA – 54.93	USA – 55.11	GER – 55.59	AUS – 55.85	DEN – 56.01	NED – 56.12
Men 100m Freestyle - World Record (48.21 Aleksandr Popov RUS 6-18-94)					Olympic Record (48.63 Matt Biondi USA 1988)		
Aleksandr Popov	Gary Hall, Jr.	Gustavo Borges	Pieter van den Hoogenband	Fernando Scherer	Pavlo Khnykin	Ricardo Busquets	Francisco Sanchez
RUS – 48.74	USA – 48.81	BRA – 49.02	NED – 49.13	BRA – 49.57	UKR – 49.65	PUR – 49.68	VEN – 49.84
Women 200m Freestyle - World Record (1:56.78 F. van Almsick GER)					Olympic Record (1:57.65 H. Friedrich GDR 1988)		
Claudia Poll	Franziska van Almsick	Dagmar Hase	Trina Jackson	Susan O'Neill	Cristina Teuscher	Julia Greville	Liliana Dobrescu
CRC – 1:58.16	GER – 1:58.57	GER – 1:59.56	USA – 1:59.57	AUS – 1:59.87	USA – 2:00.79	AUS – 2:01.46	ROM – 2:01.63

w World Record   **o** Olympic Record   **p** Preliminary Heat   **dq** Disqualified   **e** Equal to World Record   **eo** Equal to Olympic Record
dns Did Not Start   **dnf** Did Not Finish   **ac** Also Competed   **r** Relay Lead-off Split   **E** Estimated

OLYMPIAD XXVI – 1996 – ATLANTA, USA

1996 OLYMPIC SWIMMING FINALS

	Gold	Silver	Bronze	Fourth	Fifth	Sixth	Seventh	Eighth
Men 200m Freestyle - World Record (1:46.69 Giorgio Lamberti ITA) Olympic Record (1:46.70 Yevgeny. Sadovyi RUS 1992)	Danyon Loader NZL – 1:47.63	Gustavo Borges BRA – 1:48.08	Daniel Kowalski AUS – 1:48.25	Pieter van den Hoogenband NED – 1:48.36	Anders Holmertz SWE – 1:48.42	Massimiliano Rosolino ITA – 1:48.50	Josh Davis USA – 1:48.54	Paul Palmer GBR – 1:49.39
Women 400m Freestyle - World and Olympic Record (4:03.85 Janet Evans USA1988)	Michelle Smith IRL – 4:07.25	Dagmar Hase GER – 4:08.30	Kirsten Vlieghuis NED – 4:08.70	Kerstin Kielgass GER – 4:09.83	Claudia Poll CRC – 4:10.00	Carla Louise Geurts NED – 4:10.06	Eri Yamanoi JPN – 4:11.68	Cristina Teuscher USA – 4:14.21
Men 400m Freestyle - World Record (3:43.80 Kieren Perkins AUS) Olympic Record (3:45.00 Y. Sadovyi RUS 1992)	Danyon Loader NZL – 3:47.97	Paul Palmer GBR – 3:49.00	Daniel Kowalski AUS – 3:49.39	Emiliano Brembilla ITA – 3:49.87	Anders Holmertz SWE – 3:50.66	Massimiliano Rosolino ITA – 3:51.04	Jorg Hoffmann GER – 3:52.15	Jacob Carstensen DEN – 3:54.45
Women 800m Freestyle - World Record (8:16.22 Janet Evans USA) Olympic Record (8:20.20 Janet Evans USA 1988)	Brooke Bennett USA – 8:27.89	Dagmar Hase GER – 8:29.91	Kirsten Vlieghuis NED – 8:30.84	Kerstin Kielgass GER – 8:31.06	Irene Dalby NOR – 8:38.34	Janet Evans USA – 8:38.91	Carla Louise Geurts NED – 8:40.43	Sarah Hardcastle GBR – 8:41.75
Men 1500m Freestyle - World Record (14:41.66 Kieren Perkins AUS) Olympic Record (14:43.48 K. Perkins AUS 1992)	Kieren Perkins AUS – 14:56.40	Daniel Kowalski AUS – 15:02.43	Graeme Smith GBR – 15:02.48	Emiliano Brembilla ITA – 15:08.58	Frans Ryk Neethling RSA – 15:14.63	Masato Hirano JPN – 15:17.28	Jorg Hoffmann GER – 15:18.86	Alexei Akatiev RUS – 15:21.68
Women 100m Backstroke - World Record (1:00.16 He Cihong CHN) Olympic Record (1:00.68 K. Egerszegi HUN 1992)	Beth Botsford USA – 1:01.19	Whitney Hedgepeth USA – 1:01.47	Marianne Kriel RSA – 1:02.12	Mai Nakamura JPN – 1:02.33	Chen Yan CHN – 1:02.50	Antje Buschschulte GER – 1:02.52	Nicole Stevenson AUS – 1:02.70	Miki Nakao JPN – 1:02.78

1996 OLYMPIC SWIMMING FINALS

	Gold	Silver	Bronze	Fourth	Fifth	Sixth	Seventh	Eighth
Men 100m Backstroke - World and Olympic Record (53.86 Jeff Rouse USA 1992)	Jeff Rouse	Rodolfo Falcon	Neisser Bent	Martin López-Zubero	Tripp Schwenk	Emanuele Merisi	Ralf Braun	Franck Schott
	USA – 54.10	CUB - 54.98	CUB - 55.02	ESP - 55.22	USA - 55.30	ITA - 55.53	GER - 55.56	FRA – 55.76
Women 200m Backstroke - World Record (2:06.62 K. Egerszegi HUN) Olympic Record (2:07.06 Egerszegi HUN 1992)	Krisztina Egerszegi	Whitney Hedgepeth	Cathleen Rund	Anke Scholz	Miki Nakao	Anna Simcic	Lorenza Vigarani	Nina Zhivanevskaya
	HUN – 2:07.83	USA – 2:11.98	GER – 2:12.06	GER – 2:12.90	JPN – 2:13.57	NZL – 2:14.04	ITA – 2:14.56	RUS – 2:14.59
Men 200m Backstroke - World Record (1:56.57 Martin López-Zubero ESP) Olympic Record (1:58.47 Zubero ESP 1992)	Brad Bridgewater	Tripp Schwenk	Emanuele Merisi	Bartosz Sikora	Hajime Itoi	Martin López-Zubero	Mirko Mazzari	Rodolfo Cabrera Falcon
	USA – 1:58.54	USA – 1:58.99	ITA – 1:59.18	POL – 2:00.05	JPN – 2:00.10	ESP – 2:00.74	ITA – 2:01.27	CUB – 2:08.14
Women 100m Breaststroke - World Record (1:07.46 P.Heyns RSA) Olympic Record (1:07.95 T. Dangalakova BUL 1988)	Penelope Heyns 1:07.02 p/s	Amanda Beard	Samantha Riley	Svetlana Bondarenko	Vera Lischka	Guylaine Cloutier	Agnes Kovacs	Brigitte Becue
	RSA – 1:07.73	USA - 1:08.09	AUS – 1:09.18	UKR - 1:09.21	AUT – 1:09.24	CAN – 1:09.40	HUN – 1:09.55	BEL - 1:09.79
Men 100m Breaststroke - World Record (1:00.95 Károly Güttler HUN) Olympic Record (1:01.50 N. Diebel USA 1992)	deBurghgraeve 1:00.60 w/p	Jeremy Linn	Mark Warnecke	Károly Güttler	Philip Rogers	Kurt Grote	Zeng Qiliang	Stanislav Lopukhov
	BEL - 1:00.65	USA - 1:0077	GER – 1:01.33	HUN – 1:01.49	AUS – 1:01.64	USA – 1:01.69	CHN – 1:02.01	RUS – 1:02.13
Women 200m Breaststroke - World Record (2:24.76 Rebecca Brown AUS) Olympic Record (2:26.65 Iwasaki JPN 1992)	Penelope Heyns	Amanda Beard	Agnes Kovacs	Samantha Riley	Masami Tanaka	Nadine Neumann	Brigitte Becue	Christin Petelski
	RSA – 2:25.41 o	USA - 2:25.75	HUN – 2:26.57	AUS – 2:27.91	JPN – 2:28.05	AUS – 2:28.34	BEL - 2:28.36	CAN – 2:31.45

1996 OLYMPIC SWIMMING FINALS

	Gold	Silver	Bronze	Fourth	Fifth	Sixth	Seventh	Eighth
Men 200m Breaststroke - World and Olympic Record (2:10.16 Mike Barrowman USA 1992)								
	Norbert Rozsa	Károly Güttler	Andrei Korneev	Nicholas Gillingham	Philip Rogers	Marek Krawczyk	Eric Wunderlich	Kurt Grote
	HUN – 2:12.57	HUN – 2:13.03	RUS – 2:13.17	GBR – 2:14.37	AUS – 2:14.79	POL – 2:14.84	USA – 2:15.69	USA – 2:16.05
Women 100m Butterfly - World Record (57.93 Mary T. Meagher USA) Olympic Record (58.62 Qian Hong CHN 1992)								
	Amy Van Dyken	Liu Limin	Angel Martino	Hitomi Kashima	Susan O'Neill	Ayari Aoyama	Cai Huijue	Mette Jacobsen
	USA – 59.13	CHN – 59.14	USA – 59.23	JPN – 1:00.11	AUS – 1:00.17	JPN – 1:00.18	CHN – 1:00.46	DEN – 1:00.76
Men 100m Butterfly - World Record (52.32 Denis Pankratov RUS) Olympic Record (53.00 Anthony Nesty SUR 1988)								
	Denis Pankratov	Scott Miller	Vladislav Kulikov	Jiang Chengji	Rafal Szukala	Michael Klim	Stephen Clarke	Pavlo Khnykin
	RUS – 52.27w	AUS – 52.53	RUS – 53.13	CHN – 53.20	POL – 53.29	AUS – 53.30	CAN – 53.33	UKR – 53.58
Women 200m Butterfly - World Record (2:05.96 Mary T. Meagher USA) Olympic Record (2:06.90 Meagher USA 1984)								
	Susan O'Neill	Petria Thomas	Michelle Smith	Qu Yun	Liu Limin	Jessica Deglau	Mika Haruna	Trina Jackson
	AUS – 2:07.76	AUS – 2:09.82	IRL – 2:09.91	CHN – 2:10.26	CHN – 2:10.70	CAN – 2:11.40	JPN – 2:11.93	USA – 2:11.96
Men 200m Butterfly - World Record (1:55.22 Denis Pankratov RUS) Olympic Record (1:56.26 Melvin Stewart USA 1992)								
	Denis Pankratov	Tom Malchow	Scott Goodman	Franck Esposito	Scott Miller	Denis Silantiev	James Hickman	Peter Horvath
	RUS – 1:56.51	USA – 1:57.44	AUS – 1:57.48	FRA – 1:58.10	AUS – 1:58.28	UKR – 1:58.37	GBR – 1:58.47	HUN – 1:59.12
Women 200m Individual Medley - World and Olympic Record (2:11.65 Lin Li CHN 1992)								
	Michelle Smith	Marianne Limpert	Lin Li	Joanne Malar	Elli Overton	Allison Wagner	Minouche Smit	Louise Karlsson
	IRL – 2:13.93	CAN – 2:14.35	CHN – 2:14.74	CAN – 2:15.30	AUS – 2:16.04	USA – 2:16.43	NED – 2:16.73	SWE – 2:17.25

1996 OLYMPIC SWIMMING FINALS

	Gold	Silver	Bronze	Fourth	Fifth	Sixth	Seventh	Eighth

Men 200m Individual Medley - World Record (1:58.16 Jani Sievinen FIN) Olympic Record (2:00.17 Tamas Darnyi HUN 1988)

Gold	Silver	Bronze	Fourth	Fifth	Sixth	Seventh	Eighth
Attila Czene	Jani Sievinen	Curtis Myden	Marcel Wouda	Matthew Dunn	Greg Burgess	Tom Dolan	Xavier Marchand
HUN– 1:59.91 o	FIN – 2:00.13	CAN – 2:01.13	NED – 2:01.45	AUS – 2:01.57	USA – 2:02.56	USA – 2:03.89	FRA – 2:04.29

Women 400m Individual Medley - World Record (4:36.10 P. Schneider GDR) Olympic Record (4:36.29 Schneider GDR 1980)

Gold	Silver	Bronze	Fourth	Fifth	Sixth	Seventh	Eighth
Michelle Smith	Allison Wagner	Krisztina Egerszegi	Sabine Herbst	Emma Johnson	Beatrice Coada	Lourdes Becerra	Whitney Metzler
IRL – 4:39.18	USA – 4:42.03	HUN – 4:42.53	GER – 4:43.78	AUS – 4:44.02	ROM – 4:44.91	ESP – 4:45.17	USA – 4:46.20

Men 400m Individual Medley - World Record (4:12.30 Tom Dolan USA) Olympic Record (4:14.23 T. Darnyi HUN 1992)

Gold	Silver	Bronze	Fourth	Fifth	Sixth	Seventh	Eighth
Tom Dolan	Eric Namesnik	Curtis Myden	Matthew Dunn	Marcel Wouda	Luca Sacchi	Marcin Malinski	Sergei Marinyuk
USA – 4:14.90	USA – 4:15.25	CAN – 4:16.28	AUS – 4:16.66	NED – 4:17.71	ITA – 4:18.31	POL – 4:20.50	MDA – 4:21.15

RELAY EVENTS

Women 400m Medley Relay - World Record (4:01.67 CHN) Olympic Record (4:02.54 USA 1992)

Gold	Silver	Bronze	Fourth	Fifth	Sixth	Seventh	Eighth
Beth Botsford. Amanda Beard. Angel Martino. Amy Van Dyken p - Whitney Hedgepeth. Kristine Quance. Jenny Thompson. Catherine Fox	Nicole Stevenson. Samantha Riley. Susan O'Neill. Sarah Ryan	Chen Yan. Han Xue. Cai Huijue. Shan Ying	Marianne Kriel. Penelope Heyns. Amanda Loots. Helene Muller	Julie Howard. Guylaine Cloutier. Sarah Evanetz. Shannon Shakespeare	Antje Buschschulte. Kathrin Dumitru. Franziska van Almsick. Sandra Volker	Nina Zhivanevskaya. Elena Makarova. Elena Nazemnova. Natalya Meshcheryakova	Lorenza Vigarani. Manuela Dalla Valle. Ilaria Tocchini. Cecilia Vianini
USA – 4:02.88	AUS – 4:05.08	CHN – 4:07.34	RSA – 4:08.16	CAN – 4:08.29	GER – 4:09.22	RUS – 4:10.56	ITA – 4:10.59

1996 OLYMPIC SWIMMING FINALS

Men 400m Medley Relay - World and Olympic Records (3:36.93 USA 1988) & (3:36.93 USA 1992)

Gold	Silver	Bronze	Fourth	Fifth	Sixth	Seventh	Eighth
Jeff Rouse, Jeremy Linn, Mark Henderson, Gary Hall Jr. *p* - Tripp Schwenk, Kurt Grote, JohnHargis, Josh Davis	Vladimir Selkov, Stanislav Lopukhov, Denis Pankratov, Aleksandr Popov	Steven Dewick, Philip Rogers, Scott Miller, Michael Klim	Ralf Braun, Mark Warnecke, Christian Keller, Björn Zikarsky	Keitaro Konnai, Akira Hayashi, Takashi Yamamoto, Shunsuke Ito	Tamas Deutsch, Károly Güttler, Peter Horvath, Attila Czene	Mariusz Siembida, Marek Krwaczyk, Rafal Szukala, Bartosz Kizierowski	Eitan Urbach, Vadim Alekseev, Dan Kuler, Yoav Bruck
USA - 3:34.84w	RUS - 3:37.55	AUS - 3:39.56	GER - 3:39.64	JPN - 3:40.51	HUN - 3:40.84	POL - 3:41.94	ISR - 3:42.90

Women 400m Freestyle Relay - World Record (3:37.91 CHN) ... Olympic Record (3:39.46 USA 1992)

Gold	Silver	Bronze	Fourth	Fifth	Sixth	Seventh	Eighth
Angel Martino, Amy Van Dyken, Catherine Fox, Jenny Thompson *p* - Melanie Valerio	Le Jingyi, Chao Na, Nian Yun, Shan Ying	Sandra Volker, Simone Osygus, Antje Buschschulte, Franziska van Almsick	Marianne Muis, Minouche Smit, Willma van Hofvegen, Karin Brienesse	Linda Olofsson, Louise Johncke, Louise Karlsson, Johanna Sjoberg	Sarah Ryan, Julia Greville, Lise Mackie, Susan O'Neill	Shannon Shakespeare, Julie Howard, Andrea Moody, Marianne Limpert	
USA - 3:39.29 o	CHN - 3:40.48	GER - 3:41.48	NED - 3:42.40	SWE - 3:44.91	AUS - 3:45.31	CAN - 3:46.27	RUS - dq

1996 OLYMPIC SWIMMING FINALS

Men 400m Freestyle Relay - World Record (3:15.11 USA) — Olympic Record (3:16.53 USA 1988)

Gold	Silver	Bronze	Fourth	Fifth	Sixth	Seventh	Eighth
Jon Olsen, Josh Davis, Brad Schumacher, Gary Hall, Jr. *p* - David Fox, Scott Tucker	Roman Egorov, Aleksandr Popov, Vladimir Predkin, Vladimir Pyshnenko	Christian-Alexander Tröger, Bengt Zikarsky, Bjorn Zikarsky, Mark Pinger	Fernando Scherer, Alexandre Massura, Andre Cordeiro, Gustavo Borges	Mark Veens, Pie Geelen, Martin van den Spoel, Pieter van den Hoogenband	Michael Klim, Matthew Dunn, Scott Logan, Chris Fydler	Lars Frolander, Fredric Letzler, Anders Holmertz, Christer Wallin	Nicholas Shackell, Alan Rapley, Mark Stevens, Michael Fibbens
USA – 3:15.41 *o*	RUS – 3:1.06	GER 3:17.20	BRA – 3:18.30	NED – 3:19.02	AUS – 3:20.13	SWE – 3:20.16	GBR – 3:21.52

Women 800m Freestyle Relay - World Record (7:55.47 GDR) — 1896-1992 - Event Not Held On Olympic Program

Gold	Silver	Bronze	Fourth	Fifth	Sixth	Seventh	Eighth
Trina Jackson, Cristina Teuscher, Sheila Taormina, Jenny Thompson *p* - Lisa Jacob, Ashley Whitney, Annette Salmeen	Franziska van Almsick, Kerstin Kielgass, Anke Scholz, Dagmar Hase	Julia Greville, Nicole Stevenson, Emma Johnson, Susan O'Neill	Eri Yamanoi, Naoko Imoto, Aiko Miyake, Suzu Chiba	Marianne Limpert, Shannon Shakespeare, Andrea Schwartz, Jessica Deglau	Carla Geurts, Patricia Stokkers, Minouche Smit, Kirsten Vlieghuis	Luminita Dobrescu, Loredana Zisu, Ioana Diaconescu, Carla Negrea	Nian Yun, Wang Luna, Chen Yan, Shan Ying
USA – 7:59.87 *o*	GER – 8:01.55	AUS – 8:05.47	JPN – 8:07.46	CAN – 8:08.16	NED – 8:08.48	ROM – 8:10.02	CHN – 8:15.38

Men 800m Freestyle Relay - World and Olympic Record (7:11.95 RUS 1992)

Gold	Silver	Bronze	Fourth	Fifth	Sixth	Seventh	Eighth
Josh Davis, Joe Hudepohl, Brad Schumacher, Ryan Berube *p* - Jon Olsen	Christer Wallin, Anders Holmertz, Lars Frolander, Anders Lybring	Aimo Heikmann, Christian Keller, Christian-Alexander Tröger, Steffen Zesner	Daniel Kowalski, Michael Klim, Malcolm Allen, Matthew Dunn	Paul Palmer, Andrew Clayton, Mark Stevens, James Salter	Massi Rosolino, Emanuele Idini, Emanuele Merisi, Piermaria Siciliano	Marcel Wouda, Mark van den Zijden, Martin van den Spoel, Pieter van den Hoogenband	Yann de Fabrique, Lionel Poirot, Bruno Orsoni, Christophe Bordeau
USA – 7:14.84	SWE – 7:17.56	GER – 7:17.71	AUS – 7:18.47	GBR – 7:18.74	ITA – 7:19.92	NED – 7:21.96	FRA – 7:24.85

Index

H

I

J

K

T

W

Y

Z